Public Memory, Race, and Heritage Tourism of Early America

This book addresses the interconnected issues of public memory, race, and heritage tourism, exploring the ways in which historical tourism shapes collective understandings of America's earliest engagements with race.

It includes contributions from a diverse group of humanities scholars, including early Americanists, and scholars from communication, English, museum studies, historic preservation, art and architecture, Native American studies, and history. Through eight chapters, the collection offers varied perspectives and original analyses of memory-making and re-making through travel to early American sites, bringing needed attention to the considerable role that tourism plays in producing—and possibly unsettling—racialized memories about America's past. The book is an interdisciplinary effort that analyses lesser-known sites of historical and racial significance throughout North America and the Caribbean (up to about 1830) to unpack the relationship between leisure travel, processes of collective remembering or forgetting, and the connections of tourist sites to colonialism, slavery, genocide, and oppression.

Public Memory, Race, and Heritage Tourism of Early America provides a deconstruction of the touristic experience with racism, slavery, and the Indigenous experience in America that will appeal to students and academics in the social sciences and humanities.

Cathy Rex is a Professor of English at the University of Wisconsin-Eau Claire. She specializes in early American literature and material culture. Her scholarship has appeared in many journals and edited collections; her monograph was published by Ashgate in 2015.

Shevaun E. Watson is an Associate Professor of English and Director of Composition at the University of Wisconsin-Milwaukee. She specializes in rhetoric, composition, early American rhetoric, and public memory. She is working on a monograph about heritage tourism, race, and public memory in Charleston, S.C.

New Directions in Tourism Analysis
Edited by **Dimitri Ioannides**, *E-TOUR,*
Mid Sweden University, Sweden

Although tourism is becoming increasingly popular both as a taught subject and an area for empirical investigation, the theoretical underpinnings of many approaches have tended to be eclectic and somewhat underdeveloped. However, recent developments indicate that the field of tourism studies is beginning to develop in a more theoretically informed manner, but this has not yet been matched by current publications.

The aim of this series is to fill this gap with high quality monographs or edited collections that seek to develop tourism analysis at both theoretical and substantive levels using approaches which are broadly derived from allied social science disciplines such as Sociology, Social Anthropology, Human and Social Geography, and Cultural Studies. As tourism studies covers a wide range of activities and sub fields, certain areas such as Hospitality Management and Business, which are already well provided for, would be excluded. The series will therefore fill a gap in the current overall pattern of publication.

Suggested themes to be covered by the series, either singly or in combination, include: consumption; cultural change; development; gender; globalisation; political economy; social theory; and sustainability.

Being and Dwelling through Tourism
An Anthropological Perspective
Catherine Palmer

Resort Spatiality
Reimagining Sites of Mass Tourism
Zelmarie Cantillon

The Morphology of Tourism
Planning for Impact in Tourist Destinations
Philip Feifan Xie and Kai Gu

Public Memory, Race, and Heritage Tourism of Early America
Edited by Cathy Rex and Shevaun E. Watson

For more information about this series, please visit www.routledge.com/New-Directions-in-Tourism-Analysis/book-series/ASHSER1207

Public Memory, Race, and Heritage Tourism of Early America

Edited by Cathy Rex and
Shevaun E. Watson

LONDON AND NEW YORK

First published 2022
by Routledge
2 Park Square, Milton Park, Abingdon, Oxon OX14 4RN

and by Routledge
605 Third Avenue, New York, NY 10158

Routledge is an imprint of the Taylor & Francis Group, an informa business

© 2022 selection and editorial matter, Cathy Rex and Shevaun E. Watson; individual chapters, the contributors

The right of Cathy Rex and Shevaun E. Watson to be identified as the authors of the editorial material, and of the authors for their individual chapters, has been asserted in accordance with sections 77 and 78 of the Copyright, Designs and Patents Act 1988.

With the exception of the Introduction and Chapter 3, no part of this book may be reprinted or reproduced or utilised in any form or by any electronic, mechanical, or other means, now known or hereafter invented, including photocopying and recording, or in any information storage or retrieval system, without permission in writing from the publishers.

The Introduction and Chapter 3 of this book are available for free in PDF format as Open Access at www.taylorfrancis.com. It has been made available under a Creative Commons Attribution-No Derivatives (CC-BY-ND) 4.0 license.

Trademark notice: Product or corporate names may be trademarks or registered trademarks, and are used only for identification and explanation without intent to infringe.

British Library Cataloguing-in-Publication Data
A catalogue record for this book is available from the British Library

Library of Congress Cataloging-in-Publication Data
Names: Rex, Cathy, editor. | Watson, Shevaun E., editor.
Title: Public memory, race, and heritage tourism of early America/ Edited by Cathy Rex and Shevaun E. Watson.
Description: Abingdon, Oxon; New York, NY: Routledge, 2022. | Series: New directions in tourism analysis | Includes bibliographical references and index.
Identifiers: LCCN 2021017814 (print) | LCCN 2021017815 (ebook) | ISBN 9780367609986 (hardback) | ISBN 9780367610005 (paperback) | ISBN 9781003102830 (ebook)
Subjects: LCSH: Heritage tourism–United States. | Collective memory–United States–History. | Racism–United States–History. | Slavery–United States–History. | Indigenous peoples–Social conditions.
Classification: LCC G155.U6 P83 2022 (print) | LCC G155.U6 (ebook) | DDC 306.4/8190973–dc23
LC record available at https://lccn.loc.gov/2021017814
LC ebook record available at https://lccn.loc.gov/2021017815

ISBN: 978-0-367-60998-6 (hbk)
ISBN: 978-0-367-61000-5 (pbk)
ISBN: 978-1-003-10283-0 (ebk)

DOI: 10.4324/9781003102830

Typeset in Times New Roman
by Deanta Global Publishing Services, Chennai, India

The Open Access version of the Introduction and Chapter 3 was funded by University of Wisconsin-Eau Claire.

Contents

List of contributors vii
Acknowledgments ix

New directions for research: Bringing together public memory, early America, and tourism studies 1
SHEVAUN E. WATSON AND CATHY REX

1 **Revisiting the Gateway to Bondage: A comparative study of the landscape preservation and touristic interpretation at Sullivan's Island with Ellis and Angel islands** 18
BARRY L. STIEFEL

2 **Remembrance and mourning in the Native mid-South: Florence Indian Mound Museum's past, present, and future** 35
MATTHEW DUQUÈS AND BRIAN MURPHY

3 **Remembering and forgetting plantation history in Jamaica: Rose Hall and Greenwood Great House** 52
CATHY REX

4 **At the table or on the menu at Indiana's Feast of the Hunters' Moon** 68
KATHRYN FLORENCE

5 **Slavery in the Big Easy: Digital interventions in the tourist landscape of New Orleans** 86
ELLA HOWARD

6	**Don't mess with (Anglo) Texas: Dominant cultural values in heritage sites of the Texas Revolution** MARK WARD SR.	104
7	**Bulloch Hall and the movement toward a well-rounded interpretation of antebellum life in Roswell, Georgia** SARA HARWOOD	121
8	**Rendezvous with history: Grand Portage National Monument and Minnesota's North Shore** DAVID A. TSCHIDA	136
	Afterword: Memory and heritage in the "era of just redemption" SHEVAUN E. WATSON	153
	Index	159

Contributors

Barry L. Stiefel, Ph.D. is an Associate Professor in the Historic Preservation and Community Planning program at the College of Charleston. He is interested in how local preservation efforts affect regional, national, and multi-national policies within the field of cultural resource management. Dr. Stiefel has published numerous books and articles.

Matthew Duquès received his Ph.D. in English from Vanderbilt University. He has taught at Vanderbilt, North Dakota State University, and the University of North Alabama, where he received tenure. He is co-editor of *Brill's Classical Companion to Early America* (2021).

Brian Murphy works as a curator for Florence Arts and Museums in Florence, Alabama. He teaches Public History at the University of North Alabama and serves as the N.W. Alabama coordinator for the Thousand Eyes Archaeological Stewardship Program.

Cathy Rex is a Professor of English at the University of Wisconsin-Eau Claire. She specializes in early American literature and material culture. Her scholarship has appeared in many journals and edited collections; her monograph was published by Ashgate in 2015.

Kathryn Florence (B.A. Anthropology and Art History, Purdue, 2017; M.A. Art History, Concordia, 2019) is a settler scholar residing in Carmel, Indiana. Her research focuses on the expression of visual culture at the intersection of identity, polity, agency, and representation.

Ella Howard is an Associate Professor of History at Wentworth Institute of Technology in Boston, where she teaches American and Digital History. Her research interests include the history of homelessness, historic preservation, gentrification, and popular culture.

Mark Ward Sr. (Ph.D. Clemson University) is an Associate Professor of Communication at the University of Houston-Victoria. His research on religious popular culture, published in 4 books and more than 30 articles and essays (see markwardphd.com), has received multiple national awards.

viii   *Contributors*

Sara Harwood earned her Ph.D. in English at Georgia State University, her M.A. in History at the University of Windsor, and her B.A. in History at the University of Toronto. She volunteers at heritage museums in her spare time.

David A. Tschida, Ph.D., is an Associate Professor of Communication and Journalism and Director of Liberal Studies at the University of Wisconsin-Eau Claire. His teaching and research are in communication literacy, rhetoric, critical media studies, environmental communication, and intercultural communication.

Shevaun E. Watson is an Associate Professor of English and Director of Composition at the University of Wisconsin-Milwaukee. She specializes in rhetoric, composition, early American rhetoric, and public memory. She is working on a monograph about heritage tourism, race, and public memory in Charleston, S.C.

Acknowledgments

We would like to extend our thanks to both the University of Wisconsin-Eau Claire and the University of Wisconsin-Milwaukee for their support of this project. We are also grateful to all of the authors who contributed work to this book, as well as the reviewers who offered helpful guidance that improved the collection overall. We would also like to thank Jim Embke for his assistance preparing this collection.

The University of Wisconsin-Eau Claire's Office of Research and Sponsored Programs (O.R.S.P.) provided Cathy Rex with funding and support through their Faculty Sabbatical Program, their University Research and Creative Activity Grant Program (U.R.C.A.), and a Small Research Award. Cathy would also like to thank the Center for International Education, the Faculty-Led International Immersions Program, and the English Department at U.W.E.C. for the opportunities they provided which allowed her to engage in heritage tourism experiences.

The faculty sabbatical program, as well as the English Department, at the University of Wisconsin-Milwaukee afforded Shevaun E. Watson with time and resources to work on this project. Shevaun would also like to thank Jennifer Borda and Risa Applegarth for their extensive comments on various parts of the book, as well as the crucial support our writing group has provided over the years. Shevaun is grateful to Stephen and Rowan for their unending patience and encouragement.

New directions for research
Bringing together public memory, early America, and tourism studies

Shevaun E. Watson and Cathy Rex

Introduction

Outside of academic specialists and self-anointed history buffs, Americans don't know very much about early America, a period spanning roughly from Indigenous beginnings to the early 1800s. A 2019 national survey of Americans' knowledge of U.S. history by the Woodrow Wilson Foundation found that only four in ten Americans could pass a multiple-choice citizenship test, which asks about the Constitution, colonial America, and the Revolutionary War, among other things (see also Lewer). Academics have long bemoaned the troubling fact that the American public claims to learn more about U.S. history and heritage from "unofficial" outlets such as popular culture and leisure travel than from well-researched books, subject experts, or history classes (De Groot; Loewen). With more than half of adult Americans reporting travel to cultural or historical sites each year, and that number growing steadily (Patkose et al.), heritage tourism seems worryingly implicated in the disjointed understanding of America's earliest years.

Making tourism suspect are, in part, the tourists themselves, a perennially unloved lot. They are seen by more sophisticated travelers and most academics as "shallow, gullible seekers of entertainment, banal, loud, naïve, and most damning of all, uncultured" (Smith, "Cultural Work" 210). In American culture, negative views of tourists as socially ambitious and culturally superficial go back to the 1820s (Mackintosh), and the rise of mass tourism since the 1960s has only made tourists seem more manufactured and vulgar. Tourists are perceived as boorish consumers whose unbridled appetites and demands drive the commodification, appropriation, and cheapening of culture. In relation to heritage travel especially, tourists are interlopers; their very presence diminishes the historical or cultural authenticity of the places they visit.[1] Moreover, the tawdriness of tourism spills over to the study of tourism itself, outrightly dismissed in some academic circles (Urry) and "hemmed in by disciplinary limitations" in others. As Steve Watson, Emma Waterton, and Laurajane Smith observe, "the most valuable contributions to this area of research [cultural tourism] over the past two decades ... have all occurred in isolation ... whether they are based in anthropology, sociology, cultural geography, cultural studies, [and] heritage studies," not to mention history, public history, hospitality management, and communication (1). The result of all this, these scholars feel, is the prevalence of reductive analytical frameworks and lack of interdisciplinary perspectives on this very popular form of travel, which upon closer inspection, appears not tawdry but rather quite complex and far reaching in its impacts on individuals, communities, and societies. Smith, Waterton, and Watson's *The Cultural Uses of Tourism*, and Staiff, Bushell, and Watson's *Heritage and Tourism* begin to make important inroads to deepen cross-disciplinary understandings of heritage tourists and their complicated engagements with the past.

In the growing body of diverse scholarship on tourism, and heritage tourism specifically, there remains a deep chasm between social science and hospitality management research on the one hand and humanities perspectives on the other. There is simply a relative dearth of humanities-focused research on cultural, historical, and heritage forms of travel. This volume contributes this kind of needed scholarship to ongoing conversations about cultural heritage and related tourism phenomena. Rather than just writing in parallel with (or in isolation from) social scientists, the authors here build on existing tourism literature, especially from critical and reflexive theoretical perspectives, to bridge the chasm, inviting more humanities scholars to examine tourism and more tourism researchers to engage essential humanities perspectives. We do so by bringing together public memory, race, and early America through the prism of heritage travel, offering a unique and constructive combination of issues and frameworks for humanities and social science scholars alike. Together, these chapters explore the ways in which historical tourism shapes collective understandings of America's earliest engagements with race. To foster and contextualize diverse readers' understanding of the new, interdisciplinary scholarship within these chapters of *Public Memory, Race, and Heritage Tourism of Early America*, we unpack and define each term within our title. In doing so, we assume that most readers of this volume may be somewhat unfamiliar with the most current scholarship in one or more of these areas.

Early America

"Early America," or "colonial America," is an era that, traditionally defined, roughly covers

> from indigenous beginnings ... from European contact with peoples of the Americas, to the time of United States nation making, that is to about 1812, when the United States finalized its political separation from Great Britain (though not from British culture).
>
> (Mulford 1–4)

While some definitions of early America reach further into the nineteenth century—as the Society of Early Americanists defines the era until 1830, and as it is often defined in college literature and history survey courses until the end of the American Civil War—early America is most broadly conceived as the period of European colonization of the Americas, concluding in the nineteenth century.

Although sometimes misinterpreted as encompassing only the United States and Anglo-British traditions in particular, the geographic scope of early America spans from Africa to both North and South America and the Caribbean, from Canada down to the nation-states of South America, and encompasses cultures and traditions that range from the many Indigenous societies who originally inhabited the region, to African, Scandinavian, German, Spanish, Portuguese, Russian, French, British, and other European groups who settled the continents. Each of these groups brought a wide range of religious, social, cultural, and economic practices with them and a variety of methods for establishing settlements, interacting with their Native neighbors, and engaging in enslavement.

As a result, the idea of "early America" or an "early American" person was not a concrete or stable concept during the seventeenth and eighteenth centuries. It was a heterogeneous mix of cultures, identities, and settler-colonial policies and practices. Prior to the American Revolution, most Anglo-European settlers in the Americas would have considered themselves as subjects of their imperial government; they would have viewed themselves as colonists who were acting on behalf of their government and still "British" or "French" or "Spanish" in terms of their own identities and practices. For most of these settlers—particularly British ones—that imperial, European identity was carefully patrolled and anxiously maintained in the uncertainty of "New World" settlement. Because of the widely held fear of degeneration—the belief that one would become "savage" or "uncivilized" by living in a different climate and eating different foods—most Anglo-European settlers in the Americas actively and aggressively maintained the customs, mores, and social systems from their homelands and resisted hybridized or Indigenous ideas, even if they were more practical for their settler-colonialist purposes. Although some European settlers, like the French and Spanish, sometimes intermarried with and adapted practices of Indigenous groups to create kinship alliances and for practicality (and so that disenfranchisement of Indigenous groups could proceed more smoothly), they still would have maintained a sense of their identities as Christian, civilized, and European, and not "American" or Indigenous.

However, because of this variegated environment and cultural mosaic of identities, many scholars speak of the "early America*s*" and the "literature*s*" and "histor*ies*" of these regions to underscore the multiplicity and variation within them. So, while many early American scholars may focus on a singular, nationalist, or cultural thread of this heterogenous mix of identities and cultures in their research and teaching—and this was, indeed, the primary approach to the literature and history of this era in the past—scholars now also foreground the broadness and interconnectedness of the early Americas through an updated understanding of the Atlantic World, including Africa. Beginning as early as the 1970s and 1980s with a handful of books and articles about the Atlantic World and then burgeoning into a field of its own in the 1990s and early 2000s with works such as *The Black Atlantic* by literary scholar Paul Gilroy, "The Idea of Atlantic History" and *Atlantic History* by historian Bernard Bailyn, and *The Atlantic World* by historians Douglas Egerton, Alison Games, Jane G. Landers, Kris Lane, and Donald R.

Wright, the idea of the Atlantic World worked to transcend the idea of "nation/nationality" as the central unit of identification and instead examine the Atlantic Ocean and the regions surrounding it as a single, yet complex and multifaceted, body. Scholars assert that the Atlantic and the cultures touched by it are an integrated system, joined rather than separated by the Atlantic Ocean. As historian Alison Games notes, "Atlantic perspectives deepen our understanding of transformations over a period of several centuries, cast old problems in an entirely new light, and illuminate connections hitherto obscured" (741).

Within this Atlantic framework, interdisciplinary themes that transcend political, national, and even field or discipline-specific boundaries, such as exploration, imperialism and settlement, the African slave trade and slavery capitalism, and migration and diasporas, to name just a few, are used to examine the intercultural contact, exchange, and conflicts that occurred within the Atlantic World and early Americas, revealing a richer, more interconnected web of human interactions, commonalities, and convergences. This focus on the transnational nature of early America emphasizes how the settlement and conquest of the Americas reshaped Africa and Europe rather than solely on how Europe reshaped the rest of the world. It also differs from traditional approaches to colonial literature and history in that it steps away from examining events and trends through the lens of the dominant group/s (for the most part Anglo-European, Christian, educated, upper-class males) to understand the experiences of the enslaved, indentured servants, women, workers, and others from underrepresented groups along the axes of transmission, migration, and exchange. Alison Games notes,

> Atlantic history, then, is a *slice* of world history. It is a way of looking at global *and* regional processes within a contained unit, although that region was not, of course, hermetically sealed off from the rest of the world, and thus was simultaneously involved in transformations unique to the Atlantic and those derived from global processes.
>
> (748)

These more expansive, transnational perspectives point to the need for more capacious and multidimensional understandings of American heritage, especially at tourist sites.

Race in early America

Just as "American" and "early America" were fluctuating and evolving terms, so race in seventeenth- and eighteenth-century Americas was a shifting and complex idea understood in terms of multiplicity rather than binary thought. Today, race is viewed as a more concrete concept, defined as the use of physical markers deemed by society as distinct and significant, such as skin tone, facial features, and bone structure, to categorize people into groups. Race today is also largely viewed by contemporary scholars and scientists as a social construct that is loosely and often discriminatively based on phenotypical similarities within groups which have no inherent biological qualities. Prior to the nineteenth century in Western Europe and the Americas, though, race was not tied solely to bodily traits, physical appearance, and skin color in the way that it is today. Instead, it was conceived of as "a heterogeneous compound of physical, intellectual, and moral characteristics passed on from one generation to another" (Harvey). Qualities such as appearance, the enactment of gender roles, physical strength, material culture, methods of subsistence, literacy, and language were often factored into the understanding of race, with the categories of "Christian" and "heathen" being the most prominent and widely used designations to signify similarity or difference. These early Western European understandings of race were based in natural philosophies about the "humors" and theories about how geographical location and climate affected human traits and behavior (Wheeler).

During the seventeenth and eighteenth centuries, scientific thought additionally foregrounded the theory of "monogenesis," which posited that all people, based on Judeo-Christian traditions, descended from a single pair of humans, but after migration and dispersal, habits, appearances, and cultures changed based on locale and climate. So, while there was an understanding of the tapestry of differences among various cultures, racial categories based on skin color or bodily traits only did not exist with any consensus in early America or Europe. Any physical or cultural differences, as Ezra Tawil argues in his *The Making of Racial Sentiment*, were viewed as the result of "degeneration" caused by such factors as climate, geographical location, and diet. Such differences were not "permanent or immutable," and even features "such as skin color or cranial shape" were believed "to be alterable" at this time (44–5). Sharon Block similarly argues in *Colonial Complexions* that eighteenth-century British colonists would have understood complexion—the most common term used at the time—to be nonracial, and more closely tied to the framework of humoral medicine. Block posits, "Rather than being a shorthand for categorical skin color, complexion signaled individual health, character, and behavior" (11). Other early American scholars, such as Roxann Wheeler in *The Complexion of Race*, Ralph Bauer's *The Cultural Geography of Colonial American Literatures*, and Katy Chiles's *Transformable Race*, among many others, also suggest that prior to the nineteenth century race was understood as a complex and often creolized set of sociocultural symbols and that the body was changeable rather than set in an inherent biological category.

Beginning in the late eighteenth century, the growth of natural history, with its emphasis on physical attributes, began to underscore the primacy of skin color as a category of difference. The theory of "polygenesis" also began to grow in popularity, replacing earlier ideas of monogenesis and positing instead that each "race" of man developed from distinctively different forebears, a turning point in thought that, as Tawil asserts, postulated "a new kind of human body," one that is permanently and essentially "endowed with 'race'" (Tawil 48). Sharon Block notes, "By the beginning of the nineteenth century, skin color began to consistently be privileged as *the* sign of racial identity in literary, legal, and public arenas" (2). It is no coincidence that this new emphasis on skin tone and bodily characteristics as inherent and fixed came into sharper focus simultaneously with the growth of European imperial pursuits and the increasing economic power of already established colonies. Earlier constructions of Natives and Africans as "savage heathens," which served as a foil for European "civility," now worked to provide legal and moral justifications for the violent, aggressive dispossession of Native Americans and the continued trafficking and enslavement of Africans. Visual and ethnographic representations that reinscribed these savage notions of non-Anglo peoples proliferated during this time, further solidifying the connection of darker complexions and savagery, heathenism and utter otherness. These characterizations and the new science of polygenesis worked together to mitigate Anglo-European fears concerning their earlier beliefs about their own malleable identities. As Sean Harvey states, "Theories of Native inferiority in mind and body provided Europeans, simultaneously, a compelling claim to the land and reassurance that colonists would not degenerate in an alien environment" (5).

As the eighteenth century progressed, racial identities were further codified and "white" became a significant social category. Initially, non-English European immigrants were not viewed as "white." With the increase of chattel slavery, especially in the Caribbean and Chesapeake areas, and the decrease of bonded servitude of white immigrants, "whiteness" became an identity that was able to join elite planters and lower-class indentured servants under a single, united front. Ultimately, "white" became a label that excluded the enslaved, Natives, and free people of color and worked to closely patrol social boundaries, reserve privileges for a select group, and deny citizenship to all others, a system that basically remains intact today.

In sum, race as a codified concept emerged from preexisting prejudices of Anglo-Europeans, backed by ethnographic and philosophical speculation. Although racial ideas were broadly debated and morphed over time from a myriad of sociocultural traits and habits to being specifically tied to skin color and physical traits with biological fixity, race did become a stable, uniform idea carrying with it a host of social and legal significances.

It is worth noting here the unique challenges to addressing race at early American visitor sites. Tourists tend not to expect or desire treatments of race and racism during visits to heritage sites, especially at ones that don't seem obviously to pertain to such issues, which is often the case at colonial and Revolutionary sites that are assumed not to be tied to some form of oppression. Further, the ends of leisure travel are often at odds with honest appraisals of the past. There is discomfort in the latter activity that is not easily accommodated by motives of relaxation or entertainment. Moreover, if tourists are in fact open to hearing about race, the average traveler is unaware that it functioned in these very different ways in early American culture than today, leading to anachronistic assumptions about race relations and racism which do as much harm as good for public understanding and communal remembering. Early American heritage sites deserve more critical attention because, in harkening back to a more distant and less familiar era, they actually hold greater potential to shift visitors' understandings of America's imperialist past in more profound ways. It may very well be the case that tourists of seventeenth- and eighteenth-century sites are more open to challenge and change than those of sites representing more recent, visceral racial strife. The investigations here suggest that some tourists want to learn more about early American history on their travels and may be amenable to more candid treatments of colonialism, genocide, and systematic oppression during this time period.

Public memory

Public memory scholars ask not, *Is this true? Did it really happen this way?* or *Is this an authentic representation of the past?*, but instead, *Whose memories are represented here? What has been collectively forgotten, and why?* and *How are shared memories being leveraged for political or ideological purposes?* Also referred to as "collective memory," "cultural memory," and "social memory,"[2] public memory is the consolidation and circulation, and sometimes the revision, of perceptions of a shared past. Public memory scholars examine the social construction, mediation, and diffusion of communal remembrances. All groups—whether regional, national, political, religious, ethnic, linguistic, or otherwise—are formed or inhabited by people who have a collective awareness of sharing some past together. "We are a public, one might say, to the extent that we share memories," explain Matthew Houdek and Kendall Phillips (1–2). Public memory is different from history in that it accounts for more of the informal, unofficial, unsettled, or changeable ways in which communities create, maintain, and alter a sense of the past that is held in common, whereas history collects and conveys more formal, official, "singular and stable" explanations and descriptions of the past (Houdek and Phillips 1). While historical accounts and public memories are both gleaned from a similarly diverse array of archival materials and cultural texts, these are used and conceived of differently by the two groups of scholars. Historians mine artifacts from the past for facts and evidence to determine the greatest degree of probable accuracy about events, phenomena, and people, whereas public memory scholars analyze the ways that cultural artifacts and practices are used by various groups to strategically remember parts of the past that are deemed important for the collective to share and pass on. In this way, public memory is much more openly rhetorical than history, which is to say that public memory research foregrounds the vicissitudes of memory itself, and the vagaries of memories as they are purposively and suasively circulated across time and media.

Memory began to develop into a discrete area of study as early as the 1920s and 1930s, but it burgeoned in the 1990s with the work of French sociologists Pierre Nora and Maurice Halbwachs. Memory studies has animated research across social science and humanities disciplines since then, which is one reason it serves as such a useful cross-disciplinary framework featured in this collection. Some of this early scholarship was taken up by Americanists. Michael Kammen's 1991 *Mystic Chords of Memory* and John Bodnar's 1992 *Remaking America* are considered foundational texts for any scholar working on issues of American memory. These works elucidate how America became a place deeply interested in its own past, and how and why Americans' perceptions of the past shift from generation to generation. Since then, some early Americanists have used memory as an interpretative framework in several ways: to understand the lasting significance of the country's early history, to expose old and new contestations over the meaning of America's past, and to uncover cultural memory practices that shaped early America (e.g., Nash; Purcell; Seelye; Stabile; Schocket; Stoltz). It is worth noting, however, that public memory as such—which asks not how memory functioned in the past but rather how the past should be remembered now and to what ends—has not yet stimulated a great amount of research in early American studies. Thus far, some public historians notwithstanding (e.g., Devlin), the valuable perspectives of those trained as early Americanists specifically are missing from discussions about public memory of the time period in which they specialize. This points to another scholarly gap we seek to amend with the work presented here.

From another disciplinary perspective, building on Nora's and Halbwachs's insights about the processual and dialogic means by which memories are made to be collectively shared and disputed, rhetoric and communication scholars have made major inroads in public memory research of late "because it opens up avenues for exploring public meaning-making practices and contests over the past" (Houdek and Phillips 3). To name just a few key studies in this area, Barbie Zelizer examines the problems with mass-produced memories of the Holocaust; Stephen Browne explores the textuality of commemorative practices; Greg Dickinson, Carole Blair, and Brian Ott draw critical attention to places of shared memory, such as memorials, museums, and monuments; Bradford Vivian takes up the possibilities of productive forms of collective forgetting; and Katherine Mack documents the wide circulation of memories of trauma and reconciliation in South Africa.

Among the most recent and groundbreaking treatments of rhetoric and public memory is Dave Tell's *Remembering Emmett Till*, which offers an ecological and geographical understanding of memory and commemoration. Tell draws much needed attention to the "delicate balance between commerce and commemoration" facing many rural communities dying for development, but he provides his most critical insights by illustrating the many ways in which memory is "entangled" with the natural environment (103). In the case of Emmett Till, Tell argues that the Mississippi Delta is not just a place or a setting where something happened that should be remembered, but instead that the ecology and topography of the place actually play key roles in shaping the commemorative processes and practices surrounding Till. Tell's work offers new understandings of the complicated relationships between race, heritage sites, and public memory by examining the national and regional contestations over Till's commemoration, particularly as the tragic event reverberated through the Jim Crow and Civil Rights eras.

Another recent development in public memory scholarship has been attention to tourism as a significant mechanism for the circulation and consolidation of collective memory. Historical tourist destinations use narrative, landscape, built environments, and material artifacts to construct places laden with palpable and consumable memories of a shared past. Because so many of these sites are imbricated in the country's sordid history of enslavement and colonialism, the focus on tourism as a major public-memory purveyor in American culture has also entailed vital critiques of treatments of race and ethnicity at heritage destinations (Applegate and Rex; Cox; Dickinson, Ott and Aoki; Helmbrecht; Kytle and Roberts; Poirot and Watson). These researchers are raising important concerns about how the traveling public is encouraged to remember or forget the roles that race and racism played in historical events and how they animate contemporary memory practices.

Heritage tourism

Tourism as an academic field is traditionally associated with business, hospitality management, and social science researchers investigating commerce, transportation, advertising, consumer experience, tourist behavior, cross-cultural communication, regional planning, conservation, preservation, sustainability, labor, and globalization, among many other issues, as they pertain to locales all over the world and every type of travel imaginable. To keep pace with the exponential growth of leisure travel in its many and constantly proliferating forms, this body of research has exploded into a vibrant scholarly area.[3] Much of this field is built on the work of Dean MacCannell whose 1976 classic *The Tourist: A New Theory of the Leisure Class* posits tourism as a reaction to modernism, an attempt to subvert the alienation of modern consciousness, but one that ultimately succeeds in confirming it. The modern world is one large tourist attraction where "staged authenticity" draws in consumers looking for new experiences and pleasure in cultural differences. Another formative text in tourism studies is John Urry's *The Tourist Gaze*, which draws out the relationship between postindustrial capitalism and tourism, namely the commercialization of tourist destinations and the consumption of something "out of the ordinary" through visual culture and processes. Arguing that visuality is absolutely central to tourism, Urry explains that tourists mistake seeing other places and people as their own individual, autonomous acts, when in actuality these are socially organized and commercially manufactured visual experiences that establish tourists' expectations about what to see and what is worth seeing in the first place.[4] More recently, tourism studies has been (re)shaped by a "new mobilities paradigm" and the "mobility turn" in the social sciences (Sheller and Urry). Upending "sedentarist," static, territorial, and spatially fixed approaches to social phenomena, the concept of mobilities (and immobilities) directs attention to complex, interacting flows and movements of people, processes, and practices across times and spaces, of which leisure travel is only a part.

Within the field of heritage tourism more specifically, scholars from geography, anthropology, archaeology, history, and public history have joined management specialists and social theorists in helping to articulate and understand the significance of leisure travel to historic and cultural sites. These researchers offer critical perspectives on space and place; human interaction with the natural world and built environments; diasporic communities and Indigenous cultures; environmental impacts and sustainability; architecture, museums, and material culture; language and translation; and the politics of interpreting the past for diverse visiting publics (Timothy 3–4). Heritage tourists can have little interest in the culture or history of a destination, or a deep and abiding commitment to absorb information and participate in heritage displays. Dallen Timothy explains that

> Heritage tourism refers to travelers seeing or experiencing built heritage, living culture, or contemporary arts [and that] visits are motived by a desire to enhance one's own cultural self, to learn something new … to satisfy curiosity, or simply to use up excess time.
>
> (4)

Regardless of this range of desires and aims, heritage is an engine of tourism worldwide.

> The past and its resources lie at the core of much of global tourism today, and people by the hundreds of millions travel worldwide each year to seek out and experience places of historical significance … Heritage tourism is big business, and demand for it continues to grow.
>
> (Timothy 4–5; see also World Travel; World Tourism Organization)

Travel to heritage sites is among the most salient forms of contemporary tourism as global appetite for cultural experiences expands, and the enormous volume of these tourists presents an array of vexing development, management, and preservation issues for heritage destinations. Perhaps most important, at least for our explorations here, heritage tourism plays an integral role in shaping people's understandings of shared culture and collective pasts.

The "heritage" part of heritage tourism is the source of much ongoing debate, conflicting definitions, and blurry disciplinary boundaries. In his formative critique of "heritage," historian David Lowenthal argues that

> heritage is not history at all; while it borrows from and enlivens historical study, heritage is not an inquiry into the past but a celebration of it, not an effort to know what actually happened but a profession of faith in the past tailored to present-day purposes.

Whether one agrees with Lowenthal or not, his criticism points to the way in which heritage pertains as much or more to the needs and contexts of contemporary people and situations than to the past per se. Timothy concurs by embracing a straightforward distinction that "History is the past, whereas heritage is the modern-day use of the past" (3–4).

In this vein, heritage is a resource, not unlike other "natural" resources, to be leveraged and now regularly monetized for a wide range of purposes, including cultural travel, education, artistic preservation, community development, and expression of unique cultural identities. Anthropologist Celeste Ray suggests a more nuanced understanding, defining heritage as "the continually evolving and creative selection and generalization of memory that blends historical 'truths' with idealized simulacra on the individual and collective levels." She continues, "Though we may celebrate heritage as an unchanging 'thing,' it is really a process of renegotiating a past or cultural inheritance to be meaningful in the ever-changing present" (3). Ray draws out the more mutable, rhetorical, and ideological aspects of heritage. The past, or more specifically the deliberate construction of what people come to believe about a shared past, is a powerful argument for actions in the present. Along similar lines, historian Jerome De Groot in *Consuming History* confronts the growth of heritage as he grapples with the expansion of history in public domains and historians' role in mediating those historical representations. He argues that our relationship to the past has fundamentally changed from relying solely on traditional hierarchies of knowledge (in the form of academic history) to much more democratized, performative, and commodified processes and products (as in heritage). Importantly, De Groot emphasizes that popular, public engagement with history as heritage is a complex affair, neither good nor bad, but a distinct contemporary cultural phenomenon requiring much more attention.

Heritage, then, is nearly indistinguishable from cultural memory practices. As Paul Shackel notes in his Foreword to *Excavating Memory*, "Memory work is about heritage development," and the promotion of specific heritage destinations as the most highly valued sites of collective memory is essentially a "political act of remembering and forgetting" (xiii–xv). From this vantage point, analysis of heritage sites, such as those we've collected here, highlights the social construction of memory and the political stakes therein, as destinations big and small blend historical fact with negotiated meanings of cultural inheritance. Such blending and negotiation are fundamentally rhetorical processes, acts of selection and arts of presentation inevitably rooted in advocacy for a particular point of view. Some worry about the tourists' difficulty in seeing these rhetorical dimensions of heritage and memory, obfuscated as they are by the lure of entertainment, the appeal of elegance, or the gravitas of "official" history. However, other scholars like Laurajane Smith, Emma Waterton, Russell Staiff, Robyn Bushell, and Steve Watson argue that tourists are not mindless consumers of pre-packaged heritage but are active and complex co-producers of the heritage they seek to interact with and understand. As Smith explains,

> The interconnection between heritage and tourism does not reside in the macro or institutional scale with the interchange between the creation of economic resources and marketable cultural meanings. Rather, it also exists at the level of individual visits. Each visit is constitutive of the meaning of a heritage site. Heritage sites are not simply "found," nor do they simply "exist," but rather they are constituted at one level by the management and conservation processes, and at another by the visiting of visiting and engagement that people perform at them.
>
> ("Cultural Work" 213)

Such viewpoints only increase the salience of discussions about heritage, tourism, and memory among more scholars.

Overview of chapters

Shifting and more complex understandings of race and early America are combined in these chapters with deepening critical engagements of heritage tourism. Though each author focuses on a different cultural moment and set of interanimating issues, all point to ways that tourists can be rhetorically invited to understand (and possibly co-construct) more complicated dimensions of American heritage and more unsettling memories of an imperfect union. This work begins with "Revisiting the Gateway to Bondage," by preservation scholar Barry Stiefel. He examines contrasting levels of historical interpretation and tourist interest at America's three most important human entrepôts, Ellis, Angel, and Sullivan's islands. He argues that Sullivan's Island in South Carolina, which marks the point of entry and initial confinement for 40–60 percent of slaves brought to North America, is woefully underdeveloped for the millions who visit Charleston each year. Next, Matthew Duqués, early Americanist, and Brian Murphy, museum curator, explore the representation of Indigenous cultures in Alabama in "Remembrance and mourning in the Native mid-South: Florence Indian Mound Museum's past, present, and future." They illustrate how this museum shapes visitors' conceptions of Indigenous early America in this part of North America. In particular, they explain why the museum has struggled to make this a site of Indigenous-centered learning for heritage tourists and help chart a possible way forward to do so.

Building on the transatlantic focus in early American studies, literary scholar Cathy Rex moves our attention to slavery tourism in the Caribbean. In "Remembering and forgetting plantation history in Jamaica: Rose Hall and Greenwood Great House," Rex analyzes two Jamaican "great houses" and the different ways they appeal to and educate tourists. She argues that Rose Hall, the more popular of the two sites, portrays the legacies of enslavement in Jamaica in ways that sanitize and romanticize the historic spectacles of violence that occurred there, while the much less visited Greenwood Great House attempts to confront the postcolonial realities of enslavement and Anglo supremacy directly. Rex invites readers to contemplate the relationship between tourist appeal, historical accuracy, and contested memories. Returning to the continental U.S., Kathryn Florence, Executive Director of the Canadian Latin American Archaeology Society, tackles the politics of racialized reenactments in her chapter, "At the table or on the menu at Indiana's Feast of the Hunter's Moon." She critiques the historical representation of exchanges between French fur traders and the Wea Miami at an annual event hosted by the Tippecanoe County Historical Association for visitors to Fort Ouiatenon, Indiana. In striving to create an authentic experience of the past, this event ultimately undermines the historic presence of Indigenous people, it functions as a form of ongoing settler colonialism, and it dramatically skews local public memory.

We move from reenactments to apps, and from the rural Midwest to one of America's most popular tourist destinations, in Ella Howard's "Slavery in the Big Easy: Digital interventions in the tourist landscape of New Orleans." Howard, a historian, considers the New Orleans Slave Trade Marker and App Project, a digital public history initiative created for tourists to amplify the presence of slavery in the city. She analyzes the portrayal of enslavement in the eight markers developed for the app so far and finds a relatively rich and multifaceted presentation for visitors. Shifting from tourist apps to websites, Mark Ward Sr.'s "Don't mess with (Anglo) Texas: Dominant cultural values in heritage sites of the Texas Revolution" investigates the portrayal of Texas heritage for tourists. A communication scholar, Ward analyzes the collective construction of historical memory across ten websites for state-supported heritage tourism sites of the Texas Revolution (1835–6). Using a typology for cultural values, Ward asserts that these sites not only collapse a complex history into a romanticized narrative of Texan pioneer freedom fighters, but they also implicitly evoke the Anglo-American creation myth through copious analogs to the American Revolutionary War.

Next is early Americanist Sara Harwood's "Bulloch Hall and the movement towards a well-rounded interpretation of antebellum life in Roswell, Georgia." Using Eichstedt and Small's study of plantation museums, MacCannell's theory of staged authenticity, and Modlin's theory of production myths as frameworks, this chapter evaluates the interpretation of slavery at Bulloch Hall. Formerly a docent at this plantation house, Harwood explores the interplay between docents' and visitors' biases, or shared public memories, and concludes that, despite some positive changes, the overarching narrative still falls short of presenting a well-rounded understanding of enslavement. Finally, we end at a tourist destination in the northern reaches of the Minnesota–Canada border. David Tschida, an environmental communication scholar, takes readers to Grand Portage National Monument in his essay, "Rendezvous with history." Using cultural discourse analysis, he finds the heritage tourism experience at this site reflects intercultural expressions of the Anishinaabeg, European fur traders, national, state, and local governments, and the natural environment. As a result, tourists are invited to question their understandings of and relationship with Indigenous communities. The collection closes with a brief Afterword by rhetoric scholar Shevaun E. Watson that addresses how all of these collective memories shape treatments of race and racism today. She argues that heritage travel and memory need to play a more prominent and productive role in the work of racial justice.

In closing, we would like to make a final observation, brought to the fore by these case studies. Many of the colonial and Revolutionary-era heritage sites dotting the landscape are smaller places commemorating less well-known people and events. The essays presented here invite readers to contemplate the large-scale public memory impact of these more "minor" early American heritage destinations. Not only is more scholarly attention paid to the nation's biggest historical tourist draws, such as Mount Vernon, Colonial Williamsburg, and Historic Jamestown, but these major sites are relatively well-resourced with archivists, preservationists, archaeologists, historians, and deep-pocketed philanthropists who can, in theory, offer visitors higher quality public memory experiences (Lee; Handler and Gable; Devlin; Schnee). Relative to the millions who visit these principal early American history destinations each year, as many or more opt to explore the thousands of other seventeenth- and eighteen-century historical attractions along our roads and byways, such as small museums, historical markers, roadside stops, monuments, forts, houses, and parks of more local significance. These visits tend to be more affordable, spontaneous, and convenient, requiring much less commitment of travelers' time, resources, and aims. Yet these ancillary sites are no less influential in crafting shared memories of America's complicated origins and vexed racial relations.

Another way to frame the significance of these smaller sites is to consider that while top American heritage destinations garner the financial resources and scholarly expertise to offer visitors a more immersive and multifaceted experience of America's early exploits, it is also the case that these visitors' experiences are thereby more carefully curated and predetermined. The heritage encounters at the country's most developed and expensive sites are so well groomed and tightly crafted that visitors have little room for true exploration or interpretive alternatives. Ambiguity may not be well tolerated at these places, and what might that mean for changing public memories? Sites of supposedly less historical significance may hold more interpretive possibilities in their very lack of development and resources. These sites may have less control, one might say, over their historical narratives precisely because they're not all-encompassing destinations or "tourism imaginaries." There might be more slippage, more memorial "leaking," at places like Grand Portage, Minnesota and Florence, Alabama than Colonial Williamsburg, which raises interesting questions about how memories are constructed and reconstructed at the thousands of such places dotting our maps. The eight case studies presented here uncover the rhetorical and ideological power these seemingly inconsequential heritage stops and sites have.

Notes

1 Only recently have a few scholars sought to rehabilitate the conception of tourists into something more complex and significant (e.g., Sather-Wagstaff; Smith; Watson, Waterton, and Smith). It is important to note that the quote from Smith above does not represent her own view of tourists but others'.
2 See Ana Lucia Araujo's *Slavery in the Age of Memory*, especially pages 4–5, for useful distinctions of these terms.
3 See journals such as *Annals of Tourism Research*, *Journal of Hospitality and Tourism Research*, *Tourism Management*, *Tourist Studies*, and *International Journal of Tourism Sciences*, among others. See also Kirilenko, Andrei P., and Svetlana Stepchenkova for a historiographic overview of the development of the field.
4 Other key texts explicating the relationship between tourism and capitalism, and tourism and (middle) class, especially in the American context, include Aron; Chambers; Cocks; Gassan; Mackintosh; Sterngass.

References

Applegate, Cary, and Cathy Rex. "Teaching Tourism in Jamaica: Developing Students' Critical Consciousness and Intercultural Competence." *Intercultural Education*, vol. 29, no. 1, 2018, pp. 1–17. doi:10.1080/14675986.2017.1404782

Araujo, Ana Lucia. *Slavery in the Age of Memory: Engaging the Past*. Bloomsbury, 2021.

Aron, Cindy Sondik. *Working at Play: A History of Vacations in the United States*. Oxford UP, 1999.

Bailyn, Bernard. *Atlantic History: Concept and Contours*. Harvard UP, 2005.

Bailyn, Bernard. "The Idea of Atlantic History." *Itinerario*, vol. 20, no. 1, 1996, pp. 19–44. doi: 10.1017/S0165115300021513

Bauer, Ralph. *The Cultural Geography of Colonial American Literatures: Empire, Travel, Modernity*. Cambridge UP, 2003.

Block, Sharon. *Colonial Complexions: Race and Bodies in Eighteenth-Century America*. U of Pennsylvania P, 2018.

Bodnar, John. *Remaking America: Public Memory, Commemoration, and Patriotism in the Twentieth Century*. Princeton UP, 1992.

Browne, Stephen H. "*Remembering Crispus Attucks: Race, Rhetoric and the Politics of Commemoration*." *Quarterly Journal of Speech*, vol. 85, no. 2, 1991. doi: 10.1080/00335639909384252

Chambers, Thomas A. *Drinking the Waters: Creating an American Leisure Class at Nineteenth-Century Mineral Springs*. Smithsonian Institution P, 2002.

Chiles, Katy L. *Transformable Race: Surprising Metamorphoses in the Literature of Early America*. Oxford UP, 2014.

Cocks, Catherine. *Doing the Town: The Rise of Urban Tourism in the United States, 1850–1915*. U of California P, 2001.

Cox, Karen L., editor. *Destination Dixie: Tourism and Southern History*. UP of Florida, 2012.

De Groot, Jerome. *Consuming History: Historians and Heritage in Contemporary Popular Culture*. 2nd edition. Routledge, 2016.

Devlin, Erin Krutko, "Colonial Williamsburg's Slave Auction Re-Enactment: Controversy, African American History and Public Memory." Dissertations, Theses, and Masters Projects, 2003, Paper 1539626387.

———. *Remember Little Rock*. Amherst: University of Massachusetts Press, 2017.

Dickinson, Greg, Carole Blair and Brian L. Ott, editors. *Places of Public Memory: The Rhetoric of Museums and Memorials*. U of Alabama P, 2010.

Dickinson, Greg, Brian L. Ott, and Eric Aoki. "Spaces of Remembering and Forgetting: The Reverent Eye/I at the Plains Indian Museum." *Communication and Critical/Cultural Studies*, vol. 3, no. 1, 2006, pp. 27–47. doi: 10.1080/14791420500505619

Egerton, Douglas, et al. *The Atlantic World: A History, 1440–1888*. Wiley Blackwell, 2007.

Games, Alison. "Atlantic History: Definitions, Challenges, and Opportunities." *The American Historical Review*, vol. 111, no. 3, June 2006, pp. 741–757. doi: 10.1086/ahr.111.3.741

Gassan, Richard H. *The Birth of American Tourism: New York, the Hudson Valley, and American Culture, 1790–1830*. U of Massachusetts P, 2008.

Gilroy, Paul. *The Black Atlantic: Modernity and Double Consciousness*. Harvard UP, 1993.

Halbwachs, Maurice. *On Collective Memory*. U of Chicago P, 1992.

Handler, Richard, and Eric Gable. *The New History in a New Museum: Creating the Past at Colonial Williamsburg*. Duke UP, 1997.

Harvey, Sean. "Ideas of Race in Early America." *American History: Oxford Research Encyclopedias*. Oxford UP, 2016. doi:10.1093/acrefore/ 9780199329175.013.262.

Helmbrecht, Brenda. "Revisiting Missions: Decolonizing Public Memories in California," *Rhetoric Society Quarterly*, vol. 49, no. 5, 2020, pp. 470–494. doi: 10.1080/02773945.2019.1668048

Houdek, Matthew, and Kendall R. Phillips. "Public Memory." *Oxford Research Encyclopedia of Communication*, Oxford UP, 2017. doi: 10.1093/acrefore/9780190228613.013.181.

Kammen, Michael. *Mystic Chords of Memory: The Transformation of Tradition in American Culture*. Knopf, 1991.

Kirilenko, Andrei P., and Svetlana Stepchenkova, "Tourism Research from its Inception to Present Day." *PLOS ONE*, vol. 13, no. 11, 2018, pp. e0206820. doi: 10.1371/journal.pone.0206820

Kytle, Ethan J., and Blain Roberts. "Is It Okay to Talk about Slaves? Segregating the Past in Historic Charleston." *Destination Dixie: Tourism and Southern History*, edited by Karen L. Cox, UP of Florida, 2012, pp. 137–159.

Lee, Jean B. "Historical Memory, Sectional Strife, and the American Mecca." *Virginia Magazine of History and Biography*, vol. 10, no. 9, 2001, pp. 255–272.

Lewer, Brittany. "Reimagining American History Education." The Woodrow Wilson National Fellowship Foundation, May 2019, https://woodrow.org/wp-content/uploads/2019/05/WW-American-History-Report.pdf. Accessed 19 July 2019.

Loewen, James. *Lies Across America: What Our Historic Sites Get Wrong*. Touchstone, 1999.

Lowenthal, David. *The Heritage Crusade and the Spoils of History*. Cambridge UP, 1998.

———. *The Past is a Foreign Country-Revisited*. New York: Cambridge UP, 2015.

MacCannell, Dean. *The Tourist: A New Theory of the Leisure Class*. Schocken Books, 1976.

Mack, Katherine. *From Apartheid to Democracy: Deliberating Truth and Reconciliation in South Africa*. Pennsylvania State UP, 2014.

Mackintosh, Will B. *Selling the Sights: The Invention of the Tourist in American Culture*. New York UP, 2019.

Mulford, Carla. "Introduction" in *Teaching the Literatures of Early America*. The Modern Language Association of America, 1999.

Nash, Gary. *First City: Philadelphia and the Forging of Public Memory*. U of Pennsylvania P, 2006.

Nora, Pierre. "Between Memory and History: Les Lieux de Mémoire." *Representations*, vol. 26, 1989, pp. 7–24. doi: 10.2307/2928520

———, editor. *Realms of Memory: Rethinking the French Past*. Columbia UP, 1996.

Patkose, Margaret, Andrea M. Stokes, and Suzanne D. Cook. *The Historic/Cultural Traveler*. The Travel Industry Association of America, 2003.

Poirot, Kristan, and Shevaun E. Watson. "Memories of Freedom and White Resilience: Place, Tourism and Urban Slavery," *Rhetoric Society Quarterly*, vol. 45, no. 2, 2015, pp. 91–116. doi: 10.1080/02773945.2014.991879

Purcell, Sarah. *Sealed with Blood: War, Sacrifice and Memory in Revolutionary America*. U of Pennsylvania P, 2002.

Ray, Celeste, "Introduction." *Southern Heritage on Display: Public Ritual and Ethnic Diversity Within Southern Regionalism*, edited by Celeste Ray. U of Alabama P, 2003.

Sather-Wagstaff, Joy. *Heritage That Hurts: Tourists in the Memoryscapes of September 11*. Taylor & Francis, 2011.

Schnee, Clara. "One Nation, Two Founding Stories: A Study of Public History at Jamestown and Plymouth." Dissertations, Theses, and Masters Projects, 2011, Paper 1498121.

Schocket, Andrew. *Fighting over the Founders: How We Remember the American Revolution.* New York UP, 2015.
Seelye, John. *Memory's Nation: The Place of Plymouth Rock.* U of North Carolina P, 1998.
Shackel, Paul. "Foreword." *Excavating Memory: Sites of Remembering and Forgetting,* edited by Maria Theresia Starzmann and John R. Roby. UP of Florida, 2016.
Sheller, Mimi, and John Urry. "The New Mobilities Paradigm." *Environment and Planning A: Economy and Space,* vol. 38, no. 2, 2006, pp. 207–226. doi: 10.1068/a37268
Smith, Laurajane. "The Cultural 'Work' of Tourism." *The Cultural Moment in Tourism,* edited by Laurajane Smith, Emma Waterton, and Steve Watson. Taylor & Francis, 2012. 210–234.
———. *Uses of Heritage.* Taylor & Francis, 2006.
Stabile, Susan. *Memory's Daughters: The Materials Culture of Remembrance in Eighteenth-Century America.* Cornell UP, 2004.
Staiff, Russell, Robyn Bushell and Steve Watson. *Heritage and Tourism: Place, Encounter, Engagement.* Taylor & Francis, 2013.
Sterngass, Jon. *First Resorts: Pursuing Pleasure at Saratoga Springs, Newport, and Coney Island.* Johns Hopkins UP, 2001.
Stoltz, Joseph. *A Bloodless Victory: The Battle of New Orleans in History and Memory.* Baltimore: Johns Hopkins UP, 2017.
Tawil, Ezra. *The Making of Racial Sentiment: Slavery and the Birth of the Frontier Romance.* Cambridge UP, 2006.
Tell, Dave. *Remembering Emmett Till.* U of Chicago P, 2019.
Timothy, Dallen J. *Cultural Heritage and Tourism: An Introduction.* Channel View, 2011.
Urry, John. *The Tourist Gaze: Leisure and Travel in Contemporary Societies.* Sage, 1990.
Vivian, Bradford. *Public Forgetting: The Rhetoric and Politics of Beginning Again.* Pennsylvania State UP, 2010.
Watson, Steve, Emma Waterton, and Laurajane Smith. "Moments, Instances, and Experiences." *The Cultural Moment in Tourism,* edited by Laurajane Smith, Emma Waterton, and Steve Watson. Taylor & Francis, 2012. 1–16.
Wheeler, Roxann. *The Complexion of Race: Categories of Difference in Eighteenth-Century British Culture.* U of Pennsylvania P, 2000.
The Woodrow Wilson National Fellowship Foundation. "Woodrow Wilson American History Initiative 50-State Survey Data." Apr. 2019, https://woodrow.org/wp-content/uploads/2019/04/WW-AHI-50-State-Data-Pamphlet-3-20-19.pdf. Accessed 19 July 2019.
World Tourism Organization. *UNWTO Tourism Highlights, 2018 Edition.* Madrid: UNWTO, 2018. doi: 10.18111/9789284419876
World Travel and Tourism Council. "Economic Impact Reports." 2020, https://wttc.org/Research/Economic-Impact. Accessed 20 Oct. 2019.

1 Revisiting the Gateway to Bondage

A comparative study of the landscape preservation and touristic interpretation at Sullivan's Island with Ellis and Angel islands

Barry L. Stiefel

Most Americans are aware that Ellis Island in New York Harbor and Angel Island in San Francisco Bay were the points of entry for millions of immigrants from Europe and Asia, and the throngs of tourists who flock to these historic sites every year come precisely to see this history told to them. However, most Americans are unfamiliar with Sullivan's Island, near Charleston, South Carolina, where roughly between 200,000 and 360,000 enslaved people from Africa were forcibly brought to North America during the transatlantic slave trade of the eighteenth century (Clyburn 8, 176). By some estimates, 40 percent or more of Africans who were brought to North America entered through Charleston's port. An additional number of enslaved Africans were also brought to Charleston into the 1860s through the intercoastal slave trade and transatlantic slave smuggling. While Ellis Island was nicknamed the "Gateway to Freedom" (*Disposal of Ellis Island* 16) and Angel Island designated "the Ellis Island of the West" (Bamford), in a literal sense Sullivan's Island can be dubbed the "Gateway to Bondage" for the role it played in American history, and few tourists come to Sullivan's Island to learn about this past because it is so unknown.

While there have been previous histories of Ellis Island, Angel Island, and even Sullivan's Island, none have explored the interplay between the trio regarding their preservation, heritage value, and tourist experience. Sullivan's Island has been grossly understudied compared to the other two arrival locations of American ancestors and is significant for representing the African contribution to the country's population. According to the 2010 census approximately 42 million people in the United States have at least some African ancestry (Locke and Bailey 105). Indeed, as Toni Morrison commented in a 1989 magazine interview:

> [t]here is no place you or I can go, to think about or not think about, to summon the presences of or recollect the absences of slaves ... no wall, or park, or skyscraper lobby ... There's no 300-foot tower, no small bench by the road that I can visit or you can visit.
>
> (Morrison and Denard A44)

Even today, few tourists visit Sullivan's Island to think and reflect on this bench, which was installed by the Toni Morrison Society's Bench by the Road Project in

DOI: 10.4324/9781003102830-2

2008 as a response to Morrison's harsh critique, let alone engage in other activities related to this episode of the island's African migration history. Instead, visitors come to Sullivan's Island to enjoy South Carolina beach island recreation and are oblivious to the historical significance of this place for people of African descent. Thus, this chapter reveals the neglect of preservation and heritage interpretation of the African arrival experience when there are peer historic sites representing European and Asian immigrant groups as a comparison. The story presented here complicates conceptions of identity, race, and the way public memory related to the greater American arrival experience is presented to tourists, underscoring some of the economic inequality and social injustice in heritage tourism.

Contextualizing Sullivan's Island vis-à-vis Ellis and Angel islands

Athinodoros Chronis and Ronald D. Hampton have found that the public interpretation of places like Charleston is constructed to suit the tourist-based economy, itself based on a romanticized interpretation of the colonial and antebellum periods, ending with the Civil War (111–26). According to Stephanie E. Yuhl, the political elite of Charleston (who came from white privileged backgrounds) were the ones to articulate and shape the historical legacy of Charleston during the 1920s and 1930s, molding it from a private to a public memory that influenced the way visitors and other outsiders came to conceptualize the city. Only in recent years has there been an honest effort to recognize that what the public perceives as what is great about Charleston—the historic ambiance, the cuisine, southern charm, and hospitality—was built on the backs of enslaved Africans and maintained for many decades under Jim Crow rule.

Scholarly interest in the history of Africans arriving at Sullivan's Island during the eighteenth century emerged during the 1980s, as presented by Elaine Nichols in her paper "Sullivan's Island Pest House: Beginning an Archaeological Investigation" given at the Digging the Afro American Past: Archaeology and the Black Experience Conference, at the University of Mississippi. Local historian Suzannah S. Miles also discusses the experience of Africans at the Sullivan's Island pesthouse in multiple works that she self-published from the 1990s to the early 2000s. A "pesthouse" (short for pestilence house) was used to protect a community from infectious diseases, sometimes called a *lazaretto*. Most histories of Sullivan's Island focus on other stories of the island's past, only briefly mentioning the place's role within African migration history (Miles, *The Island* 1–10). The exceptions are Blain Roberts and Ethan J. Kytle, Ana L. Araujo, and Yuhl who present landscape histories of slavery and the built environment, either focusing specifically on Charleston or comparing Sullivan's Island to other significant places where enslaved people were imported, such as Rio de Janeiro, Salvador, and Recife, Brazil; New York City (not Ellis Island); and Jamestown, Virginia. These studies were published between 2012 and 2014, reflecting the growing and continued interest in African American studies. As of yet, no study has compared the preservation accomplishments (or the lack thereof) and visitor experiences of

Sullivan's Island with Ellis or Angel islands together. Charles River and Emmy E. Werner have edited books that were inclusive of Ellis and Angel islands as a pair, but these were not peer-reviewed histories and underscore that scholars have not taken this history very seriously.

River's publication presents an important observation regarding the two better-known immigrant stations:

> Angel Island is often referred to as the Ellis Island of the West, but many argue that they are extremely different in their preservation of immigrant histories. For one, Angel Island took much longer to preserve, and the preservation of Ellis Island focuses on the positive reception of European immigrants on the East Coast, which plays well to corporate sponsors and the American story. Historian John Bodnar explained that Ellis Island represents "the view of American history as a steady succession of progress and uplift for ordinary people." Ellis Island fits nicely into the narrative of the American Dream, because even though the immigrants who came through there were subject to racism, they were predominantly white. Angel Island was a much more multiracial experience, and when recounting its history, the tensions of exclusiveness and xenophobia that existed in the late 19th century and early 20th century are laid bare for all to see.
>
> (River cover abstract)

River does not discuss Sullivan's Island, but his critique has equal relevance to an expanded case that is inclusive of this historic arrival site. Moreover, the preservation and public history interpretation at Ellis and Angel islands have not always been a successful story, with both enduring their own challenges of intolerance. Tourism to Angel Island began in 1954 when a portion of the island was given by the federal government to the California State Park Commission, followed by much of the rest of the island in 1962, but the tourist experience emphasis was at first on outdoor recreational activities. Until 1970, the Angel Island immigration station was under consideration for demolition (Lai 4–5; "Angel Island History Timeline"). After a couple of years of preparation, Ellis Island opened to visitors in 1976, with more than 50,000 tourists in the first year ("Bicentennial: 'Where the Action Was'" 101; "Ellis Island Timeline"). The saving of the Angel Island immigration station and the creation of the Ellis Island tourist experience both coincided with American Independence bicentennial celebration preparations, where preserving historic places and visiting them became increasingly popular during this decade (Rymsza-Pawlowska 139–64). However, many years of political struggle, financial investment, and touristic development would ensue before the creation of the experiences tourists feel today when visiting these sites. In contrast, Sullivan's Island was completely ignored during the 1970s regarding the African arrival history, focusing instead on beach recreation and the American Revolution and Civil War history of former Fort Moultrie. Together, the hardships encountered in the preservation and public history interpretation at all three locations reflect a shortcoming within mainstream American society to embrace peoples who have come here and are culturally different. Additionally, other peoples, such as Indigenous Americans who were here prior to European settlement for thousands of years, as well as Latin Americans who arrived overland across what is now the southern border with Mexico (or experienced a border shift following the Mexican–American War after 1846–8) do not have an officially recognized site that honors their experience of arrival or origins.

Of the three gateway islands for arrival to what is the United States, Sullivan's Island is not only the oldest but also the longest serving, spanning from 1707 to 1799. Ellis Island's immigration station was not established until 1892. It was utilized until 1954, though mass immigration was cut off after 1924. Angel Island served as an immigration station for three decades, from 1910 to 1940. In contrast to the history of Africans arriving at Sullivan's Island, a substantial amount of scholarship exists on the migration experience at Ellis and Angel islands (Cannato; Lee and Yung). The facility at Sullivan's Island was also very different from Ellis and Angel islands because it was a pesthouse and not an immigration station, by technical legal definition. Moreover, Africans did not make the voyage to escape persecution or to find new economic opportunity in America, which is the story that is told at Ellis and Angel islands, but were captives forced to make the Middle Passage for a new life in bondage.

New York and San Francisco were not the only ports of entry for people immigrating from Europe and Asia to the United States, and neither was Charleston for those coming from Africa. Algiers Point, on the opposite side of the Mississippi River from New Orleans' French Quarter, was the point of disembarkation for enslaved Africans in French and Spanish Louisiana. According to Douglas B. Chambers, about 11,000 Africans were imported to New Orleans (186). Most enslaved people in Louisiana were brought from other French or Spanish colonies, or later, other parts of the United States. In the Chesapeake Bay region there was no urban center that slave traders brought Africans to for auction due to the dispersed agrarian settlement of the region. During the legalized transatlantic slave trade most Africans in Georgia came through Charleston/Sullivan's Island, South Carolina, though some arrived directly through Savannah, by way of Tybee Island. Quantifying how many enslaved people were brought from Africa to Georgia is difficult due to the smuggling that occurred here. Between 1801 and 1820 more than 2,000 people from Africa were found illegally trafficked through Georgia's Sea Islands, with the practice known to have lasted as late as 1858 (Morgan 33). Enslaved Africans were brought to mid-Atlantic and New England (and even Canadian) port cities too, but not in the same numbers as we find in the American South where there was a greater economic need for them in the cash crop economy of tobacco, cotton, sugarcane, rice, and indigo. While Sullivan's Island was used from 1707 to 1799, the transatlantic slave trade to South Carolina first ended in 1787 when the state government temporarily outlawed the commerce (the trading of enslaved Africans was still permitted between states), with a brief renewal of the importation of Africans from 1803 to 1807 (Butler). This coincided with the federal government's constitutionally mandated deadline of January 1808, permanently ending the transatlantic slave trade to the United

States. In summary, the horrific number of Africans brought to North American ports in what is now the United States between 1619 and 1807 is estimated at 650,000, with the most significant harbor being Charleston, where 40 percent or more arrived (Northrup 460).

The pesthouse at Sullivan's Island, 1707–99

During the eighteenth century the transatlantic trip from Africa to South Carolina lasted on average two months and the human cargo would likely have been dehydrated and malnourished upon arrival, not to mention terrified of the world they were about to enter and bereaved of the homes and loved ones that they would never see again. Quarantine was mandated to be at least 10 days, sometimes as long as 40 days, in order to ascertain who was sick, healthy, or dead. If the slave ship was too large to safely beach on Sullivan's Island, the newly enslaved Africans who survived the Middle Passage would have been shackled and herded in groups onto smaller watercraft, and ferried from the ship that brought them across the ocean to the pesthouse (Miles, *Island* 11). Ships that brought over enslaved human cargo to the Carolinas and Georgia would vary in size, carrying from a couple of dozen to sometimes more than 500 people (Morgan 33). Quarantine could also take place aboard ship within one mile of the Sullivan's Island pesthouse, with a frequently used anchorage location in front of Fort Johnson. Ship quarantine was generally only conducted when the enslaved cargo and crew were found to be without infectious diseases upon initial arrival (a preferred practice by ship captains). So, in these instances, the newly enslaved would have found themselves exposed to the elements on the main deck of the ship (Lucas). Therefore, the Sullivan's Island quarantine entry point was not exclusive to *terra firma* per se, but also the immediate area on the water within a one-mile radius, extending to the area in front of Fort Johnson on the opposite side of the harbor mouth by James Island.

Quarantine of infectious diseases before modern medicine and germ theory was a serious issue, with outbreaks occurring in Charleston on a periodic basis of two to three per decade starting as early as 1684. In 1728, the smallpox epidemic is specifically identified as having originated from a slave ship, and in 1763 there was an epidemic of smallpox that began among the enslaved Africans, before spreading to white colonists (Nichols 13). The colony's statute from 1752 required that for at least five of the ten days of quarantine the newly enslaved Africans had to be outside for a minimum of six hours during the cooler months and five hours during the summer for purposes of "better purifying and cleansing the said slaves and vessel from any infectious distemper" (Cooper and McCord 773). Failure to comply with these regulations could result in the South Carolina government confiscating the enslaved cargo, though the repeated postings of legislative acts requiring quarantine suggest that there were issues of evasion. Exceptions could only be granted by the Governor or Commander-in-Chief of the militia in the event of hurricane or other imminent dangers (Cooper and McCord 773). During quarantine the survivors of the Middle Passage were given water and food in order to fortify them for auction in Charleston, which during the eighteenth century frequently took place at the wharves along the city's harbor. Europeans coming from exotic places abroad or who were sick also had to undergo quarantine.

The experience of African arrivals on Sullivan's Island—whether on land or confined to the slave ship's main deck for quarantine—also contrasted greatly from Europeans and Asians on Ellis and Angel islands. To begin, upon disembarking from the light watercraft that brought those from Africa ashore there was no great building or hall for processing. Even at Charleston's wharves the auctions frequently took place on outdoor platforms prior to 1808. Few detailed illustrations or descriptions of Sullivan's Island's pesthouse survive, but according to what exists it can be inferred that the facilities were very modest. Between 1707 and 1799 a total of four pestilence houses were located in succession on southwestern Sullivan's Island, which were primarily operated by South Carolina's government (either colonial or state). They were not all built on the same location, but staggered between the contemporary parallel streets of Station 9 and Station 12, spanning a distance of half a mile (Nichols 1–10). The first pesthouse was completed in 1708 and was a 480 square foot brick building of 30 × 16 feet, and was used until 1739 when it was destroyed by a hurricane. A second pesthouse was built near the first one on Sullivan's Island between 1745 and 1747, which was also modest in size as a brick building comprising four small rooms, and without a ceiling, doors, insulation, or windows (Nichols 4, "Pestilence Houses: Immigration in Charleston"). This pesthouse was neglected and fell into disrepair. On September 15, 1752, a hurricane hit Charleston and washed away the second pesthouse several miles up the Cooper River. This lost facility housed 15 unknown persons at that moment, 9 of whom died in this terrible incident, and we do not know if they were white or Black (*The London Magazine* 567). Sometime between 1752 and 1759 a third pesthouse was built to replace the second one lost by hurricane. The third pesthouse was used until the early 1780s, when it fell into disrepair and was replaced by a fourth in 1783–4 which was instead made of lumber (Nichols 5; Miles *The Island* 29). While the precise size of only one of the pesthouses facilities is known, they were all relatively similar—better described as shacks—and at best could only accommodate a very small number of people indoors. Therefore, the lack of preservation and interpretation work at Sullivan's Island about African arrivals due to the absence of extant monumental facilities makes sense, but with the revisited awareness of this historic place the continued neglect of the site is a moral issue because it sanitizes the experience of arriving to this continent. Confronting this painful past on Sullivan's Island also challenges the type of tourism that has been developed at this place, the foundation of this community's current economy. Beachcombers and American Revolution and Civil War buffs—the bulk of visitors—come to Sullivan's Island for a carefree and enlightening experience of recreation or immersion in patriotic celebration. They are not looking for a thanatouristic experience that forces them to engage the dark history of the Middle Passage and slavery; or complicated, soul-searching reflection on the present status of social justice issues in the United States as the legacy of slavery. To change the touristic interpretation of this place to reflect the African experience would potentially threaten this island's economy (Timothy and Boyd 1–16). Therefore, there is little local public interest in exploring or interpreting the African arrival story any further (as of this moment).

When a large brigantine arrived at Sullivan's Island with Africans in the triple digits, or when multiple smaller ships overlapped in their arrival, we must therefore picture this place as one where dozens if not hundreds of enslaved Africans were bound and exposed to the outdoors for a good part of their quarantine (either on land or on the ship's main deck). An account of the quarantine from Peletiah Webster, who visited Sullivan's Island in 1767, describes more than 300 African arrivals being held there who were infected with smallpox (Miles, "Fighting"). This was simply 1 of more than 1,100 slave ships recorded as having unloaded at Charleston Harbor between 1735 and 1775, an average of 1 shipment every 13 days (Ball 190). With this frequency of shipment arrival, it was common for slave ships to overlap during quarantine. The coastal breezes would have kept biting insects at bay, but the land likely would have been compacted and denuded of vegetation from the heavy foot traffic following the visit of a large shipment, and the aroma pungent from the quantity of human waste. The enslaved Africans would have also had minimal clothing. There would have also been bodies to dispose of from those that did not survive the quarantine and were dumped in shallow or watery graves. Fatalities from the Middle Passage would have also been tossed overboard en route at sea.

Sullivan's Island is representative of the dichotomy that Barry Schwartz and Horst-Alfred Heinrich (115–46) describe as the conflict between orthodox and progressive presentations of morality in heritage interpretation. The history of the American Revolution and Civil War, as presented at Sullivan's Island, embraces an absolute definition that the Americans were good and the British were bad— that the Union and Confederate soldiers were in a struggle over federal versus states' rights. Relativism and multiple truths are peripheral, especially with the lack of discussion about slavery and the role this place played in the slave trade for more than a century under the British, Americans, and Confederates. There has been little room for a progressive evaluation of majority oppression, minority subjugation, or a ritualistic apology for tourists to experience and engage ownership over past wrongs. Interpreting the dark public history setting for tourists to Sullivan's Island would be controversial, but the truth is that this was no Gateway of Freedom of "your tired, your poor, your huddled masses yearning to breathe free" (Lazarus)—the people who were brought here and managed to survive this living hell had the very appalling future of a lifetime of chattel bondage. It was in Africa where these people had once been free and most would never see it again.

The erosion of the Charleston pesthouse and the brief use of Point Comfort

In 1776, Fort Moultrie was built near the pesthouse by American rebels to defend Charleston from a British invasion, which the British successfully accomplished in 1780. This is significant because Fort Moultrie—the original eighteenth-century fortifications as well as subsequent versions built on the same location in the nineteenth century—came to overshadow the historical significance of this part of Sullivan's Island through the roles it played in coastal defense from the Revolution through World War II. Also ignored in the interpretation of the Revolutionary War history of the site is that runaway Africans also settled on Sullivan's Island for a period in 1776 in order to harass the American rebels because the British were offering them freedom. During the Revolution years the importation of enslaved Africans was also ceased, and so the story of enslaved Africans as this site during this time period of touristic interpretation is given no space to be represented (Horne 240).

With the Sullivan's Island pesthouse in a dilapidated state in 1799, a new facility was built across the harbor on James Island, ironically at a location called "Point Comfort," relatively near Fort Johnson. According to historian Nic Butler's estimates, after 1804 as many as 75,000 of the enslaved people brought to Charleston Harbor may have actually first set foot on this location (Lucas).[1] On Sullivan's Island was also the emergence of a new settlement, called Moultrieville. The residents of Moultrieville requested the relocation of the pesthouse away from their village. During the 1830s, the pesthouse was relocated again from James Island to Morris Island, also within Charleston Harbor (Miles, *Island* 13). The illegal human trafficking in enslaved Africans that occurred between 1808 and 1861 did not use official pesthouses or other ports of entry, but instead disembarked clandestinely, often in remote or isolated locations along the coast or the navigable areas of rivers.

Contrasting the interpretation of arrival at Sullivan's Island with other locations

According to Katherine Toy, the founding executive director of the Angel Island Immigration Station Foundation, "Angel Island and Ellis Island serve as bookends to the national story of immigration, not only in geography, but also in meaning and experience" (Bayor 135). Toy's assumption is that the American arrival experience of people from abroad is binary, with people either coming from the West or the East, reflecting the strategically located immigrant stations of this time period. But non-Indigenous American migrants came not only from Europe or Asia, but also south—from Africa—and from an earlier point in history. Historians such as Ronald H. Bayor in *Encountering Ellis Island: How European Immigrants Entered America*, as well as Erika Lee and Judy Yung, analyze the visitor experiences on these islands in great detail. In contrast to what is found by visitors at Ellis and Angel islands in New York and San Francisco, none of the pesthouse facilities on Sullivan's or James islands survives.

Charleston also lacks a monumental landmark that speaks to the descendants of Africans who came through its harbor, such as the Statue of Liberty or the Golden Gate Bridge. Instead, Charleston is nicknamed the Holy City due to the church steeples on the city's skyline, representing the religious diversity that defined South Carolina's tolerance of diverse European peoples. While a few of these church steeples represent African American congregations, as a whole the skyline does not communicate a message of African inclusiveness especially when we consider that those steeples built prior to 1865 were erected with enslaved labor. Spanning across the Cooper River, from the City of Charleston to the Town of Mount Pleasant, is the imposing Ravenel Bridge (built between 2005 and 2011), but for those from outside of South Carolina this bridge is not a landmark that represents the city nor an African-origin cultural heritage. The International African American Museum is being planned and developed on old Gadsden's Wharf, a place where an estimated 30,000 enslaved Africans were brought into Charleston either after their quarantine on Sullivan's or James islands or through the intercoastal trade (Collier), but only time will tell if its exterior architecture will become an iconic representation for Charleston's skyline and its associated African American history—the needed landmark that speaks to the descendants of Africans who came through this harbor. Today, Sullivan's Island primarily serves as a recreational, beach island community and is incorporated as its own municipality, and James Island is a twentieth-century suburban extension of Charleston.

Besides Charleston Harbor being the place of disembarkation for more Africans brought over on the Middle Passage than any other place in North America, the area where the Sullivan's Island pesthouse once stood is likely the least disturbed landscape of any African slave disembarkation point located within the proximity of a city. At the southwestern end of Sullivan's Island is the Fort Moultrie historic site (next to where the pesthouses once stood), which is part of the Fort Sumter National Monument managed by the National Park Service, and on federally owned land that may afford future opportunities to consider for interpreting the arrival experience of enslaved people from Africa. The Fort Moultrie historic site and Visitor Center are located between the streets Station 12 and Station 13, just to the east of where the original pesthouses had been located between Station 9 and Station 12. Unfortunately, between Station 9 and Station 12 streets is a scattering of single-family beach housing, so there has been some contemporary development disturbance.

To the east of Fort Moultrie, near the Station 13 and Middle Street intersection, is a free-standing historical bronze plaque that was erected in partnership by the South Carolina Department of Archives and History and the College of Charleston's Avery Research Center for African American History and Culture in 1999 (Figure 1.1). Located next to the Visitor Center are the historic site's parking lot and an adjoining field where on July 26, 2008, the Toni Morrison Society placed its bench on the side of the road to mark the site, along with a small descriptive plaque that states

> placed in memory of the enslaved Africans who perished during the Middle Passage and those who arrived on Sullivan's Island, a major point of entry for Africans who entered the U.S. during the Transatlantic Slave Trade. Nearly half of all African Americans have ancestors who passed through Sullivan's Island.
>
> (Morrison and Denard, *Toni Morrison*)

Revisiting the Gateway to Bondage 27

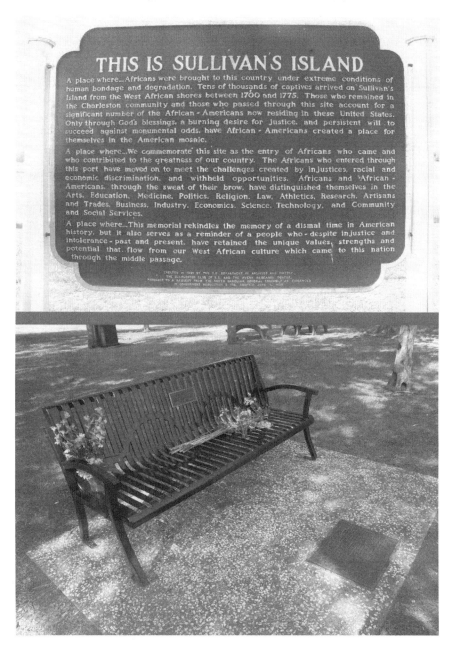

Figure 1.1 The plaque and the bench by the side of the road near Fort Moultrie identifying that this location was where Africans were brought to this country during the eighteenth century. Photographs by the author.

In 2009, a very small exhibit on *African Passages* was opened inside the Visitor Center to interpret Sullivan's Island role within the transatlantic slave trade (Stiefel) (Figure 1.2). As a matter of comparison the *African Passages* exhibit area is smaller than the 480 square feet of space that once comprised one of the pesthouses that had been nearby. This is the extent of the interpretation resources and experience on Sullivan's Island pertaining to the story of the place where so many Africans came to what is now the United States. The combined guesstimate budget is in the tens of thousands of dollars, the historical plaque being paid for by the State of South Carolina, the bench by the Toni Morrison Society, and the *African Passages* by a modest amount allocated from the National Park Service's budget for the Fort Sumter National Monument (the specific amount for this line item could not be found).[2] This shortfall is reflective of what Minoo H. Esfehani and Julia N. Albrecht discuss on how protected areas are "highly dependent on the presence of the local community, their cooperation in governance of the area, and their continuous support of existing resource" (15–29), and that Sullivan's Island boosters (both on and off the island) have selected what history they are prioritizing, which is that of their Euromerican forebears involved in the American Revolution and Civil War, over those of the African oppressed who were only transients on the island. The reason for this, as Esfehani and Albrecht conclude, is that "[t]ourism as a socio-economic driver in protected areas ... causes and

Figure 1.2 The small exhibit *African Passages* at the Fort Moultrie Visitor Center that provides further interpretation of the historical significance of Sullivan's Island to the migration of Africans to South Carolina. Photograph by the author.

requires interaction with local communities and their cultural context" (15–29). Since there are so few African American residents on Sullivan's Island to advocate for their cultural context there continues to be a disconnect between the local community and this aspect of the place's history.

In contrast the Point Comfort pesthouse on James Island, the place at the opposite end of Charleston's harbor mouth where tens of thousands of enslaved Africans were brought between 1804 and 1808 is a problematic site because the facility's location has been completely lost. Algiers Point, Louisiana, is an urbanized inner suburb of New Orleans, so the quarantine station and the rural context that enslaved Africans encountered during the French and Spanish colonial periods have long since been erased. Where the Tybee Island pesthouse in Georgia was located, US Highway 80 was built in 1960, which completely obliterated the brick ruins that survived a hurricane in 1893, as well as disturbing the historic context of the landscape (Sussman, et. al. 20). Within the Chesapeake Bay area there may be surviving remnants of the dispersed rural points where enslaved Africans disembarked as early as 1619, but this would be representative of this region's unique experience. In comparing places in Brazil with the United States, Ana L. Araujo found that "sites of arrival of enslaved Africans remained concealed in the public spaces of former Atlantic ports because most old port areas had become either abandoned, impoverished, or replaced with new construction" (76). Therefore, there is less material fabric to encounter or central places to visit "for bringing physical and spiritual closeness" for visitors to connect to the past, which is essential for preserving the "heritage of the senses," that Chronis advocates as necessary for reflection and identity articulation (267–96). In the case of Charleston's harbor, the specific issue is that the interpretation of war history at Fort Moultrie has eclipsed the story of African arrivals on Sullivan's Island. The beach resort economy of Sullivan's Island has also gentrified the community so that very few African Americans with ancestors who were brought to this place live there as a testament to how they arrived. Charleston's auction sites, such as Gadsden's Wharf, have not only undergone new construction but are also gentrified, displacing many of the previous African American inhabitants with luxury condominiums, city parks, an aquarium, and marina.

The essential person that orchestrated the few interpretive elements at Fort Moultrie on the significance of the site was Michael Allen, and for the purposes of involving the local community in its history. If it was not for Allen's efforts, who was a National Park Service employee (now retired) who went beyond his position's responsibilities, there would likely be nothing for any visitor to learn about this neglected past. Allen rightly received the South Carolina African American Heritage Commission's Lifetime Achievement Award in 2015 (Harriot). Yet, when we evaluate that Sullivan's Island history of African arrival to what is now the United States, which is on par with Europeans through Ellis Island and Asians through Angel Island, what has been established is not nearly enough despite the dark history of the African arrival experience.

While what has been commemorated at the Fort Moultrie historic site on the arrival experience of Sullivan's Island is important, it pales in comparison to what has been invested at Ellis and Angel islands. For example, in 2008 the nonprofit Save Ellis Island and the National Park Service together raised $32 million for "stabilizing and commencing renovation of the buildings" (Janiskee). This is on top of the $162 million spent in the 1990s for previous preservation work at the facility, totaling close to $200 million. According to Bob Janiskee, the preservation of Ellis Island has been "the most expensive publicly funded historic preservation project in U.S. history." A lot of money has been spent for preservation work at Angel Island too, with the State of California investing $60 million between 2005 and 2009, with great attention spent on "restoring the barracks, where many immigrants carved poems into the wooden walls" (The Associated Press).

The preservation projects at Ellis and Angel islands are important causes and money well spent on teaching tourists the arrival experiences at each location. According to the Statue of Liberty–Ellis Island Foundation more than three million tourists currently visit this location annually. The National Park Service has tabulated that the economic impact from these visitors is $364 million, sustaining 3,400 jobs (NPS "Over"). The Angel Island Immigration Station Foundation also reports that 200,000 visitors come to this location per year (Li). National Park Service statistics for attendance to its facilities in Charleston's harbor are between 800,000 and 900,000, but the tourists come to see the Civil War history of Fort Sumter and the Civil War, American Revolution, and World War II history of Fort Moultrie (NPS "Park Statistics"). They do not come to visit the location where the largest number of Africans arrived in North America, and only a very small number of visitors become aware of this significance as presented by the passive and unapparent interpretive historical plaque or small *African Passages* exhibit. As Daniel E. May argues "the conflict between landscape change and historic landscape preservation is not always present. It is important to mention that tourism itself can be a stimulus for landscape change in this paradigm" (186–90), and that perhaps effective change can happen at Sullivan's Island if sincere effort is made that is inclusive of the African arrival experience in order to address this shortfall. The Toni Morrison bench by the side of the road, at the opposite end of the Visitor Center's parking lot, is not frequented very often for its intended purpose of hosting people to contemplate African ancestors. Occasionally, one can find the dried-up flowers left by anonymous locals as a memorial (Stiefel). There is presented here a great social injustice when a disproportionately high amount of taxpayer money has been spent on preserving and interpreting the arrival experience of Americans with European and Asian ancestries to the neglect of those with African origins. Ned Kaufman has stated that "the nation's history as presented at its historic sites as lived by its people lies a significant diversity gap. How should historic preservation present racially, ethnically, and culturally diverse historical experiences? How should it serve diverse constituencies?" (75). The answer in this case on the representative ports of arrival for the ancestors of Americans from other continents is that we must equally fund, support, and value their significance—this is the socially just imperative. This is why we must understand heritage as a process instead of a physical relic (Chhabra and Zhao 94–109); and therefore, values will evolve and change as has emerged recently in the George Floyd protests demanding equality, inclusion, and rhetoric that Black Lives Matter (Bates). From a preservationist's perspective, Black ancestors also matter and they should be honored and respected in appropriate and equivalent ways as European and Asian ancestors are already recognized at Ellis and Angel islands. When we consider this, then Sullivan's Island and its role in the African slave trade merit a new-found value based on the prevalence of such movements, and the potential tourists who will want to come and see such places even if it is a thanatouristic experience (Gibson and Pendlebury 1–18). Besides the pesthouse sites on Sullivan's Island, financial investment for the purpose of preserving this history and interpreting it for the public can also take place at the developing International African American Museum on Gadsden's Wharf since the two locations are so intricately connected to each other.

Conclusion

Sullivan's Island is an idyllic coastal sea island with white sand beaches that looks out upon the crystal blue Atlantic Ocean and Charleston skyline, with its multitude of historic buildings testifying to its antebellum golden age. Fort Moultrie punctuates the tranquil island life of Sullivan's Island by offering a contrasting story of its role in warfare from the very founding of the American Republic, and at the same time, overwhelms and causes the unknowing visitor to be unaware of an even older and very significant part of this nation's history—that this is where 40 percent or more of African American ancestors were brought to this continent. When we become aware of this past, we then have an additional layer of preservation and interpretation complicity when we consider the imbalance of resources invested at peer sites like Ellis and Angel islands, especially regarding the way the sites in New York and California have become such significant tourist destinations. By itself, the improved preservation and interpretation of the African arrival experience on Sullivan's Island will not fix the contemporary issues of racism and bigotry. However, if done strategically, it could help facilitate cross-racial learning, understanding, and respect for the African experience that has often been neglected in American preservation and public history practice, and the message transferred to other places through the visitation involvement of tourists. While Ellis Island represents "the view of American history as a steady succession of progress and uplift for ordinary people," and Angel Island lays bare "the tensions of exclusiveness and xenophobia that existed in the late 19th century and early 20th century … for all to see" (River cover abstract); Sullivan's Island conversely unveils that after more than 150 years American society has so far failed to come to terms with or reconcile the ugly, lasting legacies of slavery, racism, and institutionalized social inequality—and this is something that all tourists who leave this island should come away with knowing.

Notes

1 The 75,000 enslaved people brought to Point Comfort are included within the 200,000 to 360,000 estimate brought to Charleston Harbor as a whole.

2 The amount in 2020 for a State of South Carolina historical marker is $2,200 and the bench by the Toni Morrison Society $5,000. What the costs for these items were respectively in 1999 and 2008 could not be found.

References

"About Ellis Island," *The Statue of Liberty–Ellis Island Foundation*, 2019, https://www.libertyellisfoundation.org/about-the-ellis-island. Accessed 21 March 2021.

"Angel Island History Timeline," *California State Parks*, 2020, https://angelisland.org/wp-content/uploads/2010/04/Angel-Island-Timeline.pdf. Accessed 21 March 2021.

Araujo, Ana L. *Shadows of the Slave Past: Memory, Heritage, and Slavery*. Routledge, 2016.

Associated Press, The. "Angel Island History Center Reopens," *The Denver Post*, 29 January 2009, https://www.denverpost.com/2009/01/29/angel-island-history-center-reopens/. Accessed 21 March 2021.

Ball, Edward. *Slaves in the Family*. Farrar, Straus and Giroux, 2014.

Bamford, Mary E. *Angel Island: The Ellis Island of the West*. Woman's American Baptist Home Mission Society, 1917.

Bates, Karen G. "Similarities And Differences Of George Floyd Protests And The Civil Rights Movement," *National Public Radio*, 4 June 2020, https://www.npr.org/2020/06/04/869952367/similarities-and-differences-of-george-floyd-protests-and-the-civil-rights-movem. Accessed 21 March 2021.

Bayor, Ronald H. *Encountering Ellis Island: How European Immigrants Entered America*: Johns Hopkins UP, 2014.

"Bicentennial: 'Where the Action Was'" *The New York Times*, 16 Dec. 1973, 101.

Butler, Nic. "The End of the Trans-Atlantic Slave Trade." *Charleston Time Machine*, Charleston County Public Library, 26 Jan. 2018, https://www.ccpl.org/charleston-time-machine/end-trans-atlantic-slave-trade. Accessed 21 March 2021.

Cannato, Vincent J. *American Passage: The History of Ellis Island*. Harper Perennial, 2010.

Chambers, Douglas B. "Slave Trade Merchants of Spanish New Orleans, 1763–1803: Clarifying the Colonial Slave Trade to Louisiana in Atlantic Perspective." *New Orleans in the Atlantic World: Between Land and Sea*, edited by William Boelhower. Routledge, 2013, pp. 180–191.

Chhabra, Deepak and Shengnan Zhao. "Present-centered Dialogue with Heritage Representations," *Annals of Tourism Research*, vol. 55, 2015, pp. 94–109. doi: 10.1016/j.annals.2015.09.004.

Chronis, Athinodoros, "Heritage of the Senses: Collective Remembering as an Embodied Praxis." *Tourist Studies*, vol 6, no. 3, pp. 267–296. doi: 10.1177/1468797607076674.

Chronis, Athinodoros, and Ronald D. Hampton. "Consuming the Authentic Gettysburg: How a Tourist Landscape Becomes an Authentic Experience." *Journal of Consumer Behaviour*, vol 7, no. 2, 2008, pp. 111–126.

Clyburn, James E. "Tribute to African Passages" in *Congressional Record: Proceedings and Debates of the 111th Congress, First Session. vol. 155*, part 6. U.S. G.P.O, 2009.

Collier, Melvin J. "Tales Untold," *Family Tree Magazine*, 2019, https://www.familytreemagazine.com/premium/shaped-by-the-slave-trade-charlestons-iaam-museum-tells-the-stories-of-people-and-places/. Accessed 21 March 2021.

Cooper, Thomas, and David J. McCord. *The Statutes at Large of South Carolina: Volume Third, Containing the Acta from 1716, Exclusive to 1752, Inclusive*. A.S. Johnston, 1838. Print.

Disposal of Ellis Island (new York Harbor): Hearings Before the Subcommittee on Intergovernmental Relations of the Committee on Government Operations, United States Senate, Eighty-Seventh Congress, Second Session, Pursuant to Senate Resolution 359, 87th Congress. September 26, December 6 and 7, 1962. U.S. G.P.O, 1963.

"Ellis Island Timeline," *Ellis Island Immigration Museum*, 2020, https://www.statueofliber tytickets.com/Ellis-Island/?show=timeline. Accessed 15 February 2021.

Esfehani, Minoo H., and Julia N. Albrecht. "Roles of Intangible Cultural Heritage in Tourism in Natural Protected Areas." *Journal of Heritage Tourism*, vol 13, no. 1, 2018, pp. 15–29, doi: 10.1080/1743873X.2016.1245735.

Gibson, Lisanne and John Pendlebury. "Introduction: Valuing Historic Environments." *Valuing Historic Environments*, edited by Lisanne Gibson and John Pendlebury. Routledge, 2009, pp. 1–18.

Harriot, Janie. "Kingstree native presented Lifetime Achievement award," *Kingstree News*, 27 Apr. 2015, https://www.kingstreenews.com/news/kingstree-native-presente d-lifetime-achievement-award/article_eb439a2a-e4a0-5a70-9f80-7da924443b38.html. Accessed 21 March 2021.

Horne, Gerald. *The Counter-revolution of 1776: Slave Resistance and the Origins of the United States of America.* New York UP, 2016.

Janiskee, Bob. "At Statue of Liberty National Monument, Save Ellis Island, Inc., Works to Restore Ellis Island's Time-Ravaged Buildings," *National Parks Traveler*, 26 Sep. 2008, https://www.nationalparkstraveler.org/2008/09/statue-liberty-national-monum ent-save-ellis-island-inc-works-restore-ellis-island-s-time-rav. Accessed 15 February 2021.

Kaufman, Ned. *Place, Race, and Story: Essays on the Past and Future of Historic Preservation.* Routledge, 2009.

Lai, H. M. "Angel Island," *Bridge*, vol 5, 1977, pp. 4–6.

Lazarus, Emma. *The New Colossus*. Poem is inscribed on a plaque inside the Statue of Liberty's lower level pedestal, 1903. Originally composed in 1883. Historic site.

Lee, Erika and Judy Yung. *Angel Island: Immigrant Gateway to America.* Oxford UP, 2012.

Li, Han. "Reconstruct and Illuminate: Advancing the Storytelling of Angel Island" (translation of an article which appeared in the World Journal), Angle Island Immigration Station Foundation, 16 June 2019, https://www.aiisf.org/news-articles/storytellingofa ngelisland. Internet. Accessed 15 February 2021.

Locke, Don C., and Deryl F. Bailey. *Increasing Multicultural Understanding.* Sage, 2016.

London Magazine, The. "By Letters from Charles-town." December 1752, 567.

Lucas, Jake. "Doubt cast on S.I. as slave landing point," *Moultrie News*, 24 Aug. 2016, https://www.moultrienews.com/archives/doubt-cast-on-s-i-as-slave-landing-point/a rticle_072c1759-2c79-52dc-98c5-96bfaadede12.html. Accessed 21 March 2021.

May, Daniel E. "Rethinking the Conflict between Landscape Change and Historic Landscape Preservation." *Journal of Heritage Tourism*, vol 11, no. 2, 2016, pp. 186–190, doi:10.1080/1743873X.2015.1047374.

Miles, Suzannah S. "Fighting Illness at Sullivan's Island Pest House," *Moultrie News*, Evening Post Industries Company, 21 Oct. 2014, https://www.moultrienews.com/a rchives/fighting-illness-at-sullivan-s-island-pest-house/article_2398f643-9b97-5c48-b fc3-bc42cecb9b7d.html. Accessed 21 March 2021.

———. *Island of History: Sullivan's Island from 1670 to 1860.* Historic Views, 1994.

———. *The Islands: Sullivan's Island and Isle of Palms, An Illustrated History.* Ross Printing, 2013.

Morgan, Philip D. *African American Life in the Georgia Lowcountry: The Atlantic World and the Gullah Geechee*. U of Georgia P, 2011.

Morrison, Toni, and Carolyn C. Denard. A Bench by the Road. Historical plaque and bench by the Toni Morrison Society, 26 July 2008, Sullivan's Island, South Carolina.

———. *Toni Morrison: Conversations*. UP of Mississippi, 2008.

National Park Service (NPS). "Over 940000 Visitors Came to Charleston Area National Park Sites in 2016," U.S. Department of the Interior, 16 Mar. 2017, https://www.nps.gov/chpi/learn/news/over-940000-visitors-came-to-charleston-area-national-park-sites-in-2016.htm. Accessed 15 February 2021.

———. "Park Statistics," *U.S. Department of the Interior*, 4 Sep. 2019, https://www.nps.gov/stli/learn/management/park-statistics.htm. Accessed 15 February 2021.

Nichols, Elaine. "Sullivan's Island Pest Houses: Beginning an Archaeological Investigation", *presented at the Digging the Afro American Past: Archaeology and the Black Experience Conference*, Oxford, MS: 17–20 May 1989.

Northrup, Cynthia C. editor. "Slavery." *The American Economy: A Historical Encyclopedia, vol. 1, Short Entries*. ABC-CLIO, 2003, 458–465.

"Pestilence Houses: Immigration in Charleston," *For Sumter and Fort Moultrie*, National Park Service, 14 April 2015, https://www.nps.gov/fosu/learn/historyculture/pestilence.htm. Accessed 15 February 2021.

River, Charles. *Ellis Island and Angel Island: The History and Legacy of America's Most Famous Immigration Stations*. Amazon Digital Services LLC, 2019.

Roberts, Blain, and Ethan J. Kytle. "Looking the Thing in the Face: Slavery, Race, and the Commemorative Landscape in Charleston, South Carolina, 1865–2010." *The Journal of Southern History*, vol. 78, no. 3, 2012, pp. 639–684.

Rymsza-Pawlowska, M. J. *History Comes Alive: Public History and Popular Culture in the 1970s*. U of North Carolina P, 2017.

Schwartz, Barry, and Horst-Alfred Heinrich, "Shadings of Regret: America and Germany." *Framing Public Memory*, edited by Kendall R. Phillips, U of Alabama P, 2004, pp. 115–146.

Stiefel, Barry L. 14 Aug. 2019. Site visit to Sullivan's Island.

Sussman, Richard, et. al. *Low Country Gullah Culture: Special Resource Study and Environmental Impact Statement (Public Review Draft)*. National Park Service, December 2003.

Timothy, Dallen J., and Stephen W. Boyd. "Heritage Tourism in the 21st Century: Valued Traditions and New Perspectives," *Journal of Heritage Tourism*, vol 1, no. 1, 2006, pp. 1–16. doi: 10.1080/17438730608668462.

Werner, Emmy E. *Passages to America: Oral Histories of Child Immigrants from Ellis Island and Angel Island*. Potomac Books, 2009.

Yuhl, Stephanie E. "Hidden in Plain Sight: Centering the Domestic Slave Trade in American Public History." *The Journal of Southern History*, vol. 79, no. 3, 2013, pp. 593–624.

———. *The Making of Historic Charleston: A Golden Haze of Memory*. U of North Carolina P, 2005.

2 Remembrance and mourning in the Native mid-South

Florence Indian Mound Museum's past, present, and future

Matthew Duquès and Brian Murphy

> Then thought I, "This must be the grave of one
> Who ranked among the warriors of the
> Wilderness—And when he saw his country
> Doomed, his tribe oerthrown, and his strong arm
> Grown weak before his pale-faced foes
> And when he knew his hour was come in which his soul
> Must leave the form it once had moved to noble
> Deeds, and travel to the hunting-grounds, where erst
> His fathers went, he here had dug his grave
> And singing wild his death-song to the wind
> Sunk down and died!"
>
> —John Rollin Ridge, "An Indian Grave"
> (1847)

Introduction

A wide range of Indigenous tourist sites have, in recent years, been of interest to scholars because they shed light on how American institutions and communities address their complex histories of settler colonization. These scholars have focused their research primarily on casinos, national parks, prominent monuments, and festivals.[1] Left out of the conversation to date are Indian burial mounds. These sacred sites, which are among the few places in the Americas where one can gain a deeper understanding of pre-Columbian Indigenous ecologies, matter to Indigenous people because of their ties to ancestors, homelands, philosophies, and social practices while they tend to matter more to tourists because of their archaeological and spiritual mysteries. The roots of these regularly conflicting perspectives on mounds—perspectives that are strained by the fact that mound provenance tends to be unclear—provide insight into a topic that concerns students of early American history and culture, namely the role of public memory in sustaining systematic racism. For this reason alone, they are important sites to consider. As the editors of *Heritage and Tourism: Place, Encounter and Engagement* note, tourist sites reinforce tourists' preconceived sense of heritage when they meet tourist expectations, or accord with their values as well as their

DOI: 10.4324/9781003102830-3

desires (Staiff, Bushell, and Watson 3). Tourist sites devoted to early American history support this point: when they convey an image of the past that favors tourist groups and their descendants, these groups get an affirming sense of what *their* city, region, or nation represents, a sense that is reinforced by the fact that civic and commercial interests have made this construction of the past public. This relationship between the early American tourism industry and its tourists is political, and it has been responsible for solidifying a pervasive, informal memory of the past that leaves systemic racism unquestioned in the present. Such a dynamic has characterized numerous sites devoted to early American Indian history. Ironically buttressed by a commitment to historical and material authenticity, many of these sites have perpetuated racism by indicating that Indigenous people have vanished, or are destined to vanish, thereby extending the heritage of white settlers who visit them as tourists.[2] This perpetuation is relevant for Indian mounds, as exemplified by "Indian Grave," a short poem by popular nineteenth-century Cherokee author John Rollin Ridge. "Indian Grave" presents a visitor's assumption ("this must be …") leading, without obstacle, to the idea that all Indigenous people are "doomed" to be "oerthrown." Modern histories as well as current operations of mounds suggest that there is much to learn from understanding how site purveyors advance such assumptions, how tourists embrace them, and how both work to collectively question them, in turn, creating public memories that effectively reduce the forms of systemic racism instantiated by the idea that a race of people, fortunately or unfortunately, simply does not belong in a given time and place.

The following essay examines the histories and operations of one such burial mound, a ceremonial Woodland-period mound built nearly 2,000 years ago and located on the Tennessee River in an area of northwest Alabama known as the Shoals.

The mound is adjacent to a public museum, the Florence Indian Mound Museum (F.I.M.M.). The F.I.M.M. is part of a small but unquestionably thriving local tourist industry motored by the area's remarkable late-twentieth century music history. The mound and the museum, in tandem, bring Indigenous and non-Indigenous people together to talk about a much more remote epoch in southern history and to compare that remote past with the present in ways that could help sustain tribal communities and heal persistent racial divisions in the region. Both the mound and the F.I.M.M. have an opportunity, that is, to effect positive change by educating visitors about Indigenous peoples and cultures, and, just as importantly, to share new information about historic and ongoing interracial relations in the region. To better understand why the mound and its museum have struggled to converse about race, in the first section of our essay, we locate the roots of settler misconceptions about Indigenous people in the racial fantasies of mound-building myths. The second part of the essay demonstrates how the evolution of these popular myths, which naturalized the premise that Indigenous people were removable, led locals long after to see the mound as an exotic southern attraction in the mid- to late twentieth century. This prevailing view of the mound, we explain, was facilitated by the mound's uncertain ties to a recognized modern tribal Nation—Choctaw, Chickasaw, Cherokee—making it an ideal site for visitors of all backgrounds to project their racialized fantasies about Indigeneity and for grave robbers to see it as a place to buy arrowheads and other relics. We conclude the essay by showing how the museum's recent programming has helped it begin to address the region's systemic racism.

Mound-builder myths

The F.I.M.M. sits adjacent to a middle Woodland-period (between 2,100 and 1,600 years ago) mound located on the banks of the Tennessee River in what is now the city of Florence, Alabama (Figures 2.1 and 2.2).

Likely first constructed as a burial mound, another layer of earth was added later in the Woodland period, presumably to make the place a ceremonial center. The mound does not appear to have been used during the subsequent Mississippian period, but large population centers were located nearby, suggesting that the area around the mound witnessed considerable activity (Edmond A. Boudreaux and Johnson). In the colonial and early national eras, the Chickasaw hunted in the middle Tennessee River valley around the Muscle Shoals.[3] They did not have any principal village sites in what is now Florence and apparently did not actively use the mound as a burial site or place of worship. But they did have enough control over the area to be considered its proprietors by white settlers who sought out and obtained Florence land through an 1816 treaty with the Chickasaw.[4] This treaty was signed at a moment when Euro-American

Figure 2.1 Postcard of Indian Mound.

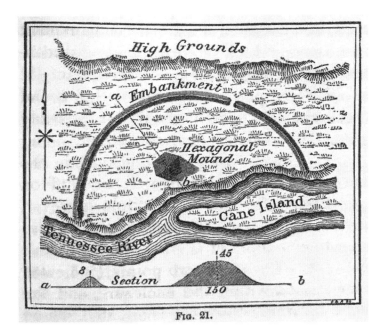

Figure 2.2 Map of the Mound, drawing from Smithsonian's Ancient Monuments of the Mississippi Valley.

immigrants were flocking to the Tennessee River valley, the decade between 1810 and 1820, a period dubbed by historians as "Alabama Fever." The quest for land brought thousands of farmers to the area, most hoping to acquire land to plant and harvest cotton. These settlers correctly identified the mound as manmade. However, they apparently did not see the mound's unknown provenance as an impediment to dividing all of the area's land, including the mound, into salable parcels. From 1818 onward, the mound became a part of the legal, physical, and cultural landscape of Florence.[5]

After the American Revolution, settlers re-examined Indigenous mounds, such as the Florence Indian mound, as a means of officially determining the history of the new nation. Caleb Atwater's account of Ohio mounds, published by the American Antiquarian Society in 1820, was one of the first major contributions to this re-examination. It helped establish the myth of the "mound builder" that would dominate the settler discourse on these ceremonial structures for decades to follow (Hinsley 182). Atwater hypothesized that the earliest Indigenous people came from northern Asia and constructed mounds across what is now the eastern U.S. before moving on to South America. Contemporary Indigenous people, claimed Atwater, were descended from a second wave that arrived more recently from southern Asia (Hinsley 183). The prevailing belief was that the Native

Americans living around Atwater could not have built the mysterious burial structures dotting eastern U.S. landscapes.

From the beginning, the mound-building discourse was racialized, as Euro-American religious leaders implied that the previous "race" was a race of white men. This theory, promoted by Joseph Smith in his *Book of Mormon* (1830), proposed that America had originally been populated by the children of Lehi, who sailed to America around 600 B.C. In Smith's version, Lehi's children split into two groups: the fair-skinned, kind-hearted, agricultural Nephites; and the red-skinned, marauding Lamanites. The Lamanites eventually overran the Nephites (Howey 442). The belief that hostile Native Americans had displaced an entire race of people helped white settlers justify federal and state-based removal policies. In 1832, esteemed white poet, William Cullen Bryant, captured this belief in verse:

> The red man came-
> The roaming hunter tribes, warlike and wild,
> And the mound-builders vanished from the earth.
> The solitude of centuries untold
> Has settled where they dwelt

In Bryant's poem, "mound builders" lived in "solitude" until the "roaming hunter tribes, warlike and wild," violently displaced them. According to anthropologist Meghan C.L. Howey, "the colonial justifications emerging from the Mound Builder myths" promoted by Smith and Bryant, among others, are obvious: "if Indians killed a white race, the white race was justified in killing or removing them" (Howey 443). Andrew Jackson acted on this belief. A champion of removal from its state-sanctioned, 1814 beginning with the infamous "Treaty of Fort Jackson," Jackson owned a plantation near Florence, purchased town lots in Florence, and had close friends who were founders of the city. In seeking support for his Indian Removal Act of 1830, Jackson spoke to Congress in December of 1830 and offered this justification: "In the monuments and fortresses of an unknown people, spread over the extensive regions of the West, we behold the memorials of a once-powerful race, which was exterminated or has disappeared to make room for the existing savage tribes" (Howey 444).

Antebellum and postbellum accounts of the mound suggest that Florence residents never explicitly made the link between a vanished white race and the mound itself. Instead, early chroniclers tied the mound to a brutal idolatry that was not white. The first published account of the Florence mound came from an 1838 article in the *Western Messenger*. Authored anonymously, the article cited Major David Hubbard, Florence resident from 1823 to 1826, as the primary informant. Hubbard provided one of the first-known descriptions of the mound and surrounding wall:

> It was probably a place of worship, a high altar upon which sacrifices were offered to some deity whom the people ignorantly worshipped. On its summit, perhaps, the blood of the victim flowed, and the smoke of the incense

ascended. May not the circular wall have been the place where these people assembled to witness the rites and ceremonies of their religion? This monument of ancient labor and skill I have contemplated with admiration, and busy fancy has pictured to the imagination the scenes which were there displayed in bygone ages—the superstitious rites which were performed, when the darkness of idolatry covered the nations of the earth.

(Ball 55)

Hubbard felt no need to consult a written study of Indigenous mounds, or consider popular theories. His account is useful, not only because it sheds light on features of the mound and wall layout before the latter was destroyed and the former altered through human use, but because it establishes a foundation of *idolatry* that would be used to describe the inhabitants of the mound for the next 150 years.

Epraim G. Squier and Edwin H. Davis penned a Smithsonian Institution publication, *Ancient Monuments of the Mississippi Valley* (1848), that used Hubbard's details but omitted his social assessment and any real theory as to the mound's use. Squier and Davis observe,

it consists of a large mound, hexagonal in form, truncated, and forty-five feet in height by four hundred and forty feet in circumference at the base. The level area at the summit is one hundred and fifty feet in circumference. It appears to be composed of the ordinary surface loam, and is carried up with great regularity. So far as it has yet been examined, no traces of bones or other foreign substances have been discovered.

(Davis and Squier 109)

Squier and Davis paved the way for more "scientific" studies of mound sites in the late 1800s to challenge the racial replacement theory of the early 1800s. Cyrus Thomas's 1894 Bureau of American Ethnology mound survey is one such "scientific" study, an impactful one that nearly put the mound-builder theory to rest. Thomas argued for an evolutionary understanding of Indigenous people as opposed to the "mound-builder" ancient race replacement myth (Hinsley 183). Thomas saw a continuum between the people who built the mounds and current Native Americans. Among other claims, Thomas rejected the idolatry theory put forth by David Hubbard. He equated the burial mound sites to the Euro-centric understanding of special cemeteries. A step in the right direction, Thomas set the stage for later archaeologists and anthropologists.

By this time though, the mound had become so embedded in the landscape of the city of Florence that citizens felt no need to change their assumptions about it. Florentines added "burying ground" of an ancient race of "mound builders" as a descriptor for the mound site. Local residents like Delos H. Bacon, who would later become Mayor of Florence, gave talks about "mound builders" referring to this "interesting race which have left many relics and mounds in the south" and describing "the big Indian mound at the river" as "one of the burying grounds of the Mound Builders" (Bacon 4). Cyrus Thomas's theory of an Indigenous continuum had not yet been accepted in Florence. Consequently, while the mound was thought to be a cemetery, it did not stop locals from farming the entire area—including the mound itself. The mound as a legal entity—a plot of land to be owned, lived on, and farmed—was not questioned. By the late 1800s, John Kachelman, a Bavarian immigrant, had built a house on top of the mound and planted crops around the base and sides of the mound. Due to sharp winter winds atop the mound, Kachelman relocated his house to the base of the mound and continued to farm the area. The mound was used as a garden or farm land until the 1930s (Boudreaux and Johnson 90). By 1890, E.F. Zinn continued what became known as the "Mound Garden." Zinn had a "model garden and truck farm" where he grew produce and sold it to local residents (*Herald* 3). This kind of mound-as-garden concept was not unique to Florence. It could be found in practice across the region as it was an effective way of maximizing the land resources in the Tennessee River valley—a byproduct of the larger cotton-dependent economy. Citizens followed this model, but they were also clearly aware that the mound had to be treated differently from regular farm land. Kachelman, for instance, did not permit the mound to be "touched" and refused to sell it even for large amounts of money (Boudreaux and Johnson 90).

The early twentieth century brought further speculation about the people who built the mound, speculation which would fuel an interest in tourism. A 1924 Smithsonian Fieldwork report commented on the Florence mound and claimed it was "the foundation of a sun-fire temple" (*Smithsonian* 99). While the meaning of "sun-fire temple" is not clear, it is different from the local belief that it was a "mound-builder" graveyard. Importantly, this is the first reference to a "temple" on top of the mound, and this interpretation of the mound lasted for nearly all of the twentieth century. Within the Smithsonian report is another reference to preservation. The report states,

> the present owner of this mound is thoroughly alive to its value as an asset to the two cities, Florence and Sheffield, and has opposed efforts to cart it away for roads. Its value as a landmark is much greater than the value of the contents for building causeways or roads.
>
> (*Smithsonian* 99)

Valued as a garden, but also coveted for its dirt, alleged to contain a "sun-fire temple," or the bodies of an "interesting race," the Florence mound elicited a variety of race-based fantasies. These fantasies, which often translated into racist attitudes, inspired increasing numbers of locals and visitors to check out the site and to spread word about this attraction across the mid-South.

Self-determination era exoticism

During the 1940s, local discourse shifted toward preserving the mound as a historic site, a shift that would lead to the mound becoming a tourist site. This move toward preservation-thinking aligned with a gradual change in federal Indian policy: U.S. termination policies had been in place to eliminate governmental assistance to, and recognition of, Native people, to dismantle Native sovereignty and provenance, and to exploit Native resources. Termination would be phased out by the end of WWII, replaced by policies of so-called self-determination, which underscored the value of Indigenous national autonomy and, at least on paper, the sanctity of Native traditions. Self-determination, in theory, recognized tribal governments, promoted individual and reservation community self-sufficiency, returned stolen Indigenous lands and artifacts, and helped maintain sacred sites. As Mark Rifkin explains, while these policies were less explicitly threatening than their forebears, they nevertheless "disabled the acknowledgement of legacies of trauma and violence while also enacting new modes of displacement and erasure" (Rifkin 2).

In Florence, as the mound began to develop into a tourist site—propelled by the city's investment in preservation—it followed the logic of erasure that unfolded nationally under federal self-determination policies, as evidenced by new theories of the site belonging to a different group of "mound builders." Mrs. R.S. Dabney, whose family owned the land around the mound, "donated" the mound to the city in 1945 with the caveat that the site be "preserved and used in a manner that would be in keeping with its historical value" (Lauderdale Deed Book 182). The deed itself showed that the people of Florence's limited knowledge of what the mound was corresponded initially with their investment in transforming the mound into a civic entity. The legal description of the mound displays the initial indecision: "the land herein undertaken to be described is an ancient Indian Monument spoken of as an Indian mound." Uncertainty in terminology and in authority ("spoken of" by whom?) led to a note in the deed: the property must be used "for the benefit of the public and to be used for park purposes and historical and educational purposes only." A year later, the interpretation of the mound shifted toward a known entity, the Cherokee, and this shift conspired to add potential entertainment value to the site, introducing the prospects of the civic and commercial elements of tourism. A radio station was constructed near the foot of the mound in 1946 as the community was still determining exactly what to do with the entire site. According to a newspaper article published in response to the new station, the site was a fit location for broadcasting as the "Cherokee Indian mound, thought to be a temple mound" once "echoed with the voices of the red men and the sound of their tom-toms as they worshipped the great sun god and made their sacrificial offerings with absolute faith" (Bailes 6). The site would now echo with another set of voices. No longer a graveyard for an ancient race, the mound took on an exotic connotation, despite the familiarity of the Cherokee in the area. The article ends: "the Indians are gone from the banks of the Tennessee, but they have left their secrets, 'pointing mutely from the present to the ages long forgotten, to a well-nigh vanished race.'" No longer a threat to the U.S., the region, or the city, the Cherokee, a tribe whose members live all over the mid-South to this day, are, consequently, romanticized by people whose ancestors had contributed to their removal. The seamless passage of the mound into, and then just as quickly out of, Cherokee provenance (on account of the fact that they have supposedly vanished for good) in this article bespeaks an underlying racism expressed through the white communities' touristic interest in capitalizing on sensationalized stories about the mysteries of *their* Indian roots.

Post-removal romanticization is a concept that permeates Shoals Native American heritage tourism to this day in ways that acknowledge Indigenous provenance and historical injustice while also ignoring or simplifying living Indigenous people and nations. A sense of loss for the Indigenous people on whose land, homes, businesses, roads, and structures in the Shoals have been built is expressed through public activities such as the annual Trail of Tears Commemorative Motorcycle Ride. This tourist event draws thousands of riders each year through Florence and across the mid-South and seeks to honor the Cherokee, Choctaw, Chickasaw, Creek, and Seminole nations without including meaningful participation from said nations.[6] Other tourist-related public commemorations in Florence illustrate this romanticization, but none more so than the city-wide use of the branding phrase, "singing river." Florence boasts a Singing River Bridge, Singing River Brewery, Singing River Statue. Other sites and businesses throughout the Shoals have also adopted the phrase. Singing river is said to be the English translation of what the "Indians" first called the Tennessee River. More specifically, the name comes from the Euchee tribe, erstwhile residents of the area, who believed that the river sounded like a "female chorus" (Reali 244). This legend was featured at the beginning of the highly acclaimed documentary about the area, *Muscle Shoals* (2013), where it was used to provide charming context to suggest a possible origin for the remarkable mid- to late-twentieth century production of popular music in the area's now world-famous sound studios. City officials and local businesses were quick to use the phrase to improve the quad-city's struggling economy, largely by promoting small, local businesses and tourism. Ubiquitous now, the term lends a mysterious, natural quality to places and services, even as it papers over American Indian dispossession and hides the fact that the Tennessee River is notorious for its high content of microplastics and mercury.

Perhaps nobody has done more, wittingly or unwittingly, to popularize the "singing river" brand than Tom Hendrix. Tom passed away in early 2017 at the age of 83 after spending nearly 30 years constructing a monument to his great-great-grandmother, a Euchee woman who was forced to travel to Indian territory but missed the "singing river" so much that she returned on her own. Tom's monument to his great-great-grandmother is the largest un-mortared rock wall in the nation and the largest memorial to a Native American woman. "Tom's Wall," as it is referred to locally, has now become a popular tourist destination, and Tom's story has been accepted by much of the community and its visitors. Romanticized versions of Indigenous history, words, and stories such as Tom's continue to tincture Florence daily life, its heritage, and, of course, its tourism.

Before the commemorative Trail of Tears event was established and the "singing river" name popularized, the F.I.M.M. helped introduce Florentines to these romantic "Indian" branding strategies—these ways of promoting a place, or various sites therein, using the trappings of an entire race of people while largely ignoring the living ancestors of those people. The F.I.M.M. opened in 1968, a year when policies of self-determination were still being implemented across the U.S. That year the city purchased the radio station at the foot of the mound and converted the space into a museum. At this time, the narrative about the mound's origins had shifted yet again. No longer assigned to the Cherokee, the mound was now believed to have been used for a "temple, a council house, a chief's house, or even an altar." With the opening of the museum, the Florence mound was subject to a promotional phase, as the city sought to draw attention to this "local attraction." An historical marker was erected at the base of the mound; concrete steps were built to the top of the mound where a picnic table was placed; and a plaque was fixed atop the mound to commemorate the white people who "donated" the mound to the city. Promotion of the F.I.M.M. centered around the phrase: "Tennessee Valley's Largest Domiciliary Mound," an allusion to the likely erroneous belief that people had once lived on top of the mound. An early brochure described the mound as a "typical example of the work of those mysterious early Indians who discovered Alabama." The brochure explained that the museum's exhibits "depict in chronological order the Paleo, Transitional, Archaic, Woodland and Mississippian age of the Redman." To add to the site's "mystique," early museum pamphlets often attach the name "Wawmanona" to the mound, claiming that the name came from the "Indians." It is not clear which "Indians" the pamphlets refers to, and no origin for this name has been identified. But the name adds an authentic air to the mound, as if it had been adopted by real "Indians." Such a pretense of Indigenous authenticity helped the museum garner tourist interest, but the effect was not simply to get tourists interested in visiting the site and seeing it as part of their birthright; it also attracted interest among artifact collectors with very specific aims of extending their heritage in mind. Into the 2000s, pamphlets promoted the museum as "Ancient. Authentic. Historic" (Figure 2.3).

The "authentic" claim in this promotion is a direct link to the monetary valuation of artifacts by collectors. Authentic in this context refers to artifacts made by Indigenous people prior to roughly 200 years ago, when Native Americans were forcibly removed from the Shoals area. These artifacts can be extremely valuable; a local legend asserts that one projectile point was sold by a Shoals area collector for $150,000. The valuation of tools, bowls, pipes, axes, etc., in monetary terms, has no place in the language, curation, and programming of the current museum. This message, however, is not universally understood. Perhaps the most egregious description of this authentic artifact fetish is the one on the Florence-Lauderdale Tourism website, which reads: "the mound rises from history—43 feet high, the largest trove of ancient tools, pottery, jewelry, and pipes in Alabama." The description continues, "climb the steps yourself, wondering if Indian priests and chiefs mounted them too, reaching for the sun." This flowery description reduces the tourist site to a "trove" of materials valuable to twenty-first-century white visitors. The artifacts are thus valued by rarity and monetary worth—and not for what they tell us about the people who made them or used them. Furthermore, this separation of the people from their artifacts serves the Euro-centric view that artifacts, cultural remains, burial mounds, and ceremonial centers can and should

Figure 2.3 Florence Indian Mound Pamphlet, Florence Department of Arts and Museums.

be owned by private, non-Native entities. Tourist promotions conclude by catering to white tourists' desires to think about "Indian" ways, a break from a tired and tedious modern reality that ultimately firms up their sense of themselves as different and better owners of Indigenous places.

During the last three decades of the twentieth century, amateur white archaeologists, not Indigenous people, were the major stakeholders at the F.I.M.M. The interpretation of the mound during this time focused on the Mississippian-era Indigenous cultures that were known to build large, flat-topped mounds. Because these ancient peoples predated the Cherokee and other Native Americans, it was possible for the activities associated with the museum to be seen as outside the realm of contemporary politics and culture. The museum had little, if anything, to do with the late-twentieth-century American Indian Movement (A.I.M.), or with the outpouring of self-determination era Native American literature, as the museum was devoted to stoking up feelings in whites for a romanticized bygone world to which current tribes likewise had little connection (Dunbar-Ortiz). Of course, this presumptive and, in many cases, actual disconnect between the Mississippian past and modern Indian nations was itself the result of an era of Removal that had, in the southeast, forcibly separated tribes from sacred places and traditions. On the basis of this national disjuncture, Indigenous people organized, wrote, and resisted while the museum became a safe haven for white collectors whose artifact gathering (also called "arrowhead hunting") became a very popular pastime in the Shoals, akin to backcountry, local touristic plundering.

For many Florentines, the "thrill of owning a piece of history," or holding something crafted thousands of years ago is the driving force behind this hobby. For others, artifacts can be sold for serious money. Unfortunately, the F.I.M.M. played an unethical role in the distribution of artifacts from the Shoals area. Artifacts were brought to the museum to be appraised, sold, or traded. Undermining the ethical obligations of museums, this system of reckless exchange went on for years and has only recently been prohibited. In keeping with this practice, if not facilitating it, the museum also acted insensitively towards Native Americans. Before 1979, collecting artifacts was legal on federal property (most of the riverbanks and islands in the middle Tennessee River valley are owned by the Tennessee Valley Authority, a federal agency established in 1933 to help manage the resources of the Tennessee River). The passage of the Archaeological Resources Protection Act (A.R.P.A.) in 1979 helped to curb the collection of artifacts from along the banks of the Tennessee River. The A.R.P.A. helped and continues to help prevent looting of Indigenous materials by forbidding the excavation or removal of archaeological resources from federal or Indian land without a permit from a land managing agency. The A.R.P.A. was particularly impactful in the Florence area.

The effort to curtail practices associated with Indian exoticism helps us understand more recent perceptions of the mound. Amateur collectors today view the mound as a potentially valuable source of artifacts that can be added to their collection or sold for great cost based on their rarity, workmanship, and authenticity. Regardless of what they do with their findings, these collectors tend to see the site as an opportunity to pretend to be, or "play" Indian, to use Phil Deloria's term. Their uncritical accumulation of material goods allows them to act out fantasies of Indigeneity, which prohibit them from learning anything about the Native people who came before them, much less those who live in their vicinity today. Archaeologists, in contrast, continue to be interested in the mound for what it can tell us about past cultures based on material remains. They typically see the actions of collectors as unsavory means of taking artifacts from their contexts, thereby depriving the professional community of a chance to study how these items relate to larger spheres of culture, environment, and habitat. For example, the result of the collectors' actions, according to archaeologist Robert Mallouf, is "a pile of objects having little or no meaning, often stored in cigar boxes in a garage or carefully mounted in geometric patterns and hung on a living room wall" (Mallouf 200). Many Indigenous people have a different perspective from either the collectors or the archaeologists. They value the mound for personal, familial, and tribal reasons. Their reaction to stolen artifacts is, as Mallouf puts it, "beyond comprehension." These three groups' perceptions of the mound index how early American tourist sites function as sites for upholding, yet also potentially critiquing or questioning, the belief systems—racist or otherwise—fostering public memory.

Complicating these differing views of the mound in Alabama is the fact that most Native Americans were forcibly removed from the state and, thus, from these cultural items. Just 0.4 percent of the population of Lauderdale and neighboring Colbert Counties are listed as Native American in the 2010 census. But among the collectors, the vast majority of whom are white, there is a tendency to minimize Indigenous suffering, sovereignty, and resistance and to establish their right to pilfer and loot artifacts based on asserted but never verified claims of Native ancestry, typically a distant Cherokee relation. In other words, whites who claim Indigenous ancestry acquire a presumptive pass for the collection of artifacts that belong to "their ancestors." On account of such typically unsubstantiated claims, collectors often have no problem speaking for Native Americans, whom they feel should not be offended by the pilfering and looting of artifacts in the lands from which their ancestors were removed. This facility with representing Indigenous people filters into the culture of the museum, making white site purveyors and white tourists feel even more at home in this Indigenous place. Claims of Cherokee ancestry, it is important to note, are hardly irrelevant here. There was, at one time, a village belonging to the Chickamauga Cherokee located in the Shoals. That said, the majority of Cherokee claims made today are not motivated by a desire to understand the history of that village or to connect to family and kinship history, and engage in cultural practices through the Cherokee language. Rather, these claims are part of a broader cultural fascination with authenticity. According to historian Gregory D. Smithers, "shifting one's identity to claim ownership of an imagined Cherokee past is at once a way to authenticate your American-ness and absolve yourself of complicity in the crimes Americans committed against the tribe across history" (Smithers). By melding purported Cherokee, or other alleged tribal national identity with artifact-collecting, white Alabamians whitewash history. They do so in order to justify their loot and firm up their provenance in the Native South, effectively carrying on a racist legacy that had its roots in the nineteenth-century epoch of federal removal, yet took on a new sheen as the F.I.M.M. became a local tourist fixture in the era of self-determination.[7]

Twenty-first-century collaborations

Recently, several federally recognized tribes with ties to Alabama and the mid-South have turned to existing historic preservation laws for inclusion in matters concerning the homelands and materials of their ancestors. Government agencies are now required to consult with federally recognized tribes on projects that may disturb burials and sacred sites outside of Indian land. The Chickasaw Nation has started the Chickasaw Explorers Program to train young Chickasaw leaders in archaeological methods.[8] In these ways, federally recognized tribes like the Chickasaw are paving the way for collaborative work between Indigenous people, museums, and archaeologists outside of tribal land. Collaboration with different tribes was not always a priority at the F.I.M.M. In the past, a human skeleton was put on display. It remained on display until 2015, well after most museums had removed human remains from their collections (Colwell). While the skeleton has been removed, the scarring from such a display will take time to heal. Illustrating the degree to which such tourist displays of supposed "Native" authenticity shape public memory, white visitors often lament the removal of the skeleton, which many remember from grade-school trips to the museum in the past. Through the repatriation of human remains once housed within the museum, the F.I.M.M. has started taking steps that will ideally allow for new opportunities for collaboration with representatives and groups from Native American nations. For example, to strengthen the collaboration among federally recognized southern tribes, archaeologists, and the museum, the F.I.M.M. has started a chapter of the Thousand Eyes Archaeological Stewardship program, which was created by the Tennessee Valley Authority to help monitor endangered archaeological sites on T.V.A.'s property. The Thousand Eyes program is built on the premise that preservation is in the public interest. Volunteers visit sites and make sure that looters are not removing cultural artifacts and that environmental destruction is not taking place. The museum serves as a hub for the Thousand Eyes group and fosters a sense of archaeological stewardship through programming that promotes responsible practices (Pritchard 304).

Another area that the F.I.M.M. has improved in is in its gift shop. Prior to 2018, the gift shop still carried items that overtly stereotyped Native Americans. From slingshots and noisemakers with Native American faces, to drums and whistles that evinced a Native American focus, the items in the gift shop ranged from outright racist materials to all-too-common, subtle forms of cultural appropriation. While this merchandise may seem like a minor point since the central subject of the site is the mound itself, gift shops do play a crucial role in commodifying the tourist experience, particularly if that experience is already tinctured by artifacts that are, in the minds of tourists, already seen as commodities. Shops, in these instances, swiftly turn the intangible features of a shared or personal tourist memory into a tangible item that can reinforce said memory. The present gift shop is working to change the sense of heritage it conveys by featuring many more educational resources, specifically books, including books by Native American authors and scholars and historians. The museum, for example, purchases books and DVDs from the Chickasaw Press and sells both in its gift shop. While the museum still does carry many non-Native items, it is working to continue to identify Native American vendors and craftspeople and to carry those items in the gift shop. In addition, the F.I.M.M. hosts Indigenous storytellers and dancers as part of the annual Oka Kappassa celebration, in which Chickasaw people return to the Shoals area for a weekend of celebration. Recently, the museum also took steps to create an advisory board made up of members of federally recognized tribes to help guide the F.I.M.M.'s focus in regard to the gift shop, programming, and exhibits. The F.I.M.M. hopes to strengthen its connections to the Native American tribes that have been removed from the area in order to incorporate their voices into the museum's narrative by working with tribal historians on exhibit panels contextualizing Removal from a native perspective, and exploring the conditions and incidents members of different tribes faced upon arriving in their new homeland west of the Mississippi.

The F.I.M.M. realizes that it has an obligation to investigate its own history and to take an honest look at its past and current actions. Future steps the F.I.M.M. hopes to enact include removing the utility poles from the mound site; acquiring more land surrounding the mound and the museum to protect potential archaeological sites from destruction; and increasing space to install interpretive panels. The museum is focused on being a good steward of the Indigenous cultural histories of the site and the area and has now become more than a traditional museum. It is a community center, focused on education, environmental and archaeological stewardship, and the cultural history of Native Americans in the Shoals area. Reconciliation is a process that takes time; the F.I.M.M. is looking to take an active and open role in that process by acknowledging its past and working collaboratively towards a better future.

Notes

1 Lisa Ruhanen and Michelle Whitford, "Cultural Heritage and Indigenous Tourism" in *Journal of Heritage Tourism* Vol. 14 (2019) Issue 3 179–91; and Bryan S.R. Grimwood, "Settler Colonialism, Indigenous Cultures and the Promotional Landscape of Tourism in Ontario Canada's 'Near North'" in *Journal of Heritage Tourism* Vol 14 (2019) Iss. 3. 233–48.
2 For pertinent studies linking quotidian views of Indians to modern-day racism see Phillip J. Deloria, *Playing Indian* (New Haven: Yale University Press, 1998) and *Indians in Unexpected Places* (Lawrence: University of Kansas Press, 2004).
3 The Muscle Shoals were a series of shallow rapids that extended roughly 40 miles in the Tennessee River between present-day Decatur and Florence, as the river flowed over a bedrock of erosion-resistant chert. The Shoals were historically unnavigable and created a natural geographic barrier along the Tennessee River. Two canals and a railroad were built to steer commerce around the Shoals before a series of dams created by the Tennessee Valley Authority in the 1930s finally obscured this defining feature of the river.
4 The 1816 Treaty of Chickasaw Council House, negotiated between Chickasaw leaders and Andrew Jackson, saw the Chickasaw cede land on the north and south sides of the Tennessee River in what is now northwest Alabama.
5 The mound is currently preserved and protected by the city of Florence, and the museum falls under the city's management. It stands 43 feet in height and has a flat top that measures roughly 145 by 95 feet. The mound itself was once surrounded on three sides by an earthen wall that reached a height of 12 to 15 feet.
6 The Trail of Tears Commemorative Motorcycle Ride is not supported by any of the federally recognized tribes with claims to the Shoals area.

7 Many people who claim Cherokee ancestry will readily assert the horrors of the Trail of Tears; some will use this tragedy to diminish the brutality of southern American slavery.
8 "Chickasaw Explorers Program," Chickasaw.net, https://www.chickasaw.net/Services/Chickasaw-Explorers-Program.aspx, accessed September 12, 2019.

References

Bacon, Delos H. "Will Lecture on the Mound Builders." *Florence Herald*, March 4, 1897, 7.
Bailes, Mary H. "New Meets Old In Shadow Of Mound." *Florence Herald*, June 14, 1946, 2.
Ball, Donald B. "Notes on an 1838 Account and Map of the Florence Mound." *Journal of Alabama Archaeology*, vol. 59, no. 1, 2013, pp. 97–153.
Boudreaux, Edmond A. and Johnson, Hunter B. "Test Excavations at the Florence Mound: A Middle Woodland Platform Mound in Northwest Alabama." *Journal of Alabama Archaeology*, vol. 46, no. 2, 2000, pp. 87–130
Colwell, Chip. *Plundered Skulls and Stolen Spirits: Inside the Fight to Reclaim Native America's Culture*. U of Chicago P, 2017.
Davis, Edwin H. and Squier, Ephraim. *Ancient Monuments of the Mississippi Valley*, Washington, D.C., 1848.
Deloria, Phillip J. *Playing Indian*. Yale UP, 1998.
Dunbar-Ortiz, Roxanne. *An Indigenous Peoples' History of the United States*. Beacon Press, 2015.
"Explorations and Field-work of the Smithsonian Institution in 1924." Washington D.C., pp. 99.
Florence Indian Mound Pamphlet, Florence Department of Arts and Museums, Circa, 2000.
"Florence Indian Mound and Museum," *Florence-Lauderdale Tourism*, https://www.visitflorenceal.com/directory/florence-indian-mound-and-museum/. Accessed 11 June 2020.
Grimwood, Bryan S. R. "Settler Colonialism, Indigenous Cultures and the Promotional Landscape of Tourism in Ontario Canada's 'Near North'." in *Journal of Heritage Tourism* vol 14 no. 3, 2019, pp. 233–248. doi: 10.1080.1743873X.2018.1527845
Hinsley, Curtis M. "Digging for Identity: Reflections on the Cultural Background of Collecting." *American Indian Quarterly: Special Issue: Repatriation: An Interdisciplinary Dialogue*. vol. 20, no. 2, 1996, pp. 181. doi: 10.2307.1185699
Howey, Meghan C.L. "'The question which has puzzled, and still puzzles': How American Indian Authors Challenged Dominant Discourse about Native American Origins in the Nineteenth Century." *American Indian Quarterly*, vol. 34, no. 4, 2010, pp. 435. doi: 10.5250.amerindiquar.34.4.0435
"Indian Mound is Donated to City by Mrs. Dabney." *The Florence Times*, March 2, Florence, 1945, 1.
Lauderdale County Deed Book 352, Florence, 1945, pp. 182.
Mallouf, Robert J. "An Unraveling Rope: The Looting of America's Past."*American Indian Quarterly*, vol. 20, no. 2, 1996, pp. 199. doi: 10.2307.1185700
"Personal," The Florence Herald (Florence, AL), May 3, 1890, p. 3.
Pritchard, Erin E. "The Future of Archaeology and Stewardship at TVA." in *TVA Archaeology*, edited by Erin Pritchard and Todd Ahlman, U of Tennessee P, 2009, pp. 299–308.
Ruhanen Lisa and Whitford Michelle. "Cultural Heritage and Indigenous Tourism" in *Journal of Heritage Tourism* vol. 14 no. 3, 2019, pp. 179–191. doi:10.1080.1743873X.2019.1581788

Reali, Christopher. "Muscle Shoals." *The New Encyclopedia of Southern Culture*, vol. 24, edited by Thomas C. Holt, Laurie B. Gree, and Charles Reagan Wilson, U of North Carolina P, 1996.

Ridge, John Rollin. "Indian Grave" *Changing is not Vanishing: A Collection of American Indian Poetry to 1930*, edited by Robert Dale Parker, U of Pennsylvania P, 2011, pp. 70.

Rifkin, Mark. *Erotics of Sovereignty: Queer Native Writing in the Era of Self-Determination*. U of Minnesota P, 2009.

Smithers, Gregory D. "Why do so Many Americans Think they have Cherokee Blood?" *Slate.com*, 1 October 2015, https://slate.com/news-and-politics/2015/10/cherokee-blood-why-do-so-many-americans-believe-they-have-cherokee-ancestry.html. Accessed September 12, 2019.

Staiff, Russell, Robyn Bushell, and Steve Watson, editors. *Heritage and Tourism: Place, Encounter, Engagement*. Routledge, 2013.

Tributaries of the Muscle Shoals Heritage Area, Commissioned by the Muscle Shoals Heritage Society, Circa 1970.

3 Remembering and forgetting plantation history in Jamaica
Rose Hall and Greenwood Great House[1]

Cathy Rex

When most people imagine a vacation to Jamaica, they often picture things like lounging on a pristine beach at an all-inclusive resort, eating jerk chicken and drinking rum punch, listening to reggae, and perhaps enjoying some adventurous activities, like hiking to a waterfall or parasailing above the turquoise waters of the Caribbean Sea. In short, they imagine "getting away from it all" and having a deluxe tourist experience. They typically do not imagine focusing on the fraught colonialist history of slavery and the sugar trade that shaped Jamaica into Britain's wealthiest colony by the start of the American Revolution; legacies that to this day still define the country in many ways.[2] As a result of this history, Jamaica has a surprising number of great houses—plantation homes—that are open to the public for touring and events, such as weddings and receptions. The 2017 *Lonely Planet Guide* to Jamaica, for example, lists 11 different great houses around the island that are open to the public for tours, meals, or even overnight stays. The Jamaican National Heritage Trust has declared 30 different great houses as national monuments across the island, although neither of these numbers accounts for great houses that have not yet passed the National Heritage Trust's assessment, remain closed to the public, or lie in partial ruins ("Greathouses" [sic]).[3] The number of these plantation homes on an island the size of Jamaica—a country slightly smaller in land mass than the state of Connecticut—is a testament to the overwhelming domination of the sugar industry, slavery, and the plantation economy that directed the island's development. However, despite this, many tourists don't visit these historic homes—or if they do, they do so selectively—because Jamaica's tourist industry, for the most part, shies away from addressing this legacy of chattel slavery.

The tourist industry, which is Jamaica's top source of revenue—tied with remittances from expatriates, and then in descending economic importance: agriculture, bauxite and alumina mining, and manufacturing—works to cultivate an image of Jamaica as a "sun, sea, and sand" getaway with a "No problem, mon" attitude.[4] According to the Jamaica Tourist Board, tourism brings in nearly four million visitors a year because of year-round activities and the balmy tropical climate ("Tourism in Jamaica"); and with cruise ship ports in Ocho Rios, Montego Bay, Falmouth, Port Antonio, and Kingston, it is no wonder Jamaica is

DOI: 10.4324/9781003102830-4
This chapter has been made available under a CC-BY-ND 4.0 license.

considered one of the "World's Leading Cruise Destinations" ("Quick Facts About Jamaica").[5] Jamaica is also the largest English-speaking island in the Caribbean, which explains why the highest number of tourist arrivals come from the United States, followed by Canadian arrivals as a distant second, and finally, visitors from the United Kingdom (*Annual Travel Statistics:2018*).[6] However, the slick promotional advertisements, tourist activities, and luxurious, well-manicured resorts that idealize Jamaica create a "tourism imaginary," which Athinodoros Chronis identifies as productions of place that exist in an ambiguous temporal space between a locale's present and past. This tourism imaginary is rooted in "the projected or desired departure from the ordinary" (Blair, Dickinson, and Ott 26) and allows for "the playful permissiveness of a liminoid experience" in which everyday obligations are suspended (Gmelch 5). These imagined frameworks "attract tourists and invite them to participate in a fantasy that propels a visitor's escape from his/her ordinary preoccupations" and, in the case of Jamaica, often overwrite the fraught and complex transnational, colonial history, culture, and identity of Jamaica in order to reanimate North American Anglo supremacy and the tourist industry (Poirot and Watson 98).

Two Jamaican plantation houses—Rose Hall and Greenwood Great House—both located in St. James parish a short distance outside of Montego Bay and Falmouth (port cities that are huge tourist destinations) solicit and attract tourists in very different ways. Rose Hall conceptualizes the tourism imaginary and the legacies of slavery in Jamaica in ways that sanitize and romanticize the historic spectacles of racialized violence that occurred there through the gothic-style tale of Annee Palmer, the "White Witch of Rose Hall."[7] However, Greenwood Great House rejects the performance of that tourism imaginary and instead confronts the postcolonial realities of slavery, imperialism, and Anglo supremacy directly, asking visitors to remember these forgotten and suppressed legacies of Jamaica's past.

Before tourism became the major industry in Jamaica—and the "number one foreign exchange earner for Jamaica since 1983" (Stupart and Shipley 11)—slavery, sugar, and plantation systems dominated the economy. Approximately 1.5 million Africans were brought to Jamaica over the course of the Atlantic slave trade (beginning with the Spanish and continuing through English rule), heavily influencing the demographics of Jamaica's modern population of approximately 2,808,570 people, of which approximately 92 percent are Black, with large numbers of multiethnic populations, and growing numbers of East Indian residents ("Central America: Jamaica"). Because of Jamaica's dominant Black population, the ubiquitous presence of rum (made from sugar), and the elegant British-style (and some Spanish-style) buildings and great houses visible around the island, one would think the legacies of colonialism and slavery would, seemingly, be difficult to overwrite or suppress when welcoming tourists to the island and informing them about its culture and history. However, the Rose Hall Great House manages to do just that, providing visitors with a titillating, escapist, and entertaining engagement with Jamaica's history as a heritage experience.

Rose Hall Great House

On the official Rose Hall website, beneath a large banner image of the home's façade and the tagline "Experience the Magic," the great house is described as "a restored 18th-century architectural masterpiece" rather than as a plantation home ("Rose Hall Great House"). Most likely completed around 1780, the three-story great house is of Georgian architecture, consisting of cut-stone on the first two levels and stucco on the uppermost level. The main entrance to the home—and the vantage point through which all tours enter and where many bridal parties pose for pictures—is on the second level of the building and is reached by ascending a cut-stone, symmetrical grand staircase which leads to a veranda with impressive views of the Caribbean Sea (Figure 3.1).

Built by the Honorable John Palmer, a slaver as well as the Custos and Chief Justice of the Common Pleas of St. James parish, and named in honor of his wife, Rosa, the building, at its zenith, had been described as "the finest private residence in Jamaica" (*The Legend of Rose Hall* 7). During its prime as a working plantation, Rose Hall was adjoined to its neighboring plantation, Palmyra, and together they covered about 6,000 acres, which were divided among sugar cane, grass, and pasture for cattle; it is estimated that approximately 250 enslaved Africans worked the joined properties of Rose Hall and Palmyra. The Palmer family occupied Rose Hall until 1831 when enslaved people across Jamaica united in the Christmas Rebellion under the leadership of Baptist preacher, Samuel Sharpe, and the home, along with many other plantations across the island, was destroyed.[8] Rose Hall lay

Figure 3.1 Rose Hall façade, photo by author.

in disrepair until the 1960s when it was purchased and restored by John Rollins, an American entrepreneur and former Lieutenant Governor of Delaware, and his wife Michelle, a former Miss USA. The Rollinses have since developed the plantation to include two award-winning golf courses, a resort community where private individuals can buy lots and build their "dream homes" in what the Rose Hall website refers to as a "vacation colony of the highest quality [... filled with] kindred spirits," and of course, the Rose Hall Great House, where tours are given, weddings held, and the ghost of Annee Palmer—the infamous White Witch of Rose Hall—is the celebrated focus ("About Rose Hall Developments, Ltd.").

The story of Annee Palmer, which has mostly been proven false, but still heavily circulated, is that of a "black widow"—a woman who killed three husbands and then killed her subsequent sexual partners (mostly enslaved men) through a combination of witchcraft and cruelty.[9] As a child, Annee had spent time in Haiti where, as the legend states, she "became a favorite of a high voodoo priestess ... who taught Annee to believe in spirits ... The priestess convinced Annee she had the powers of a god" (*The Legend of Rose Hall* 12). After marrying a grand nephew of the plantation's original owner in 1820, Annee came to be the "haughty, cruel, impatiently bored, and easily provoked" mistress of Rose Hall (*The Legend of Rose Hall* 11). Legends about her state that after her first and second husbands died mysteriously, her third husband discovered she was having a sexual liaison with a young enslaved man on the property and flew into a rage. Annee poisoned him and then allowed the young man to be flogged to death, because he was ultimately blamed for the murder. Annee then became the manager and overseer of the Rose Hall estate, never remarrying. She was said to be a "particularly cruel overseer, making frequent use of the spikes and iron collars, the stocks and flogging posts" that were common in plantation management (Thomas 113). She also supposedly used bear traps to keep the enslaved people on the property and enjoyed watching their torture from her bedroom balcony each morning. When one of the enslaved tried to poison her and was condemned to death, legend states that Annee had "the head delivered to her ... [and] stuck onto the end of a bamboo pole, and placed above the corn house a short distance from the great house itself" (Thomas 113). It was rumored that even the area practitioners of black magic (*obeahmen*) were afraid of Annee and her magical powers. Until her death due to a fall from a horse, Annee purportedly tortured the enslaved at Rose Hall, ran her plantation with an iron fist, and took multiple sexual partners, both enslaved and white, who she then killed with a mysterious fever (Black 22).[10]

Tours at Rose Hall revel in this lurid tale, despite its historic inaccuracies, undoubtedly because it reads a like a gothic novel and is a titillating story for tourist consumption. Guides at Rose Hall Great House, who are mandatory on the tour and all of whom have been Black women each of the three times I've visited the site, are dressed in colorful peasant-style skirts with crisp, white, off-the-shoulder tops.[11] They take tourists up to the house by way of the grand, carved stone staircase, pausing for a professional photo opportunity with a staff photographer, because as the group is told, no personal photography is allowed once the home has been entered. The guides then lead tourists through the house, room by room, relating carefully scripted stories about Annee's childhood in Haiti, her personality quirks, her marriages, and her cruel, sexual reign over the plantation. Guides whisper at appropriate times and point to all the places where Annee's ghost has been seen or screams of her tortured sexual partners have been heard. None of the great house's original furnishings or décor remain, due to the Christmas Rebellion and looting that occurred at other times, but the home has been redone imaginatively, if not anachronistically, in ways that highlight the glamor and wealth of plantation living and showcase Annee's lascivious story. Visitors, for example, are shown Annee's bedroom, which has been redone entirely in shades of inauthentic crimson with heavy brocade fabrics and red velvet, indicative of the macabre "bloodiness" of Annee's tale, and taken to the old cellar where Annee supposedly imprisoned her sexual partners, which has now been converted to an English-style pub that serves rum punch and Red Stripe, among other beverages.

Each time I have visited Rose Hall (in 2014, 2016, and 2020) our guide, after allowing us special opportunities to snap forbidden photos and touch wallpapers and textiles in the home—a scripted and approved privilege undoubtedly intended to increase visitor satisfaction and the intimacy of the tour, as well as tips for the guides—took our group at the very end of the tour to the stone crypt on the property where Annee is supposedly buried and heavily hexed by the enslaved to keep her soul from escaping, although it did anyhow according to legend.[12] There, the guides sang us a few verses from Johnny Cash's song, "The Ballad of Annee Palmer," which focuses on Annee's dead husbands and asks as part of the refrain, "Where's your husband, Annee?" before dismissing us to wander in the gardens and visit the multiple gift shops on the property.[13]

The main narrative emphasis of the great house tour is placed on Annee Palmer's "witchiness" and black magic leanings, her wanton sexuality, and her cruelty to her sexual partners through that insatiable sexual appetite. The enslaved men that Annee seduces and then executes are framed during the tour as wronged paramours in a long line of wronged sexual partners and husbands (both white *and* Black—something the tour highlights repeatedly), instead of as chattel property within a plantation system; these men are often referred to during the scripted tour as Annee's "lovers" rather than as her property or as enslaved. This focus on the sexual misconduct and unhinged violence of a singular individual—and a woman, at that; misogyny is definitely at play here—works to overwrite and obscure the violent, systemic inequalities of slavery and the wealth and privilege that white planter society in Jamaica gained from it. Instead, emphasis on the tour is placed on the fact that Annee was an outlier; her mastery of voodoo and her mercurial nature which thrived on engendering terror and maintaining iron-fisted control mark her as an aberration rather than as an archetype of enslavers within the plantation system. Anthropologist Deborah Thomas has posited that the myth of the White Witch "renders legible … the corruption of plantation societies [,] the complex but fundamentally unequal relationships that develop within them [, and] the violence that structures these relationships" (113–14). I would counter, however, that the tour of Rose Hall artfully and salaciously repackages the myth of the White Witch to obscure the violence of the chattel slavery system and instead, reassign them to a white woman's sexuality and power gone awry. It is Annee Palmer who is the villain in this story, not the larger system that encompasses her. While the ugly legacies of Jamaica's history with slavery are certainly acknowledged on the tour and cannot be overlooked by even the most uninformed visitor to the site, they are made barely legible and are certainly not the focus of the great house tour. Instead, tourists at Rose Hall are offered an opportunity to visit a famous landmark and to engage with a sanitized "history" of Jamaica. The tour enables them to detach themselves from any guilt or discomfort about the historic realities of chattel slavery by focusing on the story of the White Witch, the beautiful view, and maybe having a Red Stripe or two before playing a round of golf on one of the beautiful Rose Hall courses.

The escapism provided by the Rose Hall tour is extremely appealing for white tourists, Americans in particular, I would argue, because of the way in which slavery and North American and European ties to the plantation economy—any potential "guilt" for visitors from these regions—is removed from focus. As Barry Schwartz and Horst-Alfred Henrich have observed in their study of American and German citizens' reactions to shameful events from their cultural histories, Americans are typically unwilling to "express regret for past wrongs" due to their particular cultural beliefs in individualism and exceptionalism (118). They are often resistant to accepting responsibility for shameful events of the past, like slavery, and are "hard-pressed to understand ... that people can be morally responsible for events in which they did not participate" (Schwartz and Heinrich 119). Further, Americans "typically reject moral responsibility for the misconduct of others, especially their ancestors" (Schwartz and Heinrich 119). Because the Rose Hall tour plays into these frameworks, laying the blame for the atrocities that occurred on the property at the feet of a cruel, deviant, white woman rather than on an entire system of enslavement, which would potentially carry uncomfortable implications for white visitors, particularly Americans, guests at Rose Hall ultimately get a free pass—a heritage experience without the guilt or personal reckoning.

A secondary, but equally telling focus of the tour of Rose Hall is on the lavish plantation lifestyle Annee led, as well as the extensive and expensive renovations made to the home by the Rollinses after they purchased the property. Throughout each room of the tour, visitors are regaled with information about how much maintaining the wallpaper in the home costs due to Jamaica's humid climate or the long distances from which various exquisite replacement materials had to be imported. Extravagant and high-end decorative items, from china sets to chandeliers to heavy furnishings made of mahogany, are pointed out every step of the way. This emphasis on the luxurious living standard of Jamaica's planter society is further promoted on the Rose Hall website, so that before visitors have even set foot on the property, they are prepared for a glamorous, escapist tour. Under the tab about the "Day Tour" where patrons would purchase their online tickets for a 20% discount, visitors are urged to

> Immerse [themselves] in the heritage of the island as your expert guide shares the story of this colonial ruin restored to its former majesty in the

1960's. Learn about the *lifestyle of the European bourgeoisie* in the isles of the Caribbean in the Eighteenth Century. The tale of the Annee Palmer, the famed White Witch of Rose Hall is sure to delight. Beautiful tropical gardens and personalities will colour your experience with fun along the way!

("Rose Hall Great House"—emphasis mine)

Nothing about slavery, the corruption of plantation societies, or the violence that structured them—the actual history of this site—is mentioned on the Rose Hall webpage, and they are barely touched upon in the actual tour itself. Instead, the focus is on the majesty of the home, the "bougie" lifestyles of planters in the Caribbean, and the "delightful" story of Annee Palmer. As Deborah Thomas states, this sanitized version of historic memory functions to "present the luxury and grandeur of the life of plantation owners but neither the excruciatingly hard labor nor the forms of terror and torture that were the daily lot of slaves" (114). As within any tourism imaginary, reality is suspended and obligations are removed at Rose Hall; idealized versions of the past replace the actual historic narrative of origin, and visitors are able to leave feeling edified and guilt-free. They are able to "experience the magic," just as the Rose Hall website enjoins, without having to grapple with the harsh, historical truths of the plantation economy or how those legacies have structured the tourism-centric Jamaica they are currently enjoying.

Greenwood Great House

Greenwood Great House, which is literally just minutes down the road from Rose Hall in St. James parish, is far less popular in terms of the numbers of cruise ship visitors and tourists it sees, but, I would argue, this is because of the way this site approaches its own historic place within the plantation economy and the way it edifies and interacts with visitors. Built in 1800 as a guest house by Richard Barrett, a slaver, Speaker of the House, and part of the wealthy and influential Barrett family that included Elizabeth Barrett Browning, Greenwood Great House survived the Christmas Rebellion of 1831 and consequently still has many of its original furnishings, artwork, and unique musical instruments, all of which are on display in the home and discussed on the tour.[14] The two-story stone and timber structure has a cedar-shingled roof, cut-stone floors, mahogany doors, and a detached kitchen that is connected to the main house by a covered walkway (which is now a small pub and the ticket office) (Figure 3.2).

Although certified as a national monument and having received a Musgrave Medal of Excellence in Heritage Preservation, a National Association of Returning Residents plaque, and the Berger Paints Heritage in Architecture award, Greenwood Great House is unique in that it still functions as a private residence ("Plan a Visit"). The plantation home is owned and lived in by Bob and Anne Betton, who purchased the property in 1976 as a sort of homecoming for Bob, who is originally from Jamaica, and Anne, a white New Zealander, after the couple had lived in England for many years. The Bettons have worked to maintain the home in as original a condition as possible, and they display historic heirlooms,

Figure 3.2 Greenwood Great House façade, photo by author.

antiques, and even found items from around the property throughout the great house. Greenwood, like Rose Hall, also seeks to bring in cruise ship passengers and tourists from all-inclusive resorts by advertising with tour companies and having write-ups in travel guides like *Fodor's*, *Rough Guide to Jamaica*, and *Lonely Planet* (a publication which lists Greenwood as a "Top Choice" on their website). They also have similar operating hours to Rose Hall, a similar entry fee, and provide tour guides who follow a carefully scripted program, including a tale about a "duppy" or ghost that appears in a photograph featured on the tour. However, unlike Rose Hall, Greenwood allows its guides (both men and women) to dress in street clothes and lets visitors linger in rooms as long as they would like, taking pictures; they do, however, enforce a strict "no touching" policy due to the value and rarity of the original items in the home. The most striking difference between the tours at Rose Hall and Greenwood, however, is the fact that at Greenwood, they directly address the history of the home as a slave plantation without glamorizing or sanitizing the structural violence of the plantation economy and the imperialism that buttressed it, and they do so without coddling or "entertaining" visitors with elaborate backstories about the property or its previous owners.

The tour of Greenwood Great House, which begins at wrought iron gates that lead into the property's gardens, introduces visitors, first, to the famous lineage of the Barretts, including Elizabeth Barrett Browning, but then immediately follows with details about the massive nature of the Barrett's plantation operation:

> The Barretts were the largest plantation owners [in Jamaica]; they owned from Little River to Falmouth, that is about twelve miles along the coast, and this was one of many of their estates. They owned over 2,000 slaves and 84,000 acres of land.
>
> ("Greenwood Tour")

The tour guide then points out an antique two-man, hand-pump fire cart and a water canon that sit on a side porch of the residence, noting, "Just before the slaves got their freedom, they started a spate of burning, so naturally these were their form of insurance against fire" ("Greenwood Tour"). These opening lines from the tour not only acknowledge the massive holdings of plantation elites in Jamaica—particularly the Barretts'—of both land and enslaved humans, but also the active resistance of the enslaved populations to that system, as well as its volatility and instability. This is all before visitors have even entered the home and within minutes of the tour's start. Throughout the remainder of the tour, guests are continually reminded of the home's plantation legacy. They are told of features of the home such as the gun slots that are still visible in the basement level to defend the home, shown items like weights and metal cauldrons that would have been used in sugar production, and directed to various indentures and legal documents that are framed and on display, one of which is a list of enslaved people that includes the moniker "Trouble," something the guides always remark upon. The violent legacies of the plantation economy, including its roots in sugar production, enslavement, violence, and dehumanization, are never far from the mind during the tour.

There are also more overt and direct engagements with the home's history, and Jamaica's more generally, as a plantation and as a site of systemic violence and resistance. For example, early in the tour, guests are shown the framed last will and testament of the Reverend Thomas Burchell. Burchell was a white British Baptist missionary and abolitionist who worked in Jamaica for 22 years building churches and working closely with Samuel Sharpe, an enslaved man who was Burchell's Deacon and a major leader in the Christmas Rebellion of 1831. While pointing out the document, the tour guide notes,

> In 1831, he [Burchell] and William Knibb were accused of inciting the slaves under Sam Sharpe to rebel. It became the bloodiest rebellion in Jamaica's history. It led to the slaves getting their freedom three years later. Sam Sharpe is now one of Jamaica's national heroes.
>
> ("Greenwood Tour")

This statement not only snaps visitors out of their tourism imaginary by shifting attention away from the luxurious planter lifestyle and incredible wealth of the enslavers, things the Rose Hall tour focused on intensely, but it also redirects attention to the legacy of Samuel Sharpe, the enslaved man who was executed for his role in the largest slave rebellion in Jamaica history, instead of on the historic document of the will, the Anglo abolitionist who created it, or the wealthy Barrett family and their luxurious home that is full of artifacts such as Burchell's will. The traditional focus of great house or plantation home tours across the U.S. and Caribbean is flipped here, placing the emphasis on the enslaved and their resistance to that enslavement rather than on the "gracious" lifestyle of the enslavers.

Near the end of the Greenwood Great House tour, when visitors are being walked from the main house to the home's original kitchen in a separate building, which has now been converted to a pub called "The Level Crossing," the guide relates that the covered walkway between the two buildings is called the

Rose Hall and Greenwood Great House 61

"Whistler's Walk," because "to stop the slaves [from] eating the food from the kitchen to the great house, they [slaves] were instructed to whistle because you can't chew and whistle at the same time" ("Greenwood Tour"). Guests are then deposited in the pub where there is a wall display of glass cases that contain leg (leg irons), whips, shackles, and other artifacts of the plantation spectacle of violence, including a full-sized man trap directly below the display, which have been found on the property or purchased elsewhere in Jamaica (Figures 3.3 and 3.4).

Exhibited without a lot of commentary or contextualizing information beyond what has already been offered as part of the tour, it makes a sobering, stark statement about the great house's—and Jamaica's—origins.[15] This final display at the end, as Deborah Thomas asserts, "places Greenwood Great House within a more general dialogue about a history of violence in Jamaica and the impact of that history on the present" (115). It also, I would argue, forces tourists out of their "sun, sea, and sand getaway" fantasy to grapple with the historic context that first created Jamaica as the wealthiest colony in the British Empire and then as a tourist destination for mostly white, American visitors. It ruptures the tourism imaginary and places issues of racism, white supremacy, imperialism, colonialism, and enslavement at the forefront of the visitor's mind. Greenwood Great House offers, as the *Lonely Planet* guide notes, "one of the few direct references … found in any Jamaican historical home to the foundations of the plantation labor market, i.e. slavery" (126). This may explain why the Bettons see far fewer international

Figure 3.3 Glass display case at Greenwood Great House; photo by author.

Figure 3.4 Man trap at Greenwood Great House; photo by author.

and cruise ship visitors than their counterpart, Rose Hall. They instead receive a "steady stream of Jamaicans, many of whom tour Greenwood Great House as part of a high school, university, or church field trip," groups that are undoubtedly more interested in the actual historic origins of the home and their own identities as Jamaicans than in an interpretive heritage experience that excises the home's significance within the plantation economy (Thomas 115).

The rare and invaluable furnishings and décor within Greenwood Great House are a featured part of the tour, much as they were at Rose Hall. Because the home was never destroyed or looted as many other plantation sites around the island have been, including Rose Hall, Greenwood is a virtual museum that has one of the most extensive collections of antique furniture, artwork, china, and fixtures in Jamaica and perhaps in the entire Caribbean. Throughout every room of the house, guides point out the age and provenance of items such as a beautifully inlaid piano that once belonged to King Edward VII and was made by Thomas Broadwood (who made pianos for Beethoven), busts of Queen Victoria and Prince Albert, and the largest intact plantation library on the island containing over 300 books—the oldest one being published in 1697 and many of them signed by members of the Barrett family ("Greenwood Tour").[16] Unlike Rose Hall, however, Greenwood has also been painstakingly maintained in as close to original condition as possible, with no creative redecorating or replacement of original fixtures to amplify the home's appearance and glamor or to obscure its origins within imperialist, transatlantic systems of the slave trade.[17] In fact, a key emphasis within the Greenwood tour is on the rarity of items and furnishings as well as their provenance—rather than their value—because many of the home's contents were procured by or gifted to the Barretts as a part of the British crown's far-reaching imperialist conquest of the world.

At various points throughout the tour, visitors are told about items such as a unique set of library steps that convert to a chair of Spanish origin, a bronze Chinese punch bowl, a Chinese watercolor and a Japanese wood block print on silk, a Flemish cupboard, Tibetan religious horns "used for hunting wild pigs," and a Sicilian platter ("Greenwood Tour"). There are also various tapestries and carpets from all over the globe including a Turkish floor runner, an Indian rug, and a set of Casa Pupo rugs; the home even has an American-made platform rocker with a base that doesn't move so that the valuable carpets beneath it would not be destroyed. Each of these material items signifies the imperial and commercial circulation of bodies, products, power structures, and wealth throughout the Caribbean and the larger Atlantic World. They speak to Britain's imperial dominance and engagement in the slave trade in the eighteenth and early nineteenth centuries as well as the Barretts' participation within and financial benefit from those systems. Greenwood's vast collection of items that are described on the tour are a collective snapshot of Atlantic history and the ways in which the plantation economy enabled and bolstered that transatlantic development of wealth and power for a limited few. Greenwood Great House exposes not only these historic systems but also their legacies within the modern tourist industry of Jamaica in ways that visitors to this site cannot help but recognize.

Coda

Ultimately, these great houses consciously construct very different versions of public memory and race in the early Americas/Caribbean for very different audiences. Whereas Rose Hall works to engage the tourism imaginary and shape visitors' understandings of the plantation economy in ways that centralize whiteness and decentralize "white guilt" or tourist "shame" over Jamaica's plantation-economy origins, Greenwood rejects the tourism imaginary and instead produces a more capacious understanding of the country's history that is more historically sound and decolonial in its representation of and confrontation with racialized power structures within empire and the modern tourism industry.

Rose Hall performs a twentieth-/twenty-first-century version of imperialism in which Anglo-American settlers "move in" and revive an "architectural masterpiece" with opulent, top-of-the-line furnishings to create not only a popular and profitable tourist hotspot, but also an exclusive Anglo tourist community and enclave. It presents Jamaica as "naturally colonial"—as a modern-day recreation of the very system through which Annee Palmer and other white, wealthy transplants to the island were able to exploit the Jamaican landscape and people—only now it is through the racialized tourism industry rather than the plantation economy of slavery (Gordon 41). As Communications scholar Nickesia Gordon has argued, the tourism industry and its advertisements work to assure contemporary guests in Jamaica that they can still "expect to be served, not unlike how colonial elites were once waited upon. The servitude of the locals [is] part of the authentic experience tourists can expect when they visit" (41). Sociologist Karen Wilkes more concisely states, "the consumption of Black labor in the Caribbean is sold as a luxury" (9). As a participant within these systems of consumption and neocolonialism, the Rose Hall tour produces for its mostly white, American visitors a fanciful and titillating narrative about plantation life in Jamaica which, because of its focus on the singular instance of Annee Palmer where power, violence, and extreme cruelty overrode the humanity of one individual, does not challenge or disturb the surety of its visitors that they are "good" people who are free from any implications or benefits of the colonialist legacies of slavery and racism that ensnared Annee. Because these visitors do not—and cannot—identify with Annee, they are able to eschew any connections with the White Witch of Rose Hall and her subsequent ties to the transatlantic slave trade and its contemporary colonialist repercussions in the tourism industry. They depart feeling edified and engaged with Jamaica's history, but ultimately unchallenged in their own understandings of race, power, and imperialism in the Caribbean and their own implication within these systems.

Greenwood Great House, however, places the focus of its tour on the spectacular violence of slavery, as well as the imperialist, racist frameworks that enabled and maintained that system, rather than the aberrant, white identities and posh lifestyles it engendered. The emphasis of the Greenwood tour is placed on systems of oppression—racism, imperialism, chattel slavery, economic dominance—that still clearly have long-lasting impacts on present-day Jamaica—the very Jamaica tourists are consuming and enjoying. Greenwood confronts its visitors with the web of power structures that not only enabled Jamaica's foundation as Britain's wealthiest colony in the Caribbean, but also currently maintains it as a tourist-driven economy that still relies on white American patronage and tourist dollars, and Black Jamaican servitude. As a result, guests are less easily able to separate themselves from and reject the narrative about the long-lasting and far-reaching implications of slavery that Greenwood is telling. Greenwood makes explicit the connections between the plantation economy of the eighteenth and nineteenth centuries and the continuing tourist economy today, which creates a challenging and resistant heritage narrative that does not align with the tourism imaginary. Greenwood demonstrates that it is possible to tell decolonized stories about race, power, and the legacies of colonialism in the Caribbean, and to create more nuanced and substantial narratives about how a place like Jamaica, which often seems so distant and inconsequential to white American visitors' understanding of their own histories and identities, is actually foundational—rather than tangential—to understanding the Atlantic World and the complex and fraught nature of race, slavery, and neocolonialism in the contemporary United States and tourism industry.

Notes

1. An earlier, condensed version of this essay appeared in the spring 2019 issue of the *Society of Early Americanists' Newsletter* (S.E.A.N. 31.1). I would like to thank the University of Wisconsin-Eau Claire's Office of Research and Sponsored Programs (O.R.S.P.) for their support of my research through a semester-long sabbatical and travel funding through a University Research and Creative Activity (U.R.C.A.) grant. I would also like to thank my Jamaican immersion program students throughout the years (2014, 2016, 2020) and my faculty co-leader of the 2020 immersion, Dr. Joel Pace, who lent his unfailing support and enthusiasm to this project.
2. T.G. Brunyard notes in his 2001 article, "'Prodigious riches,'" that estimates of the capital and income of Jamaica demonstrate that it was the wealthiest colony in British America, both in terms of total wealth and in regard to the wealth of individual white settlers (507).
3. Some sources estimate that there may have been as many as 700 great houses in Jamaica by 1838 when slavery was abolished. Today, perhaps only 400 of those survive, with many lying in ruins or being used as makeshift housing in poorer communities around the island.
4. See Stupart and Shipley for discussion of the origins and historic development of the tourist industry in Jamaica. For analysis of Jamaica's tourism-centric efforts at "nation branding," see Johnson and Gentles-Peart's *Brand Jamaica*. For information about the socio-economic impacts of tourism in Jamaica, see the work of Ibrahim A. Ajagunna and Ann P. Crick.
5. The newest cruise ship port was opened in January 2020 in Port Royal, Kingston, after a more than 40-year absence of cruise ships in this area. Jamaica now has five ports around the island.
6. The *Annual Travel Statistics: 2018* report for Jamaica more specifically notes that 1,628,402 Americans visited the island in 2018 versus 399,969 Canadians and 217,978 citizens from the United Kingdom during the same time frame. Americans clearly constitute the bulk of Jamaica's tourist arrivals.
7. Although Palmer's name is sometimes spelled "Annie," most Jamaican sources about her, including materials from Rose Hall and Rollins, Ltd., such as their self-published booklet *The Legend of Rose Hall*, their coffee table book, *Rose Hall, Jamaica*, and their website, spell her name "Annee," so that is the spelling I will utilize here.
8. The Christmas Rebellion of 1831–2, also called the Great Slave Rebellion or the Baptist War, was ignited when Blacks, under Sharpe's leadership, demanded more freedom and a working wage of "half the going wage rate"; they took an oath to stay away from work until their demands were met by the plantation owners. It became the largest uprising of enslaved people in the British West Indies, mobilizing as many as 60,000 of Jamaica's 300,000 enslaved. Fourteen whites were killed by armed battalions of enslaved people during the course of the rebellion, and 207 rebelling enslaved were killed. It is estimated that an additional 300–350 enslaved people were executed after the war in reprisals. For further reading, see the work of James A. Delle.
9. Most scholars attribute the legend of the "White Witch of Rose Hall" as originating in a 1929 novel by Herbert G. de Lisser, a Jamaican journalist and author, aptly titled *The White Witch of Rose Hall*.
10. Other sources claim Palmer died from being strangled by one of her lovers in her own bed (*The Legend of Rose Hall*, 11).
11. See Gentles-Peart for analysis of the white supremacist trope of Black Jamaican women "being built for servitude (the perennial slave[s])" and its role within the tourism industry (60).
12. Ajagunna and Crick have theorized that these kinds of special privileges work to create feelings of warmth and welcoming for tourists; they require "employees in the hospitality industry [to] imagine that the customer is a guest in their private home" and then treat them accordingly (181).

13 Johnny Cash was a one-time owner of the nearby Cinnamon Hill great house and supposedly quite taken with Annee's story. He wrote and recorded "The Ballad of Annee Palmer" in the 1970s shortly after purchasing the Cinnamon Hill property, where he and June Carter Cash resided part-time for nearly 40 years. Cinnamon Hill was purchased by the Rollinses, the owners of Rose Hall, shortly after the Cashes' deaths in 2012 and has just recently been opened to the public for tours through Rosehall.com.
14 Hersey Barrett (sometimes spelled "Hercie") had been granted the property for the Greenwood estate by King Charles II because of his role in the British takeover of Jamaica in 1655. The Barrett family also owned Cinnamon Hill (the Johnny Cash home now owned by Rose Hall, Ltd.), and Barrett Hall, which is no longer standing. Elizabeth Barrett Browning is a descendant of these planter Barretts, the daughter of Edward Moulton Barrett, although she never visited Jamaica.

Greenwood Great House is said to have survived the Christmas Rebellion due to the Barrett family's "kinder" dealings with enslaved people, including assisting them with literacy efforts, which was a criminal offense.
15 The script from the Greenwood tour only makes a passing comment on the man trap: "[T]here is a man trap. It was used for capturing runaway slaves" ("Greenwood Tour"). Individual guides will often comment further on the display and point out the additional items in the cases. Of the four times I have taken the Greenwood Great House tour (2014, 2016, 2019, 2020), three of the four guides talked further about the display; one of those guides was Bob Betton himself.
16 Other unique and rare items in the Greenwood collection include a 1626 map of Africa, one of three working barrel organs in the world, and two polyphones.
17 To clarify, Greenwood has been maintained as much as possible in its original décor and configurations in the public areas that are open for tours. Obviously, updates have been made for plumbing, electricity, and other modern facilities, but areas of the home where extensive changes have been made are not featured on the tour.

References

"About Rose Hall Developments Ltd." *Rosehall.com*. Rose Hall Development, Limited. Last modified 2019, https://www.rosehall.com/. Accessed 20 April 2020.

Ajagunna, Ibrahim A., and Ann P. Crick. "Managing Interactions in the Tourism Industry—a Strategic Tool for Success: Perspectives on Jamaica Tourism Industry." *Worldwide Hospitality and Tourism Themes*, vol. 6, no. 2, 2014, pp. 179–190. doi: 10.1108/WHATT-12-2013-0051

Annual Travel Statistics: 2018. Jamaica Tourist Board. Last modified December 3, 2019. https://www.jtbonline.org/report-and-statistics/. Accessed 15 April 2020.

Black, Clinton. *Tales of Old Jamaica*. Collins, 1967.

Blair, Carole, Greg Dickinson, and Brian L. Ott. "Introduction Rhetoric/Memory/Place." *Places of Public Memory: The Rhetoric of Museums and Memorials*, Eds. Greg Dickinson, Carole Blair, and Brian Ott. U of Alabama P, 2010, pp. 1–54.

Brand Jamaica: Reimagining a National Image and Identity. Eds. Hume Johnson and Kamille Gentles-Peart. U of Nebraska P, 2019.

Brunyard, T.G. "'Prodigious Riches': The Wealth of Jamaica before the American Revolution." *Economic History Review* vol. 54, no. 3, 2001, pp. 506–524.

"Central America: Jamaica." *Central Intelligence Agency: The World Factbook*. Last modified March 15, 2020. https://www.cia.gov/library/publications/resources/the-world-factbook/geos/jm.html Accessed 20 April 2020.

Chronis, Anthinodoros. "Between Place and Story: Gettysburg as Tourism Imaginary."*Annals of Tourism Research* vol. 3, no 4, 2012, pp. 1797–1816. doi: 10.1016/j.annals.2012.05.028

de Lisser, Herbert G. *The White Witch of Rose Hall*. Humanity Press, 1982.
Delle, James A. *The Colonial Caribbean: Landscapes of Power in Jamaica's Plantation System*. Cambridge UP, 2014.
Gentles-Peart, Kamille. "Women of 'Paradise': Tourism Discourses and the Lived Realities of Jamaican Women in the United States." *Brand Jamaica: Reimagining a National Image and Identity*. Eds. Hume Johnson and Kamille Gentles-Peart. U of Nebraska P, 2019, pp. 51–73.
Gmelch, Sharon Bohn. "Why Tourism Matters." *Tourists and Tourism: A Reader*. 2nd ed. Ed. Sharon Bohn Gmelch. Waveland Press 2010, pp. 3–24.
Gordon, Nickesia. "Branding the Nation: A Rhetorical Analysis of the Jamaica Tourist Board's Commercial Campaigns." *Brand Jamaica: Reimagining a National Image and Identity*. Eds. Hume Johnson and Kamille Gentles-Peart. U of Nebraska P, 2019, pp. 31–49.
"Greathouses (Plantation Houses)." Jamaica National Heritage Trust. Last Modified 2011. http://www.jnht.com/greathouses.php Accessed 30 June 2020.
"Greenwood Great House Tour." Tour script. Emailed to author 15 January 2020.
The Legend of Rose Hall. Rollins Jamaica, Ltd., 1967.
Lonely Planet: Jamaica. 8th edition, written and researched by Paul Clammer and Anna Kaminski. Lonely Planet Global Ltd. 2017.
"Plan a Visit." *Greenwoodgreathouse.com*. Greenwood Great House. Last Modified 2015. https://www.greenwoodgreathouse.com/plan-a-visit Accessed 25 April 2020.
Poirot, Kristan and Shevaun Watson. "Memories of Freedom and White Resilience: Place Tourism, and Urban Slavery." *Rhetoric Society Quarterly*, vol. 45, no. 2, 2015, pp. 91–116. doi: 10.1080/02773945.2014.991879
"Quick Facts about Jamaica." Jamaica Tourist Board. Last Modified 2016, https://www.jtbonline.org/tourism-in-jamaica/quick-facts-about-jamaica/, Accessed 15 April 2020.
"Rose Hall Great House." *Rosehall.com* Rose Hall Development Limited. Last modified 2019, https://www.rosehall.com/, Accessed 20 April 2020.
Rose Hall Limited. *Rose Hall, Jamaica: Story of a People…a Legend…and A Legacy*. Kingston Publishers, Limited. 1973.
Schwartz, Barry and Horst-Alfred Heinrich. "Shadings of Regret: America and Germany." *Framing Public Memory*, Ed. Kendall R. Phillips. U of Alabama P, 2004.
Stupart, Copeland A. and Robert Shipley. "Jamaica's Tourism: Sun, Sea, and Sand to Cultural Heritage." *Journal of Tourism Insights* vol. 3, no. 1, 2012, pp. 1–19. doi: 10.9707/2328-0824.1028
Thomas, Deborah. *Exceptional Violence: Embodied Citizenship in Transnational Jamaica*. Duke UP, 2011. doi: 10.15695/amqst.v12i1.4112
"Tourism in Jamaica." Jamaica Tourist Board. Last Modified 2016, https://www.jtbonline.org/tourism-in-jamaica/, Accessed 15 April 2020.
Wilkes, Karen. *Whiteness, Weddings, and Tourism in the Caribbean: Paradise for Sale*. Palgrave Macmillan, 2016. doi: 10.1057/978-1-137-50391-6

4 At the table or on the menu at Indiana's Feast of the Hunters' Moon

Kathryn Florence

Introduction

Indiana is known as the Crossroads of America. Before statehood it was the epicenter of trade in the Northwest Territories, bringing together British, French, Canadian, and Indigenous agents along the river routes that carved across the land. Every October, tourists from across the country converge on the small town of West Lafayette for the Tippecanoe County Historical Association's (T.C.H.A.) Feast of the Hunters' Moon, held at the historic site of Fort Ouiatenon. The two-day exposition of traditional trades, historical regalia and costumes, and the arrival of re-enactors from the Wabash River by canoe draws in tens of thousands with the expectation of experiencing an authentic interaction between these pioneers and the various Indigenous inhabitants of the state. However, by looking at how the Feast operates within the heritage tourism industry and how history, heritage, identity, and place are negotiated there, we are presented with the understanding that the exchanges between the original inhabitants of Indiana and the encroaching entrepreneurial explorers were never meeting on equal ground and are no more equal today because of how this re-enactment overwrites the realities of history. I propose that, in striving to recreate an authentic experience of local past meticulously focused on the naturalization of white settlers to the Indiana territory, the T.C.H.A. has simultaneously undermined the historic presence of the Indigenous that called the land home and contributes to a historicized view of First Nations today. As such, the modern revival of the Feast of the Hunters' Moon as a tourist experience is the product of ongoing colonization in the Midwest, obfuscating the racial prejudices and cultural genocide that undergird the very creation of the state.

Let me be clear about one thing; this critique is not motivated by disappointment or disdain for the Feast. I looked forward to attending the Feast every year during my undergraduate years and have worked with the T.C.H.A. as a student and as an intern and mourn the struggles the T.C.H.A. will face with the unfortunate cancellation of the 2020 edition. I intend this chapter as a chance to bring exchange and education to the table, to renegotiate how authenticity and history are served at the Feast. Critical reflexivity as suggested by Noah Nielsen and Erica Wilson (1) allows for constructive dialogues and opens the way for the possibility

DOI: 10.4324/9781003102830-5

of addressing problematic features of this form of heritage tourism that might or might not have been evident to organizers. The Feast is but one product of a dispossession that is pervasive at the institutional level, beyond the managerial capabilities of the T.C.H.A. or even the conglomeration of historical societies across Indiana. It is a microcosm of the larger nature of heritage tourism sites that has not been represented much in the discourse and therefore provides a good case study for the theme of this volume.

Fort Ouiatenon and the Feast of the Hunters' Moon, while well known in some circles, are not quite as popular in academic writing. The fort itself, on the other hand, features more presently in the realms of history and archaeology. Primary sources include pioneering accounts like Charles C. Royce's *Cessions of Land by Indian Tribes to the United States: Illustrated by Those in the State of Indiana* (1881), William Monroe Cockrum's *Pioneer History of Indiana: Including Stories, Incidents, and Customs of the Early Settlers* (1907); "THE LAST OF AN INDIAN VILLAGE" (1908), and "The Wabash and Its Valley: Part I—The Earlier History" (1905). These accounts are equally good and bad. There are receipts or records that can be corroborated across texts leading to relative veracity. They are enormously helpful for detailing trade, for example what was being sought and how it was procured. White men sure did love to write about their trade routes. On the observations of Indigenous groups, the texts devolve into blatant racism and overt mudslinging. Needless to say, one has to consult pioneering accounts with a handful of salt.

Recent literature provides more understanding of the sociocultural frameworks presented from both sides of the river. Kelsey Noack Myers's dissertation, "Indigenous Landscapes and Legacy Archaeology at Ouiatenon, Indiana" (2017), cumulates over 50 years' worth of archaeological investigation at the site which relays a history not recorded in primary accounts. Myers—and additionally the history monographs of Patrick Bottiger (2016) and Susan Sleeper Smith (2018)—recount both sides of the story by tracing history in conjunction with qualitative resources, problematizing the binary categorization often associated with settler narratives and providing a view of life on the frontier. The Ohio River Valley was being reshaped across social, political, and economic systems within Indigenous groups leading up to the construction of Fort Ouiatenon (Myers 16, 123). The history presented through Myers's findings, while not egalitarian, affirms the agency of Indigenous groups within the area and their position of power within the wider social network of trade. Moreover, the text requires us to acknowledge the discrepancy between history and the archaeological record as well as the bias of the existing Ouiatenon narrative that is perpetuated by the current knowledge system (Myers 15, 95, 121).

Jerome De Groot's *Consuming History: Historians and Heritage in Contemporary Popular Culture* (2009) informs the rudimentary understanding of the framework of heritage and history which is employed throughout the rest of this chapter. De Groot considers how heritage is conceptualized and by extension engaged with as an object and process, negotiated on the stage of public history between said public and the historians who study it. History, in this theory, is a socially and culturally constructed and consumed entity, able at once to hold within itself difference and sameness, to represent otherness and familiarity, and to remind the individual of their distance from the past while enabling them through that difference to understand themselves somehow in a way more complex than hitherto.

(5)

The commercialization of history and heritage is especially relevant to the topic of this chapter in that it acknowledges that the museum is constrained by the competition of the leisure market (De Groot 241–3; Simine 2), which has yet to be considered in relation to the Feast. De Groot's text stresses the careful consideration of the implications of such heritage commoditization, stating, "Consumption practices influence what is packaged as history and work to define how the past manifests itself in society" (2). In this chapter we have to not only question the veracity of the history re-enacted at Fort Ouiatenon, but also consider how the public engages with the past as a whole in terms of racialized performances of public history.

The notion of history and past in relation to the present forms the focus of David Lowenthal's *The Past is a Foreign Country—Revisited* (2013). While De Groot explores how the ways in which the public engages with the past has changed with the inclusion of new technologies and practices, Lowenthal questions how the past is constructed in the first place, including how we relate to it as a foundation of identity and an orienting experience. Lowenthal's text underscores the importance of how the past is conceptualized in relation to the present through memory, history, and relics (Lowenthal 292). Most importantly for considering re-enactment, how we have framed the past as something separate from the present, yet never negating the ability it has to validate the present (Lowenthal 4). The projected rupture between past and present plays a major role in the narrative of the Feast of the Hunters' Moon, as it dictates the impact of re-enactment at the site and negotiation of the historical narrative. He observes that, "Seldom do we recognize that such residues stem from the past, or that camouflaged bygones continue to shape and direct our behaviour" (290). Lowenthal's observations highlight how the dichotomy between history and contemporaneity strains against notions of linear and embedded history, communal heritage, and belonging. How we portray history, not just the events that have occurred, but also their lingering legacies, is something that must be interrogated at sites of heritage tourism.

Setting the table: Race, place, and power at Ouiatenon

In order to discuss Feast of the Hunters' Moon, we first need to know about the site where it takes place and the historic relationships memorialized in the present. I would like to begin by acknowledging that Indiana was originally home to the Lenape (Delaware), the Shawnee (Sewanee), the Neshnabe (Potawatomi), and the distinct Wea, Piankashaw, and Atchatchakangouen bands of the Miyaamiaa (Miami) Nations. Today, it is home to a diverse population of Indigenous and other peoples. I respect the continued connections with the past, present, and future in our ongoing relationships with Indigenous and other peoples within the Hoosier community. I start with this land acknowledgment not out of habit or procedure, but out of awareness. It is as much to un-settle myself, as it is to re-insert a presence that has been erased through the tides of colonialism.

During the pioneering period, race was not structurally ingrained as it is in today's societal institutions, though it was nonetheless problematic. Yes; race existed and so did racism. However, the relationships between settlers and Indigenous were not cleanly or completely defined by it (Jeffrey Ostler 590). Racial distinction is noted predominantly through settler accounts, specifically in constructing the dichotomy of white-civilized-us/red-savage-them in regard to Indigenous. Beyond that, national identity (such as French, English, and later still American) appeared to have colored settler–Indigenous relations more than race (Bottiger xvi). This is possibly because it aligned more closely with how Indigenous peoples conceptualized their relationships based on lineage or polity. Michael McDonnell, professor of early American history at Sydney, warns that though tribal labels

> became a convenient way for the new republic to organize and deal with the peoples of the *pays d'en haut* in the nineteenth century, it is still not clear when, how, and to what extent diverse Native peoples themselves adopted and embraced these labels.
>
> (99)

Wea, Kickapoo, Mascouten, Potawatomi, Piankashaw, Sauk, Fox, Seneca, Miami, Delaware, Shawnee, and smaller groups converged routinely at the site and immediate area (Myers 13, 102, 131; S. Sleeper-Smith 9). Settlers did not recognize this multiplicity, instead collecting the various groups under the label of "Ouiatenons" or "Wabash Indians" (Sleeper-Smith 118). They were categorized according to race, but that did not reflect the heterogeneity of their population. Indigenous groups constructed their identity around community, which in turn influenced how they related their identity to the land and their place within it and to each other.

The Ohio River Valley was essentially a trade highway that connected Montreal to New Orleans. The *waapaahšiki siipiiwi* or Wabash River (Figure 4.1) "formed the backbone of the Algonquian imagined landscape in this region" (Myers 6). Fort Ouiatenon (also written as Ouiatanon) was constructed around 1717 somewhere along the Wabash River near modern-day Lafayette, Indiana (Bottiger 23; Myers 1), as one of three French garrison posts serving as trade hubs for the fur industry which had begun the previous century (Cockrum 18). During the initial phase of French occupation the fort housed a dozen traders along with their families and a handful of militia men stationed there to protect said traders (Bottiger 23; Cockrum 20, 25; Myers 108). It became one of the largest population centers in the valley (Sleeper-Smith 57; Myers 15; Heath 174). On the other side of the river was *Waayaahtanonki* (Anglicized into the French fort's name) (Myers 5), an Indigenous settlement which also boasted a fort, setting it apart from other

72   Kathryn Florence

Figure 4.1 Wabash River Map. Kmusser, CC BY-SA 3.0, via Wikimedia Commons.

Indigenous centers in the Ohio River Valley (Sleeper-Smith 57). The number of residents in Waayaahtanonki and within the vicinity was in the thousands (Myers 15). Though structured as a permanent settlement, these villages were incorporated into seasonal patterns of summer gathering and winter scattering (Heath 186). Settler views of land ownership clashed with this notion of stewardship which prioritized permanent residence as an indicator of title.

Indiana is envisioned as a great middle ground where settlers imagined themselves to be pioneering into unknown land, honing their influence over extant Indigenous populations and nature itself. This was not the case. "The creation of this middle ground, in turn, was dependent on a rough balance of power, a mutual need or desire for what the other side offered, and an inability by either side to compel change" (McDonnell 79). The construction of Fort Ouiatenon was a part of a larger negotiation of power worked out through trade agreements and physical presence. In some accounts, the fort was initiated by the French as a claim to the land and as a demonstration of authority (Cockrum 19–20; S. Sleeper-Smith 112; Myers 15). As the fort changed to British and then American hands, so too did settlers mark a change in the ownership of the land, though they did not maintain the obligations that Indigenous people understood to be tied to occupation of the fort. Other accounts state that it was the Wea who petitioned for the post to be built as a display of their sovereignty, a demonstration of commitment by the foreign government, and to ease trade with Detroit (Myers 95–6). Within this landscape the Indigenous had the clear advantage over settlers as it required the other to adjust to the Native networks (Bottiger 29). There was next to no centralized leadership uniting Wea or other Miami under a singular person (Bottiger 5; Heath 178). Even though there was a Miami "capital" at Fort Wayne (Kekionga) that negotiated treaties, the satellite groups were independent actors in their own local interests ("The Wabash and Its Valley: Part I—The Earlier History" 63). Though several communities could be found in gathering centers, the Nations themselves retained autonomy as a political entity within it (Myers 121). There were tribes who affiliated with the British but were also trading with the French, which ultimately confused many settlers, "because they often interpreted Indian behavior through homogeneous tribal identities; if one Miami polity favored the British, then they must all be so inclined" (Bottiger 28). This too, was a show of power and clever diplomacy that maintained trade in accordance with the Miami rules while repelling Imperial pressures (Bottiger 24). These realities would have ramifications as the eighteenth century progressed and into today.

Sitting down at Feast of the Hunters' Moon

Dallen J. Timothy and Stephen W. Boyd (2006) describe tourism as "a complex system of supply and demand wherein destinations provide different products and the traveling public desires diverse experiences" (1). Heritage tourism specifically provides the experience of sites "where historic events occurred and places where interesting and significant cultures stand out" (Timothy and Boyd 2). The Feast itself is

> a re-creation of the annual fall gathering of the French and Native Americans which took place Fort Ouiatanon, a fur-trading outpost in the mid-1700s. It is held annually in early autumn on the banks of the Wabash River, four miles southwest of West Lafayette, Indiana.
> (Tippecanoe County Historical Association, "Welcome")

The modern Feast of the Hunters' Moon was first rolled out in 1968, ironically during the period of marked Indigenous/Native American Civil Rights movements and strengthening presence (Clifford 9; Lowenthal 6). Rounding on its 53rd installment (as of 2020), the Feast is a major event in the northern area of Indiana. The battlegrounds see upwards of 40,000 visitors over the 2 days, who come to see over 6,000 re-enactors and peruse 206 vendors (Figures 4.2–4.3). The air is constantly choking with smoke, military commands, gunpowder, petrichor, hammers on black iron, spinning wheels whirling, sweet cider, and bustling movement. In the scope of pioneering heritage sites, it ranks on the smaller side and the temporary nature of the Feast pales in comparison to year-round excursions like Conner Prairie, located 70 miles away in Fishers.

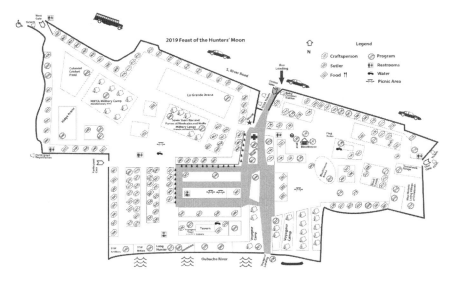

Figure 4.2 Grounds map 2019. Courtesy of Tippecanoe County Historical Association, Lafayette, IN.

Figure 4.3 Fort Ouiatenon trappers. John Schanlaub, CC BY-SA 4.0, via Wikimedia Commons.

The appeal of the Feast is that the visitor gets the chance to step back into a past that is wholly disconnected from their own lives as if it were a foreign country, with their admission ticket serving as their passport for the adventure. De Groot posits that witnessing re-enactment emphasizes the "otherness of history" from the safe distance of the present (105). This othering is predicated on the imposition of a binary wherein the past becomes mutually exclusive to the present (Shaw 159; Baillie et al. 60). So, what defines the inexorable past? Where does the present begin along the timeline? From a holistic framework, history is a cumulative affair rather more like an ocean wave where actions and encounters build upon each other. The past is never truly past (Lowenthal 1, 123). The past informs the present so that it is co-present with it. For the re-enactors, the Feast is a stage on which to perform their heritage and thus assure their authenticity (de Bernardi 252). Re-enactment becomes a way to engage in a search for continuity (Simine 57; Baillie et al. 57; Lowenthal 25) A paradox: at the Feast, the past is strange and distant, yet here it is presented before us to touch and see and taste. The Feast is thus a Foucauldian heterotopia where the paradox of these two time periods can safely co-exist outside of the bounds of normative performance (De Groot 108). Through the encounter within this liminal space, heritage (and equally history) becomes something that can be claimed in the present. Brenda Trofanenko, Canada Research Chair in Education, Culture and Community at the School of Education at Acadia University, observes that,

> These acts of declaring or telling, whether in the service of evidence or proof, reveal how we connect with, commemorate, and contest the past ... I suggest, however, that oral history is less about the event and its telling and more concerned with what is remembered and the meaning made through that memory for those telling and those listening.
>
> (150)

Here is where history is made and remade, shaped to fit present desires.

In order for this last action to be possible, there must be the acknowledgment that the past is not a concrete entity and the past they are engaging with is not strictly accurate. To this end I must address the idea of authenticity. Authenticity is a word—a concept—that carries great weight in heritage and tourism studies as well as anthropology (Timothy and Boyd 5–6; de Bernardi 251). Soojung Kim et al. (2019) synthesize that "authenticity involves traditions, techniques, spirit, feeling and historic and social dimensions of cultural heritage which together, represent a sense of historical and cultural continuity" (2), yet Timothy and Boyd (2006) assert that it is simultaneously relative being, "a subjective notion that varies from person to person depending on one's own social conditioning" (6). It is precisely that plasticity that fuels heritage tourism at these little-known sites: the untold stories, the common person who stands in the shadow of historical figures (Lowenthal 502). The past is played with by re-enactors who take bare-bone facts and then flesh out the impersonal event into something more human and relatable. History and heritage then become mediated through memory, both collective

76 *Kathryn Florence*

and personal, which cedes that we shape that past to fit the needs of the present (Simine 16; De Groot 110; Lowenthal 14; Jensen 50). This malleability means that things can be shifted in re-enactment, battles can end differently, tensions can be improved upon (Lowenthal 477).

Forty thousand visitors walk the Feast grounds over 2 days; however, according to Myers's research, the fort would have only seen a fraction of that at its height. "The largest number of Euro-Americans recorded during the duration of New France control of Ouiatenon was 70 individuals in 1746, resulting in a ratio of Native to Euro-American residents in the area of Ouiatenon ranging from 100:1 to 20:1" (109). In addition, the paper trail documenting the interaction between Indigenous and settlers (both English and French) makes almost no mention of any feast save for one mention in the *Ouiatanon Documents* by Nicolas-Marie Renaud (d'Arnaud) Davenne de Desmeloises (1696–1743) who was commander of the fort in 1732 (Sleeper-Smith 124). Perhaps, the factuality does not even matter. It is unlikely that traders coming to Fort Ouiatenon set up tarp-covered booths with their wares out for anyone to gander at, nor did they likely arrange themselves in neat rows along the field. Understandably, experiencing trade as it was carried out at the time would not be as practical or enjoyable, let alone pass safety code. There is usually at least one visitor wearing a Faire dress. British and French military would hardly be occupying the same space without trying to throttle each other. Not to mention that "In the mid-18th century, Ouiatenon was known as an epicenter of interpersonal conflict, and near constant fatal encounters occurred between Native people and Euro-Americans" (Myers 103), which is thankfully absent in the jovial atmosphere. This is a sanitized past, an idealized vision of history, what would be categorized as "inauthentic heritage" (Timothy and Boyd 5–6). Yet, this is heritage none the less. Visitors come for the *feeling* of authenticity, not the stipulation of accuracy (García-Almeida 8; Domínguez-Quintero et al. 12).

On the menu: Ongoing colonialism

There has been a shift in priority for museological function in recent decades, from authoritative preservation to community relevance. The institutions literally become "engagement zones" (Onciul 72). So too has the heritage institution shifted practice to embody the role of entertainment as well as educator (Simine 8). Like other sites of heritage re-enactment, the Feast utilizes applied theatrics

> to facilitate experiential learning, elicit emotional responses from visitors and make them empathize and identify with people from the past. One way to encourage visitors to engage with the past is to transform it into "their" past, even if they did not live actually through it.
>
> (Simine 12)

The heritage site becomes a space for invention or affirmation (Simine 8, 14). The Feast is a social space, innately tied to the production of norms, upholding of worldviews, and enculturation, for experimenting with personal and community identity that is still ultimately tied to the real life that visitors return to at the end of the day (De Angelis et al. 7; Hansen 389; Eley 556). At the core is the organizer's ability to make meaning, aware or not (Finegan 283). Chance Finegan (2019) points out that

> Interpreters un/knowingly become complicit in ongoing colonial processes if they are working in an Indigenous context and do not critically question the research on which they base their work and do not represent the multiple meanings that inhabit the resources they interpret.
>
> (284)

While this paper will not tell interpreters or scholars how to do so, it will give insight into how the institution has been perpetuating colonialism by catering to visitors' and re-enactors' desires for inauthentic heritage.

The Feast always begins with the arrival of the *coureurs de bois* from the tepid waters of the Wabash River. Upon arrival the participants hoist their canoes overhead and parade them between the corridor of spectators. Once the final vessel has docked, the grand entry shifts to the military battalions who form rank and march to the reconstructed fort for the raising of the flags that concludes the opening ceremony. Likewise, the story presented here places the beginning of history at contact with European settlers rather than with the original peoples. This narrative says, this is settler land, and before that it was empty; a notion echoed in Bryan Grimwood et al.'s (2019) examination of Canadian Near North tourism (236). The emphasis on the arrival and permanence of settlers conveys that settlers have been here since the beginning and this heritage thereby affirms the visitor's ties to the land (Lowenthal 92). In turn, re-enactment at the Feast of the Hunters' Moon ultimately feeds and fuels *hiraeth* (Lowenthal 464; Simine 54). Hiraeth is a Welsh term for a specific type of nostalgic longing that goes beyond homesickness (Kielar). It is the missing of something that may no longer exist or may have never been, the yearning for an ancestral homeland that was never yours. The history storied through the Feast and its re-enactors attempts to assuage that longing by acting out a narrative that reaffirms their connection to it (Timothy and Boyd 3; Kim et al. 3; Erb 159; Grimwood et al. 235).

Staging the Feast at Fort Ouiatenon continues to dictate how the people relate to the land on which they stand, as visitors and as Hoosiers, Americans, or settlers. There is a persistence of American nationalism at the Feast, despite the fact that the United States as an entity would not exist until 1776 and Indiana would not enter that union until 1818. These future notions were projected onto the pioneering era easily at the fort because it had been an important location across these time periods. The Feast—by presenting the fort as the enduring centerpiece and in conjunction with the raising of a temporary Wea village (Figure 4.4)—is itself is an imagining of history that provides a naturalization of settlers while simultaneously dispossessing Indigenous inhabitants according to European notions of land ownership.

Figure 4.4 The shaman's wikiiami. Dina-Roberts Wakulczyk, CC BY-SA 2.0, via Flickr.

The predominant tribal group recorded at Waayaahtanonki was the *waayaahtanwa*, or Wea, related to the contemporary Miami of Indiana and the Peoria Tribe of Indians of Oklahoma. Growing up in the state and around the heritage sites of Fort Ouiatenon, Spring Mill, Prophetstown, and Connor Prairie, there was a distinct notion that this Indigenous population was extinct. William Heath, Professor Emeritus of English at Mount Saint Mary's University, explains that

> a people cannot proceed with any kind of land claim, or other legal process, until they have established an identity for themselves, and that a demonstration of their existence is primary to such further action ... if museums, tourist facilities, books, and films present groups of people as if they no longer exist, then they may have a serious problem trying to convince others that they do.
> (156)

The Indiana Miami, or eastern Miami, received federal recognition on June 5th, 1854; however, its federal recognition was terminated 43 years later. In 1980 the Indiana legislature voted in support of federal recognition of the eastern Miami (Rafert 291). The Miami of Indiana have been petitioning for state/federal recognition as a First Nation for years now on the basis of their persistent inhabitation of the land around Peru, Indiana. The bill introduced in 2011 to grant state recognition died in committee. As of 2019, Indiana still has no state or federally recognized tribe. The historicizing dissociation of Indigenous presence in Indiana presented through the Feast does not aid in dislodging the idea from the popular imagination, as the only chance that the public has to encounter these contemporary realities is in the arena of history, which teaches them to project living incarnations onto an ahistorical narrative that removes them from the contemporary moment (Carpio 622; Shaw 156; Simpson 35; Hendry 2; Grimwood et al. 233; Erb 160).

Though the notion of race was applied more so from the settler side than the Indigenous side during the original occupation, it has since become more prevalent in the negotiation of heritage during the modern Feast. The grouping of the countless ethnicities under the umbrella label of "Indian" provides an easy binary to the white settler across time at the site, further reinforced by the manipulation of heritage that obscures the nuances of community identity that had colored the original relationships (Bottiger 10; Clifford 30; Hollinshead 48). The primary sources are evidence of an

> "othering" that occurred when colonizers created a narrative that placed themselves at the center of focus and Native people on the outside of their own history as onlookers, and this literary history was then valued above the oral histories once maintained by tribes.
>
> (Myers 121)

The Feast does attempt to confront this notion by including a handful of Indigenous performers and participants (Harper). Of the 46 performance groups in 2019, only 6 represent Indigenous cultures, flying directly in the face of the reality recovered by Myers.

What is seen is equally concerning. The re-enactment guidelines stipulate that "All items worn, displayed, or offered for sale must be appropriate to the 1717–91 time period and our location on the colonial frontier" and "Indian portrayals should wear Eastern Woodlands Indian dress of the period" (Tippecanoe County Historical Association, "Clothing Tips"). When the period in question spans over seven decades, a great deal of dress can change, a fact that is often in conflict with the notions of authenticity that heritage tourism espouses (Iverson and Davies 3), and could possibly make it more difficult for First Nations to participate in the Feast as re-enactors and interpreters. Indigenous participants are expected to conform to a certain image of "traditional," "unchanged," or "pristine" indigeneity that is uniquely for tourist consumption (Grimwood et al. 235–9; de Bernardi 250–1; Hollinshead 43–4; Erb 159; Ruhanen and Whitford 4; Abascal 265; García-Almeida 6). This historicization has little impact on non-Indigenous visitors. They know that they exist in the contemporary moment and gain from being supplanted within the narrative of the past as explained previously. Indigenous people do not because if they are to be deemed "authentic" they must exist according to traditions and unchanged, but in doing so they forfeit their place as contemporary persons; if they resist historicization then they are deemed inauthentic

80　*Kathryn Florence*

and denied the space to speak about their own history (Grimwood et al. 239; Hollinshead 55).

When looking at the presentation of history, we have to interrogate why a story is being told in addition to how it is being told. Because "For generations, stories have staked claims to history, to land, to authority, and to identity, each tale emphasizing its own particular views at the expense of competing interpretations" (Evans 222). The story presented at the Feast overwrites history in the minds and imaginations of its visitors. This event is to celebrate the coming together of settlers and Indigenous peoples, yet it neglects to inform the visitors of the unequal footing they had at the time, and the new inequalities created in the present.

Representation matters

With the rise of inclusion and reconciliation initiatives, the development of more community-oriented museological paradigms (Simpson 1; De Angelis et al. 2, 13; Heath 63; Clifford 28; Baillie et al. 66), and the shift of First Voices from being subjects to the authors of history, we are beginning to see that we still have a lot of work to do. Grimwood et al. state that "Tourism is an especially potent social force through which such settler stories can be perpetuated and resisted" (Grimwood et al. 233). Heritage tourism events, such as the Feast of the Hunters' Moon, have been tools in maintaining the status quo institutionalized by colonialism (Ruhanen and Whitford 2–3), yet they can likewise serve as places where we can renegotiate the relationships between public, subject, institution, and community by centering the role of the historic past in the present and the role we all play in the creation of that narrative. At these events visitors can be guided in considering the present and future (Simine 56; De Angelis et al. 12). It is not a pleasant process because it requires the acknowledgment that specific voices have been (un)intentionally silenced and that we do not yet live in a post-colonization age. It requires un-settling history, heritage, and memory which can only be addressed as part of de-centering settler narratives and deconstructing the systematic injustices ingrained within institutions born from colonialism (Grimwood et al. 235; de Bernardi 251; Gerberich 78).

The place to start is with the organizers themselves. A look at the website, brochures, and media releases reveals the telling absence of tribal liaisons or representatives for the event as a whole. According to Hinch and Butler's (1996) four types of Indigenous tourism activity, the Feast is firmly within *culture dispossessed tourism* (cultural themes present; low control by Indigenous people) (Butler and Hinch 6). Nielsen and Wilson (2006) expanded upon the previous model to examine the roles Indigenous peoples have across the spectrum of control in tourism research. The Feast identifies Indigenous people—in that they are present agents—"but no real involvement, action or empowerment ensues" (Nielsen and Wilson 4). There is a need to offer the means and space for Indigenous persons to become *stakeholders* (Nielsen and Wilson 5; Kim et al. 4; Ryan, "Introduction" 9) in the organization of the Feast because it benefits from the display of their culture. To be clear, I do not mean consultation over completed interpretive programs, but active and equal collaboration from the start. That is how we develop a successful cultural experience for both sides (Ruhanen and Whitford 6). Furthermore, "Tourism has the capacity to shape or transform the culture of an Indigenous community by influencing the way individuals in a community see themselves and how they perceive their identity and in particular, their intangible cultural heritage" (Ruhanen and Whitford 3). In arenas, such as the Feast, where there is an undercurrent of naturalization of settler dominance and historicization, special attention must be given to how Indigenous participation is being regulated. White western scholars and tourism leaders should not have the power to determine what is or is not authentic/traditional heritage for communities they do not belong to (Nielsen and Wilson 2). The Feast presents a space where Indigenous stakeholders can challenge the prevailing stereotypes of "Otherness" and represent their own heritage reality (de Bernardi 251; Ruhanen and Whitford 4–5). This reality might not adhere to the step-back-in-time experience the Feast usually sports because heritage is encapsulated in the adaptation of the past to the present, the growth from seeds planted by generations before us (de Bernardi 254; García-Almeida 3). In this way Indigenous stakeholders have the freedom to express their contemporaneity and reaffirm their claim to the land too as well as pride in their performance on a mainstream stage (Ryan, "Who Manages Indigenous Cultural Tourism Product—Aspiration and Legitimization" 70).

This brings me to my final point: underlying the entire Feast is the claiming of space. Claiming the territory of history, the ownership of the land, and the authority of authenticity. So, if "settler colonialism is about taking space from Indigenous peoples, unsettling settler colonialism must be about making space" (Grimwood et al. 245). This does not have to be at the exclusion of some participants. Heritage is not a zero-sum system. Making space creates the possibility for dialogue, encouraging the dissemination of knowledge through Indigenous methodologies. Primarily, an Indigenous methodology is not about product, but process, meaning that we are created by the network of relationships we are a part of, as opposed to our actions within those relationships (Wilson 80; Kahn 237; Finegan 289). On the green of Fort Ouiatenon we can have intermedial dialogues, which "serve the purpose of positioning the performer in relation to other performers, to the past, to society at large, and to possible future shifts in thinking" (Evans 222).

Conclusion: Pulling up a chair

The Feast of the Hunters' Moon was established in the middle of a public heritage boom and reflects the desire of a community to celebrate a perceived period of peace and foundational identity. The intention brought together hundreds of people who shared the vision of a living history event that would educate and entertain in equal parts. This chapter then explained who was invited to sit at the table to construct the narrative of history as it is served at the Feast. The politics of re-enactment have framed the presence of Indigenous persons as transient participants rather than as the original stewards of the land who were engaged in a contest of sovereignty. The way that visitors are encouraged to interact with the

Feast likewise perpetuates the perception that the history of the site has little to no connection to their present. The Feast reiterates the naturalization of white settlers while dispossessing Indigenous communities of their claim to the land. While unintentional, the impact of the Feast ripples out as a product of ongoing colonialization that dislocates First Voices in the historical past. The result is that Indigenous voices tend to be on the menu: cut up, discarded, or consumed when it appeals to the narrative. Examining the Feast of the Hunters' Moon has revealed that sometimes there is not a place at the table, but in this case there is room to pull up a chair and make room for decolonization in heritage tourism.

References

Abascal, Trinidad Espinosa. "Indigenous Tourism in Australia: Understanding the Link between Cultural Heritage and Intention to Participate Using the Means-End Chain Theory." *Journal of Heritage Tourism*, vol. 14, no. 3, May 2019, pp. 263–81. doi:10.1080/1743873X.2018.1549053.

Baillie, Britt, et al. "Packaging the Past: The Commodification of Heritage." *Heritage Management*, vol. 3, no. 1, Apr. 2010, pp. 51–71. doi:10.1179/hma.2010.3.1.51.

Bottiger, Patrick. *The Borderland of Fear: Vincennes, Prophetstown, and the Invasion of the Miami Homeland*. U of Nebraska P, 2016.

Butler, Richard, and Thomas Hinch, editors. *Tourism and Indigenous Peoples: Issues and Implications*. 1st edition, Butterworth-Heinemann, 2007.

Carpio, Myla Vicenti. "(Un)Disturbing Exhibitions: Indigenous Historical Memory at the NMAI." *American Indian Quarterly*, vol. 30, no. 3/4, 2006, pp. 619–31.

Clifford, James. *Returns: Becoming Indigenous in the Twenty-First Century*. Harvard UP, 2013.

Cockrum, William Monroe. *Pioneer History of Indiana: Including Stories, Incidents, and Customs of the Early Settlers*. Press of Oakland City Journal, 1907, http://books.google.com/books?id=hhEVAAAAYAAJ.

De Angelis, Alessandra, et al. "Disruptive Encounters–Museums, Arts and Postcoloniality." *The Postcolonial Museum*, 2014, pp. 1–24.

de Bernardi, Cecilia. "Authenticity as a Compromise: A Critical Discourse Analysis of Sámi Tourism Websites." *Journal of Heritage Tourism*, vol. 14, no. 3, 2019, pp. 249–62. doi:10.1080/1743873X.2018.1527844.

De Groot, Jerome. *Consuming History: Historians and Heritage in Contemporary Popular Culture*. Routledge, 2009.

Domínguez-Quintero, Ana M., et al. "The Role of Authenticity, Experience Quality, Emotions, and Satisfaction in a Cultural Heritage Destination." *Journal of Heritage Tourism*, vol. 14, no. 5–6, 2019, pp. 491–505. doi:10.1080/1743873X.2018.1554666.

Eley, Geoff. "The Past Under Erasure? History, Memory, and the Contemporary." *Journal of Contemporary History*, edited by Jan Palmowski and Kristina Spohr Readman, vol. 46, no. 3, 2011, pp. 555–73. doi:10.1177/0022009411403342.

Erb, Maribeth. "Limiting Tourism and the Limits of Tourism: The Production and Consumption of Tourist Attractions in Western Flores." *Indigenous Tourism*, Elsevier, 2005, pp. 155–79. doi:10.1016/B978-0-08-044620-2.50017-1.

Evans, Michael Robert. "Artistic Courage in Small Groups: Identity, Intermediality, and Indian Country." *The Individual and Tradition: Folkloristic Perspectives*, 2011, pp. 219–34.

Finegan, Chance. "The Interpreter as Researcher: Ethical Heritage Interpretation in Indigenous Contexts." *Journal of Heritage Tourism*, vol. 14, no. 3, May 2019, pp. 282–94. doi:10.1080/1743873X.2018.1474883.

García-Almeida, Desiderio Juan. "Knowledge Transfer Processes in the Authenticity of the Intangible Cultural Heritage in Tourism Destination Competitiveness." *Journal of Heritage Tourism*, vol. 14, no. 5–6, Nov. 2019, pp. 409–21. doi:10.1080/1743873X.2018.1541179.

Gerberich, Victoria L. "An Evaluation of Sustainable American Indian Tourism." *Indigenous Tourism*, Elsevier, 2005, pp. 75–86. doi:10.1016/B978-0-08-044620-2.50012-2.

Grimwood, Bryan S. R., et al. "Settler Colonialism, Indigenous Cultures, and the Promotional Landscape of Tourism in Ontario, Canada's 'near North.'" *Journal of Heritage Tourism*, vol. 14, no. 3, 2019, pp. 233–48. doi:10.1080/1743873X.2018.1527845.

Hansen, Gregory. "Vernacular Interpretation in a Public Folklore Event: Listening to the Call of Florida Fiddlers, Three." *The Individual and Tradition: Folkloristic Perspectives*, Special Publications of the Folklore Institute, Indiana University, Indiana UP, 2011, pp. 378–408.

Harper, Hannah. "Native Voices Resonate at Annual Feast of the Hunters' Moon." *Journal & Courier*, 4 Oct. 2018, https://www.jconline.com/story/entertainment/2018/10/04/native-voices-resonate-annual-feast-hunters-moon/1508477002/.

Heath, William. "Re-Evaluating 'The Fort-Wayne Manuscript': William Wells and the Manners and Customs of the Miami Nation." *Indiana Magazine of History*, vol. 106, no. 2, 2010, pp. 158–88, doi:10.5378/indimagahist.106.2.0158.

Hendry, Joy. *Reclaiming Culture: Indigenous People and Self-Representation*. Palgrave Macmillan, 2005.

Hollinshead, Keith. "'White' Gaze, 'Red' People — Shadow Visions: The Disidentification of 'Indians' in Cultural Tourism." *Leisure Studies*, vol. 11, no. 1, Jan. 1992, pp. 43–64. doi:10.1080/02614369100390301.

Iverson, Peter, and Wade Davies. *"We Are Still Here": American Indians since 1890*. 2nd ed., John Wiley & Sons, 2015.

Jeffrey Ostler. "'To Extirpate the Indians': An Indigenous Consciousness of Genocide in the Ohio Valley and Lower Great Lakes, 1750s–1810." *The William and Mary Quarterly*, vol. 72, no. 4, 2015, p. 587. doi:10.5309/willmaryquar.72.4.0587.

Jensen, Bernard Eric. "Usable Pasts: Comparing Approaches to Popular and Public History." *People and Their Pasts: Public History Today*, edited by Paul Ashton and Hilda Kean, Palgrave Macmillan UK, 2009, pp. 42–56, doi:10.1057/9780230234468_3.

Kahn, Joel S. "Encountering Extraordinary Worlds: The Rules of Ethnographic Engagement and the Limits of Anthropological Knowing." *Numen*, vol. 61, no. 2/3, 2014, pp. 237–54. JSTOR, https://www.jstor.org/stable/24644780.

Kielar, Samantha. "Hiraeth." *Word of the Week*, 2 Apr. 2016, https://sites.psu.edu/kielarpassionblog2/2016/04/02/hiraeth/.

Kim, Soojung, et al. "Development of Intangible Cultural Heritage as a Sustainable Tourism Resource: The Intangible Cultural Heritage Practitioners' Perspectives." *Journal of Heritage Tourism*, vol. 14, no. 5–6, 2019, pp. 422–35. doi:10.1080/1743873X.2018.1561703.

Kmusser. "Wabash River Map." Wikimedia Commons, Wikipedia, June 3, 2008, https://commons.wikimedia.org/wiki/File:Wabashrivermap.png. Accessed February 2, 2021.

Lowenthal, David. *The Past Is a Foreign Country - Revisited*. Revised and Updated edition, Cambridge UP, 2013.

McDonnell, Michael A. "Rethinking the Middle Ground: French Colonialism and Indigenous Identities in the Pays d'en Haut." *Native Diasporas: Indigenous Identities and Settler Colonialism in the Americas*, edited by Gregory D. Smithers and Brooke N. Newman, University of Nebraska Press, 2014, pp. 79–108.

Myers, Kelsey Noack. *Indigenous Landscapes and Legacy Archaeology at Ouiatenon*, Indiana UP, 2017.

Nielsen, Noah, and Erica Wilson. "From Invisible to Indigenous-Driven: A Critical Typology of Research in Indigenous Tourism." *Journal of Hospitality and Tourism Management*, vol. 19, no. 1, 2012, pp. 67–75. doi:10.1017/jht.2012.6.

Onciul, Bryony. *Museums, Heritage and Indigenous Voice: Decolonising Engagement*. Routledge, 2015.

Rafert, Stewart. *The Miami Indians of Indiana: A Persistent People, 1654–1994*. Indiana Historical Society Press, 2003. *Open WorldCat*, https://www.overdrive.com/search?q=244E873D-8335-450F-BDF8-8FCBB0BA5FF0.

Ruhanen, Lisa, and Michelle Whitford. "Cultural Heritage and Indigenous Tourism." *Journal of Heritage Tourism*, vol. 14, no. 3, 2019, pp. 179–91. doi:10.1080/1743873X.2019.1581788.

Ryan, Chris. "Introduction: Tourist-Host Nexus — Research Considerations." *Indigenous Tourism*, Elsevier, 2005, pp. 1–11. doi:10.1016/B978-0-08-044620-2.50006-7.

———. "Who Manages Indigenous Cultural Tourism Product — Aspiration and Legitimization." *Indigenous Tourism*, Elsevier, 2005, pp. 69–73. doi:10.1016/B978-0-08-044620-2.50011-0.

Schanlaub, John. "Fort Ouiatenon Trappers." Wikimedia Commons, Wikipedia, August 27, 2011, https://commons.wikimedia.org/wiki/File:Fort_Ouiatenon_Trappers.jpg. Accessed 2 Feb. 2021.

Shaw, Wendy M. K. "Preserving Preservation: Maintaining Meaning in Museum Storage." *Museum Storage and Meaning: Tales from the Crypt*, edited by Mirjam Brusius and Kavita Singh, Routledge, 2018, pp. 152–68.

Simine, Silke Arnold-de. *Mediating Memory in the Museum*. Palgrave Macmillan UK, 2013. doi:10.1057/9781137352644.

Simpson, Moira G. *Making Representations: Museums in the Post-Colonial Era*. Routledge, 2012.

Sleeper-Smith, Susan, editor. *Contesting Knowledge: Museums and Indigenous Perspectives*. U of Nebraska P, 2009.

Sleeper-Smith, Susan. *Indigenous Prosperity and American Conquest: Indian Women of the Ohio River Valley, 1690–1792*. Omohundro Institute of Early American History and Culture; University of North Carolina Press, 2018.

"The Wabash and Its Valley: Part I—The Earlier History." *The Indiana Quarterly Magazine of History*, vol. 1, no. 2, 1905, pp. 59–67. JSTOR, https://www.jstor.org/stable/27785227.

Timothy, Dallen J., and Stephen W. Boyd. "Heritage Tourism in the 21st Century: Valued Traditions and New Perspectives." *Journal of Heritage Tourism*, vol. 1, no. 1, 2006, pp. 1–16. doi:10.1080/17438730608668462.

Tippecanoe County Historical Association. "Clothing Tips." *Feast of the Hunters' Moon*, http://feastofthehuntersmoon.org.

———. "Welcome." *Feast of the Hunters' Moon*, http://feastofthehuntersmoon.org.

———. "Grounds Map 2019." Feast of the Hunters' Moon, 2019, http://feastofthehuntersmoon.org/schedule/2019-event/. Accessed February 2, 2021.

Trofanenko, Brenda. "Displayed Objects, Indigenous Identities, and Public Pedagogy." *Anthropology & Education Quarterly*, vol. 37, no. 4, 2006, pp. 309–27. JSTOR, https://www.jstor.org/stable/4126368.

Wakulczyk, Dina-Roberts. "The shaman's wikiiami." Flickr, October 8, 2006, https://www.flickr.com/photos/littlesister/268215162/in/album-72157594325629049/. Accessed 2 Feb. 2021.

Wilson, Shawn. *Research Is Ceremony: Indigenous Research Methods*. Fernwood, 2008.

5 Slavery in the Big Easy

Digital interventions in the tourist landscape of New Orleans

Ella Howard

Introduction

Each year, millions of tourists flock to New Orleans to visit historic areas, listen to live music, and enjoy themselves. Tripadvisor users' ten top-rated New Orleans attractions reflect the city's deep history, including the Garden District, City Park, Jackson Square, and the French Quarter (New Orleans Attractions). The list also includes twentieth- and twenty-first-century landmarks integral to the history of jazz, such as Preservation Hall and Frenchmen Street. The city's "Voodoo Queen" Marie Laveau appears as St. Louis Cemetery No. 1, home to her tomb, ranks number ten. As this simple metric demonstrates, New Orleans's complex history of race relations has created an urban landscape where the history of Black and white Americans is deeply intertwined. Despite this attention to history, including Black cultural history, however, little to no information about the history of slavery in New Orleans is presented at these major tourist sites.

To close this gap in the city's interpretive landscape, the City of New Orleans Tricentennial Commission, in conjunction with historians, curators, and educators, launched the mobile app, "New Orleans Slave Trade" in 2018 (New Orleans Slave Trade Marker Tour and Audio Guide). As part of the New Orleans Slave Trade Project which set out to add six physical markers on relevant historical sites, the app invites users to explore the history of the slave trade across the city. Informed by the Black Lives Matter movement, some tourists are seeking more information about the history of slavery and inequality in America. Their interest aligns with renewed critical attention being paid to the city by historians. A brand of New Orleans exceptionalism has framed the city as a site of idealized multiculturalism and interracial cooperation, stunting much earlier public dialogue on the topic of slavery. The New Orleans Slave Trade mobile app challenges the traditional treatment of slavery in public programming, reflecting shifting standards of interpretation in public history and tourism studies.

Traditional presentations of slavery in tourist sites

Historians and tourism scholars have elucidated the construction of meaning in tourist sites. Historians Anthony Stantonis and J. Mark Souther have analyzed in

DOI: 10.4324/9781003102830-6

detail the ways in which New Orleans's twentieth-century tourist culture developed within racist frameworks that left Black workers both symbolically and materially in subservient roles. Focusing on the history of New Orleans, Kevin Fox Gotham used the concept of "tourism authenticity" to study the process through which elite government and commercial actors structured the narrative presented to city visitors (322). Carefully selected images of the past are reified through circulation in tourist media, over time becoming popularly accepted versions of history.

Across the American South, historic sites have been curated largely with tourists in mind and slavery has traditionally been ignored or marginalized. One notable exception is the Old Slave Mart Museum in Charleston, South Carolina, opened in 1938 by Miriam Wilson, who purchased the Chalmers Street property that had served as a jail and auction site for the enslaved (Yuhl). Under her leadership, the museum displayed artifacts she claimed had been made by enslaved people. Many Charleston elites denied the building's history and found the museum inappropriate, although historian Stephanie Yuhl described Wilson's museum as echoing the rhetoric of the Jim Crow South. Wilson was succeeded by Louise Alston Wragg Graves and Judith Wragg Chase, who ran the museum similarly from 1960 to 1987. After a 20-year closure, the Old Slave Mart re-opened in 2007 under the leadership of Nichole Green, who has focused the site on the history of slavery in Charleston and on the specific building housing the museum.

Although slavery was practiced throughout America, research on its presentation in heritage tourist sites has centered on Southern "plantation tourism" (Buzinde and Santos). Such sites have traditionally presented a "whitewashed" vision of plantation life (Butler). Tours typically focused on the architecture and furnishings of the house and the lives of the plantation owners. Site operators managing these largely for-profit enterprises made these narrative choices to meet the expectations of their predominantly white tourist patrons. These priorities correlate to survey data about visitors, who have expressed interest in learning about all of those topics, as well as the Civil War and the tools and material artifacts used by the enslaved (Carter et al., "The House That Story Built" 552–3). When slavery has been incorporated into heritage tourism, the results have sometimes been disastrous. A now infamous 1994 re-enactment of a slave auction at Colonial Williamsburg drew criticism for being overly entertaining and insufficiently educational (J. Horton 50–1).

Given slavery's centrality to the history of Louisiana, its omission from the tourist landscape may at first appear surprising. Scholars of tourism studies and public history offer several explanations for these interpretive choices, citing both business and intellectual factors. As profit-generating enterprises, plantation tours and Southern house museums have traditionally offered programming that site operators and curators anticipated would resonate with their target audiences. Key to these decisions were their perceptions of audience demographics. Traditional programs were written for wealthy white audiences, reflecting generalizations borne out by scholarly research into tourist demographics. Studies conducted in 2002 and 2013 found the average plantation visitors to be white, educated, middle-aged women with high incomes (Dwyer 433; Bright and Carter). Curators and tour guides avoided alienating these visitors with content that might challenge their views on race or interrupt their vacation (Nelson 301).

Slavery has also been marginalized in much of the city's academic scholarship. In *Slavery's Metropolis*, Rashuana Johnson argued that New Orleans has too often been characterized as a city exempt from racial divisions. The large population of free people of color during the antebellum era has led many to "romanticize" New Orleans, Johnson cautioned (17). Instead, Johnson encouraged a critical approach to the city's complex past: "Rather than considering free blacks, people of so-called mixed race, or interracial sex as evidence of a comparatively lenient race regime, this book instead examines the contingent lived experiences of racism across all levels of a complicated society" (16).

Lynnell L. Thomas analyzed the ways this perceived interracial harmony warped the tourist landscape of New Orleans. She noted that the tourist narrative focused extensively on the French Quarter and the city's French and Spanish heritage, largely avoiding the topic of slavery, despite the city's role as a major center of the slave trade (43–4). When slavery was discussed, the city's history was framed as one in which enslaved people enjoyed more freedoms than they did in other cities (36–7). Thomas characterized the tours offered by the 1990s as "multicultural tours," or "gumbo pot 'history,'" which described the mixing of cultures in the city in ways which downplayed the horrors of slavery and the slave trade (45–8).

The exclusion and minimizing of the history of slavery from the tourist narrative had many devastating effects. With the exception of those few Black-operated heritage tours that presented information about slavery, Black guests were rhetorically excluded from much of the tourist experience (Kytle and Roberts; D'Harlingue 75). Most tourist narratives encourage visitors to identify with the dominant actors, often rendering Black tourists invisible. Such exclusion also cultivated ignorance of the horrors of slavery in white tourists, who might come away with romanticized and false understandings of the past (Carter et al., "The House That Story Built" 554–5). More broadly, such conceptual gaps in the tourist landscape matter because, as noted by tourism scholars, public history is typically less about the past than the present and is shaped by current power relations (Buzinde and Santos). After visiting historic sites, tourists apply the knowledge they gain (whether it is true or false) to our current world, where it influences their thoughts and actions.

Recent changes in the interpretation of slavery

The past five years have witnessed major debates over the Civil War's legacy and monuments. After the war, both Northern and Southern cities erected generic monuments to "common soldiers" (Savage). These monuments, routinely featuring white figures, called upon observers to respect the sacrifices made by soldiers in both armies. After Reconstruction, as the nation's Jim Crow racial politics hardened, many more monuments to the Civil War era were erected. Some were installed by veterans' organizations, but many were the work of the United Daughters of the Confederacy, established in 1894 (Cox). Such monuments often celebrated the era's Lost Cause ethos, evoking a mythic, genteel white Southern past while refusing to address the realities of human bondage. Although historians like Karen Cox have long published critical accounts of such monuments, their work has drawn more attention from the media and the general public in recent years as the debate over such monuments has intensified.

The 2015 Charleston church shooting prompted a national dialogue over the legacy of the Confederacy. As the Black Lives Matter movement called attention to ongoing racism, many communities lobbied for the relocation of the nation's prominent monuments to the Confederacy. The New Orleans City Council voted to remove four monuments, but Mayor Mitch Landrieu struggled to find area firms willing to remove the statues. Landrieu remarked, "This is the very definition of institutionalized racism." Ultimately, the monuments were removed (Wendland). Liberty Place Monument, commemorating a White League attack, fell in April 2017, followed by statues of Confederate President Jefferson Davis, General P.G.T. Beauregard, and General Robert E. Lee (Litten; Nystrom).

After the 2020 murder of George Floyd and the reinvigoration of the Black Lives Matter movement, more Confederate monuments have been toppled, even in Richmond, the heart of the Confederacy (Ortiz). Even statues of Lincoln, such as the famous work by Thomas Ball in Washington, D.C., and its copy in Boston, are being removed due to their racist iconography (Guerra). As artist Ekua Holmes said,

> What I have heard today is that it hurts to look at this piece. And I feel like on the Boston landscape we should not have works that bring shame to any group of people that are citizens, not just of Boston, but of the United States.
> (Guerra)

Some historic sites have also reconsidered their treatment of the history of slavery. Most significantly, lawyer and real estate mogul John Cummings established Louisiana's Whitney Plantation, dubbed by the *New York Times Magazine* "the first slavery museum in America" (Amsden). Located 35 miles from New Orleans, the site's progressive and groundbreaking interpretations, including several memorials to the enslaved, challenge traditional tourist narratives (Rosenfeld; "Whitney Plantation Museum"; Keller). Cummings said,

> I mean, you start understanding that the wealth of this part of the world—wealth that has benefited me—was created by some half a million black people who just passed us by. How is it that we don't acknowledge this?
> (Amsden)

Tourism studies scholars have analyzed the reactions of various groups of site visitors to changing interpretations of the history of slavery, finding that one's reaction depends on the knowledge, values, and interpretive frameworks one brings to the site. Reactions range from those who prefer to hear nothing about slavery while touring a plantation house, and those who are ambivalent, to those who want to hear about slavery and those who also want to hear about race relations (Alderman and Modlin 280–3). As the Whitney Plantation, the National Museum of African American History, and other organizations have ushered in new ways of contextualizing slavery for the public, some visitors have been angered. One Tripadvisor reviewer called the Whitney Plantation, "a race baiter's paradise," stating, "Never have I come to a place more determined to spread race hatred than Whitney, whose guides try to foment historical resentment among the mostly black patrons of the tour" (Whitney Plantation review).[1] Plantation tour guide Margaret Biser explained that tourists fail to grasp the horror of slavery, often equating it with poverty and thinking the lives of "house slaves" were "pretty all right." They repeat familiar tropes from Lost Cause propaganda and Hollywood films such as *Gone with the Wind*, romanticizing the relationship between enslaved people and plantation owners as structured by "loyalty." Tourism scholars have characterized approaches to slavery in museum interpretations as ranging from annihilation (absence), to marginalization (partial inclusion) and inclusion (parity) (Small). Even as more coverage of slavery has been provided in recent years, most sites have not achieved interpretive inclusion, in which equal time is spent on the stories of the enslaved and the slaveowners (Hanna et al.).

Twenty years ago, some scholars framed slavery's history in the context of "thanatourism" or dark tourism (Dann and Seaton). More recent studies have challenged that framework, criticizing it as neglecting the broader historical context of slavery (Yankholmes and McKercher). Some tourist sites do present slavery within a darkly voyeuristic narrative (Raymen). Historian Tiya Miles found that "haunted tours" in New Orleans and Savannah often include more attention to slavery than do traditional history tours, although their narratives are often romanticized. In New Orleans, Miles argued, such tours often present the city as "a good place to be a slave," emphasizing local laws allowing enslaved people some liberties such as Sunday afternoon gatherings in Congo Square. Miles noted that the abuse endured by enslaved people presented on haunted tours often focuses on Madame Delphine Lalaurie, whose sadistic mistreatment of enslaved workers outraged New Orleans society so much that her Royal Street mansion was attacked by a mob. Miles explains that this story at once offers guests the salacious details of human suffering as entertainment, while also distancing such abuses from the city's mainstream history.

Tourism scholars remind us that collective memory can either silence or recall past events (Buzinde and Santos 483). The change to tourist programs prompted by the current national dialogue over racism and shifting scholarly interpretation has created a highly uneven tourist landscape, in which some sites continue to ignore slavery, while others frame it in limited ways. Even in areas where monuments have been toppled, creating new ones remains a bureaucratic process. Increasingly, historians and curators are using more nimble digital tools to share updated and accurate information with interested visitors.

Mobile apps as intervention in the urban landscape

Digital tools facilitate the creation of tourist experiences that extend beyond any specific museum or site, enhancing the tourist experience (Di Pietro et al.). Through websites and mobile apps, tourists can interact with historical content on city streets, fostering broader heritage tourism interventions in the built environment (UNESCO). Self-guided audio tours, in particular, allow guests to take in content at their own pace (Van Winkle and Backman). Tourism scholars have noted that the varying interpretations presented by individual tour guides make consistency of approach nearly impossible (Hanna et al. 62). Audio tours allow the creation of a carefully crafted and edited narrative.

Mobile apps have allowed museums, universities, and historic sites to curate content about the historical significance of various sites and areas, which are then geographically located. Users download these apps onto their phone or other mobile device, and then interact directly with narratives about history and relevant primary sources and visual materials. Such apps can be used on-site, or the content can be accessed remotely. The Clio, developed at Marshall University, allows users to contribute historical content about thousands of sites to a single website. More focused projects have been carried out by historians in many areas of the country using Curatescape, a theme for Omeka, an open-source database and exhibition platform developed and distributed by the Center for History and New Media at George Mason University.

Digital exhibits are sometimes one aspect of a massive reinterpretation of a major historic site, as was the case at Monticello, the Thomas Jefferson estate. The interpretation of Monticello has grown more inclusive over the course of several decades, beginning with the extensive architectural research programs carried out in the 1970s and 1980s (Hallock 3; Kelso and Deetz). In the 1990s, publicity surrounding Jefferson's rape of Sally Hemings, an enslaved woman, forced site visitors to confront the abusive nature of plantation life. Historian Lois Horton has described the tension this causes for many site visitors, who hope to continue seeing Jefferson as benevolent, loving, and tragic, rather than cruel, domineering, and vengeful.

In 1999, the year after the public announcement of D.N.A. evidence connecting the Jefferson and Hemings families, historians Lois and James Oliver Horton studied Monticello visitors' reactions to the subject. They found little difference between the perspectives of white and African American visitors to the site. Instead, the primary distinctions were generational, as senior citizens proved more resistant to an emphasis on slavery in public programming about Jefferson (L. Horton 148–9). Raised to believe that Jefferson embodied the values of the United States, such visitors sometimes struggle to accept the more nuanced realities of his life. As Gardiner Hallock has observed, "Jefferson's role as a leading Founding Father of his young nation was exceptional, but his status as a slave owner was typical" (3).

The 2011 exhibit "Landscape of Slavery: Mulberry Row at Monticello" reframed the area around the experiences of the enslaved, bringing formerly neglected narratives to the fore (Hallock 5). In 2015, Monticello launched a mobile app, "Slavery at Monticello: Life and Work on Mulberry Row," as part of the Mountaintop Project, "a multi-year effort to restore Monticello as Jefferson knew it and to tell the stories of the people—enslaved and free—who lived and worked on the 5,000-acre plantation" ("Monticello Launches New 'Slavery at Monticello' App"; Clozel). The app features animations, maps, brief audio tracks, historic photographs and documents, and a timeline of Jefferson's relationship with the Hemings family.

Although the app makes a useful contribution to the Monticello visitor experience, the content developers missed an opportunity to take a strong stand on the cruelty and abuse inherent to plantation slavery. In the audio track, "Sally Hemings: An Historian's Perspective," Lucia Stanton, Shannon Senior Historian Emeritus, Monticello states,

> Certainly a relationship between a master and his slave is one that's incredibly unbalanced in terms of power. I have no idea what kind of affection or love was involved. But he made a promise that he would free her children when they became 21. And he did so. And Madison Hemings talks about this several times. He also talks about how most white people broke their promises. So that Jefferson is portrayed as someone who kept his promises. And that suggests a relationship of mutual trust.

This track undercuts much of the app's potential, re-inscribing Jefferson within the familiar context of benevolent exceptionalism.

The app incorporates data visualizations to convey quantitative information. This is a creative approach, but the execution here does not always lend itself to the app's educational value. A user intrigued by the question, "How many Monticello slaves were separated from their families?" who clicks the accompanying link reads a bar graph showing that 607 slaves were owned and 400 were separated by sales or gift. Was this a remarkable number? More context information would help users understand the significance of these facts. Some of the audio tracks convey some of the atrocities carried out against those enslaved at Monticello. "Separated from Her Husband" tells the story of Priscilla and John Hemings, a couple who were often forced to live apart. The track "Overseers and Violence" includes Monticello guide Brandon Dillard's powerful description of a violent overseer:

> the person that Jefferson values most as an overseer was a white man named Gabriel Lilly. We have many indications of Lilly's behavior at Monticello. He was a violent man. There's one story in particular where he beats a young enslaved man who's so ill that he could not rise from bed, and Lilly beats him about the head to force him to work.

Such personal narratives communicate the terrors of slavery in a far more immediate way than does abstract statistical data.

The creators of the New Orleans Slave Trade app benefited from these earlier, pioneering digital projects and were poised to make a critical intervention in the city's tourist programming.[2] The app represents the next phase of projects interpreting the history of slavery in a digital format, integrating various types of data into a relatively smooth narrative. Focusing the app on the city's slave trade brings needed attention to a topic fully understood by few city residents or visitors. Over 135,000 enslaved people were sold in New Orleans, their lives forever altered by the transaction. The structure of the app also ensures that users learn about the ways in which the slave trade shaped the city, and the vast number of city residents who profited from it.

Educators presenting the history of slavery strive to convey both its oppressive horrors and the ways in which enslaved people resisted domination (Heim). This mobile app does an admirable job of incorporating both perspectives. The slave trade is described in economic, geographic, and social terms, but also in psychological ones, with several audio tracks devoted to readings of first-person narratives of people who were enslaved. One track focuses specifically on the ways in which enslaved people rebelled, which ranged from work slowdowns, broken tools, arson, and food tampering, to running away and leading slave revolts (Green).[3]

This tour's authors describe the roles of a wide-ranging number of individuals who were involved in the slave trade. When imagining a slave auction, one might picture an auctioneer and financiers, but not notaries, agents, judges, clerks, and lawyers. The app reminds users that those involved in the industry occupied their own business area along Exchange Alley.

The tour consists of eight physical locations and main audio tracks. The tour's main tracks also contain supplemental audio tracks providing further details about relevant themes or additional first-person narratives from those who were enslaved. This format allows the audio tracks to remain between one and four minutes in length, keeping the tour easy to manage, even when users are also navigating crowded city streets. Specific instructions indicate when the listener should play each of the supplemental tracks, often during the walk from one site to another. Each track also features contextual images, such as prints, slave ads, bills of sale, and contemporary site photographs.

This abbreviated narrative structure also presents challenges for the tour's authors, who must condense expansive historical events and trends into brief, straightforward audio narratives. The "middle passage" of the journey from Africa to North America, for instance, is covered by only a single audio track. The authors commendably mention key themes, such as the cultural groups from which the enslaved were taken and the usefulness of their skills to the building of the city, but nuances are inevitably lost.

The narrow focus of the tour on the slave trade in New Orleans allows users to learn a great deal about the subject. Little time is available for broader analysis of relevant topics such as the daily life of the enslaved in New Orleans, the relationships between the enslaved and free people of color, or the experience of those who escaped slavery. Hopefully this pioneering tour will garner the attention necessary to inspire others to create much-needed complementary programming, both in New Orleans and in other cities. Such future apps would benefit from including transcriptions of the audio tracks for the purpose of accessibility, a feature included in the Monticello app, but not the New Orleans Slave Trade app.

Touring New Orleans with the Slave Trade app

Tourism studies scholars have shown that effective public programming around slavery should foreground individual narratives where possible, lest visitors lose sight of the humanity of enslaved people (Cook 299; E. Johnson). This approach also avoids overwhelming visitors with abstract quantitative data (Blevins). The New Orleans Slave Trade app appropriately centers much of the tour on the experiences of individuals, providing participants with an emotionally compelling narrative. The first audio track introduces the slave trade in human terms, opening with the names of 11 children who were aboard the slave ship, *The Ajax*, which arrived in New Orleans from Virginia in September 1835. This vignette reflects the approach taken throughout the tour. Although broader contextual information is provided, the tour maintains a careful local focus, highlighting the slave trade in New Orleans, particularly after its expansion following the 1808 federal ban on international slave trading, and with specific interest in the lived experience of the enslaved. The opening track reminds listeners that over one million enslaved people were sent further south after 1808, and that the scale of the regional slave trade was vast. The tour's authors urge users to focus less on the quantitative dimension of these events, arguing instead for contemplation of the human suffering that ensued (Figure 5.1).

The tour proceeds to the Merieult House on Royall Street, now a property of the Historic New Orleans Collection. Commissioned by French immigrant Jean Francois Merieult, and completed in 1794, the house served as the centerpiece of his business trading goods and enslaved people. Users learn that Merieult profited from the international slave trade, sending slave ships to West Africa, bringing over 750 individuals to the United States in a single year.

Few tourists will be familiar with the 1808 ban on the international slave trade, which is the subject of supplemental audio tracks at this stop. The 1791 invention of the cotton gin and 1803 Louisiana Purchase led to high profits for slaveowners, who continued buying and selling enslaved people after 1808. Another track conveys additional information vital to understanding the historical development of New Orleans. In 1809, Spanish military forces ejected from Cuba French-speaking settlers from Saint-Domingue, 9,000 of whom came to New Orleans. Approximately one-third of the group were white, and one-third people of color, with the largest number being enslaved people. Congress granted an exemption to the 1808 ban, allowing the arrivals from Cuba to be sold in New Orleans. The free people of color who remained in the city helped to create the significant population of free African Americans (R. Johnson 34–7).

Tourists frequently visit the Cabildo, built by the Spanish and used as a court facility by the Spanish, territorial, and Louisiana governments, but slavery is

Slavery in the Big Easy 95

Figure 5.1 The Moonwalk, the tour's first stop, photo by author.

not the focus of the site's interpretation. The app directs users to the portico, the site of late eighteenth-century slave auctions, when the building was the center of local Spanish government. When a slaveowner died without a will or went through bankruptcy proceedings, their property (including any enslaved people) was auctioned on the portico of the Cabildo.

The present-day context of this stop on the tour contrasts starkly with the historical information provided by the app. Jackson Square, the heart of the French Quarter, is the centerpiece of the city's tourist landscape, housing the New Orleans Welcome Center, restaurants, and retail shops. The real life of the square is outdoors, where local jazz and rock musicians frequently stage impromptu performances for tourists and locals alike and tarot card readers and assorted psychics offer inexpensive readings at portable tables. As the scent of incense wafted by and lively jazz music was performed, I struggled as a user of the app to reconcile the square's upbeat atmosphere with the suffering of the enslaved being described. Users of audio tours occupy the same physical space as others, while having a completely different experience. As historian James Oliver Horton cautioned, "Slavery is a sobering subject, too difficult to interpret in the atmosphere of a shopping mall or any place in which education is not the obvious intent" (53). This challenge is faced by tour operators, not only in New Orleans, but also in Savannah and Charleston, all of which are major tourist hubs drawing bridal parties and other raucous groups.

Supplemental audio tracks at this stop orient users to the role of coffeehouses or "exchanges" in the city, which served as sites for business meetings, transactions, and the purchase of enslaved workers. One track focuses on Maspero's Exchange, located at Chartres and St. Louis Streets. The site of slave auctions from 1811, when it was rented by Bernard Tremoulet, it was later operated by auctioneer Pierre Maspero from 1814 until his death in 1822 (Campanella 16–17).

Hewlett's Exchange was also run on the site by auctioneer John Hewlett from 1826 through the mid-1830s. During these years, the exchange was the city's most important location for business meetings and slave auctions, also serving as a tourist destination. App users learn that even future president Abraham Lincoln may have observed a slave auction there when visiting the city. The tour includes rich descriptions of the expensive renovations carried out by 1832, yielding a posh interior featuring four chandeliers, a circular bar, and the capacity to serve up to 300 guests. Even this structure would prove insufficient to accommodate the growing 1830s slave trade, leading to the construction of a new merchants' exchange inside the Saint Charles Hotel across Canal Street, the traditional division between the French and American districts. This stop effectively conveys the profitability of the slave trade and the callousness of not only those who bought and sold individuals but also those who enjoyed the sale as spectacle.

The St. Louis Hotel, opened in 1838, served as not only a hotel, but also a bank and trading exchange, home to multiple near-daily auctions of enslaved people until well into the Civil War. Supplemental audio tracks provide users with details about the experiences of enslaved people being sold. Drawing on the powerful testimony of John Brown, one track describes the tests enslaved people were required to perform at auction, including walking, dancing, and jumping to demonstrate their agility, and responding cheerfully to questions, in order to convey their upbeat personality. A supplemental track at a later stop shares William Wells Brown's account of the hair dyeing and plucking done to ensure enslaved people appeared younger than their age. The effective use of personal testimony and details in these tracks meets the goals of tourism scholars who call for more individualized narratives. Many tourists will be surprised to learn of the ways in which enslaved people were forced to participate actively in their own sale (Figure 5.2).

The tour successfully situates the growing slave trade in the broader context of urban history. A track explains that as the slave trade expanded from the 1830s to the 1850s, enslaved people in need of health care were sent to area institutions such as Charity Hospital. City elites tried to keep the slave trade out of the public eye even as it became more prominent. City officials banned public displays of slave auctions or the lodging of enslaved people for sale within the city limits in 1829. Slave traders responded by establishing auction sites outside the French Quarter and into the Faubourg Marigny, some of which are also included in the New Orleans Slave Trade app.

Few tourists will be familiar with Isaac Franklin and John Armfield, although they were among the wealthiest domestic slave traders in America in the 1820s and 1830s (Natanson). Historians such as Joshua Rothman (a contributor to the

Slavery in the Big Easy 97

Figure 5.2 Plaque mounted on the St. Louis Hotel, photo by author.

app) have documented their tremendous callousness and cruelty; they frequently raped enslaved women in their care. The app conveys this through slightly veiled references to invasive bodily inspections and acts of cruelty and abuse, a logical approach given the fact that many families may follow the audio tour as a group. This example highlights the tension between the need to convey accurately the

98 *Ella Howard*

horrible violence that structured the system of slavery and the pressure to produce a narrative suitable for all members of the public (Figure 5.3).

Two supplemental audio tracks feature first-person testimony from Solomon Northrup, author of *Twelve Years a Slave* (this text is also used at Frogmore Plantation). The recent Hollywood dramatization of his narrative ensures that many users will be familiar with his experience, giving them a frame of reference for the tour (Cook 299).

The Banks' Arcade, built by Thomas Banks, was located in the contemporary Central Business District. Now home to a hotel, the building was the site of some of the city's largest slave auctions, including one at which 178 enslaved people were sold. Similarly, the Slave Depot on Common Street accommodated 300 enslaved people awaiting sale in 1856. These stops help visitors understand the massive scale of the slave trade.

After clearly establishing the brutality of slavery and the slave trade, the tour's final tracks remind tourists of the role of people of African descent in creating New Orleans' vibrant culture. The French codes governing the lives of the enslaved designated Sundays a holiday and the tradition of granting a partial day of rest continued. An 1817 ordinance limited enslaved people to gathering in Congo Square (Evans). The tour concludes there, the historic heart of the city's Black community. In the antebellum period, the area remained the only officially sanctioned space for enslaved people to gather to socialize, exchange goods, worship,

Figure 5.3 Plaque marking the Franklin and Armfield stop, photo by author.

or create music. The tour narrative here emphasizes the cultural production of the African American community by discussing the history of music. Early in the city's history, the West and West Central African origins of the population of color strongly influenced the music that was composed and performed. After the ban on the international slave trade led to the expansion of the domestic slave trade, migrants from the Upper South brought influences to the region, including reels, jigs, and the harmonica, developing the distinctive musical style for which New Orleans would become known.

The tour's last audio track fittingly describes the end of the slave trade in 1862, when Union forces took control of New Orleans. Users are reminded that some enslaved people were sold to buyers in Cuba and Brazil, while others began new lives in the United States. As the tour ends, users find themselves in the Trème, a historically significant, once predominantly African American community. Concluding the tour here stands out from most of the city's other tours, which generate revenue by ending at a bar or shop. Rather than being plunged back into the commercial revelry of the French Quarter, users of the app are reminded to contemplate the continuing legacy of slavery in contemporary American society.

Conclusion

The New Orleans Slave Trade app makes a significant contribution to the public history of slavery, transcending many of the previous limitations of digital as well as physical exhibitions and tours related to the slave trade. Drawing on quantitative research as well as first-person accounts, the tour conveys a rich and multifaceted vision of slavery in the city. Particularly in the current political climate, in which any discussion of the antebellum South is fraught with controversy, public history projects of this type serve a vital purpose, ensuring that the general public has access to factually correct and engaging historical materials.

The app also helps users navigate the seeming paradox of African American autonomy within the brutal regime of slavery. Apologists for slavery long promoted a narrative that New Orleans slaveholders were less repressive in their treatment of enslaved people than were those in other cities. Scholars in recent years have pushed back against this rhetoric, arguing instead that New Orleans was a site of both limited autonomy and stark social control. The city's large population of free people of color challenged the strict racial boundaries enforced in other cities. As Rashauna Johnson argued in *Slavery's Metropolis*, however, white city residents used legislation such as the 1806 Black Code to limit African American mobility, requiring all people of color to provide documentation when asked (85–124). Johnson described New Orleans as a dynamic city in which profits were generated through trade in goods, services, and enslaved people, and in which relative spatial mobility could take place within a context of cruelty and violence. The New Orleans Slave Trade app conveys to the public the spirit of such scholarship, encouraging users to move beyond the tired tropes often perpetuated by popular media and tourist guides.

The Black Lives Matter movement is prompting heightened interest in Black history among tourists from all backgrounds, as evidenced by the dominance of antiracist titles on the June 2020 bestseller lists (Ward). African American heritage sites are also quite popular with Black tourists, who often seek out heritage tourist sites. A recent market analysis estimated that Black tourists contribute $63 billion to the American economy (Mandala Research). This rising popular interest and economic potential make it likely that more tours, exhibits, websites, and mobile apps will focus on the history of African Americans and slavery in the years to come. If developed carefully, such cultural experiences may motivate visitors not only to empathize with the past experiences of African Americans, but also to work toward contemporary social justice (Cook 292).

Notes

1 See also Carter, "Where are the Enslaved?" and Behre.
2 The New Orleans Slave Trade Project Group included representatives from the Tricentennial Commission and its Cultural and Historical Committee, as well as noted academic and public historians Erin Greenwald (New Orleans Museum of Art), Freddi Williams Evans (consultant), Luther Gray (Congo Square Preservation Society/Ashé Cultural Arts Center), Cathe Mizell-Nelson (the Historic New Orleans Collection), Joshua Rothman (University of Alabama), and Ibrahima Seck (Whitney Plantation).
3 On audience desire for stories of resistance, see Cook.

References

"THE 15 BEST Things to Do in New Orleans—2020 (with Photos)." Tripadvisor, www.tripadvisor.com/Attractions-g60864-Activities-New:Orleans_Louisiana.html. Accessed 12 July 2020.

Alderman, Derek H., and E. Arnold Modlin Jr. "On the Political Utterances of Plantation Tourists: Vocalizing the Memory of Slavery on River Road." *Journal of Heritage Tourism*, vol. 11, no. 3, 2016, pp. 275–289. doi: 10.1080/1743873X.2015.1100623.

Amsden, David. "Building the First Slavery Museum in America." *The New York Times Magazine*, 26 Feb. 2015.

Behre, Robert. "Despite Pushback, Charleston Historic Sites Expand their Interpretation of Slavery." *Post and Courier*, 1 Sept. 2019.

Biser, Margaret. "I Used to Lead Tours at a Plantation. You won't Believe the Questions I Got About Slavery." *Vox*, 28 Aug. 2017, https://www.vox.com/2015/6/29/8847385/what-i-learned-from-leading-tours-about-slavery-at-a-plantation. Accessed 21 March 2021.

Blevins, Cameron. "American Panorama: Part I." *Cameron Blevins*, 29 Mar. 2016, www.cameronblevins.org/posts/American-panorama-part-i/. Accessed 21 March 2021.

Bright, Candace Forbes, and Perry Carter. "Who Are They? Visitors to Louisiana's River Road Plantations." *Journal of Heritage Tourism*, vol. 11, no. 3, 2016, pp. 262–274. doi: 10.1080/1743873x.2015.1100627.

Butler, David L. "Whitewashing Plantations: The Commodification of a Slave-Free Antebellum South." *Slavery, Contested Heritage, and Thanatourism*, edited by Graham M. S. Dann and A. V. Seaton, Taylor & Francis Group, 2002. doi: 10.4324/9780203062586-10.

Buzinde, Christine N. and Carla Almeida Santos. "Representations of Slavery." *Annals of Tourism Research*, vol. 35, no. 2, 2008, pp. 469–488. doi: 10.1016/j.annals.2008.01.003.

Campanella, Richard. "On the Structural Basis of Social Memory: Cityscapes of the New Orleans Slave Trade Part I." *Preservation in Print*, Mar. 2013.

Carter, Perry, et al. "The House That Story Built: The Place of Slavery in Plantation Museum Narratives." *The Professional Geographer*, vol. 66, no. 4, 2014, pp. 547–557. doi: 10.1080/00330124.2014.921016.

Carter, Perry. "Where Are the Enslaved?: TripAdvisor and the Narrative Landscapes of Southern Plantation Museums." *Journal of Heritage Tourism*, vol. 11, no. 3, 2016, pp. 235–249. doi: 10.1080/1743873X.2015.1100625.

Clozel, Lalita. "An App Tells Painful Stories of Slaves at Monticello's Mulberry Row." NPR: All Tech Considered, 2 Aug. 2015, www.npr.org/sections/alltechconsidered/2015/08/02/428126511/an-app-tells-painful-stories-of-slaves-at-monticellos-mulberry-row. Accessed 21 March 2021.

Cook, Matthew R. "Counter-Narratives of Slavery in the Deep South: the Politics of Empathy along and beyond River Road." *Journal of Heritage Tourism*, vol. 11, no. 3, 2016, pp. 290–308. doi: 10.1080/1743873X.2015.1100624.

Cox, Karen L. *Dixie's Daughters: The United Daughters of the Confederacy and the Preservation of Confederate Culture.* UP of Florida, 2003.

Curatescape, www.curatescape.org/. Accessed 21 March 2021.

Dann, Graham M. S., and A. V. Seaton. "Slavery, Contested Heritage and Thanatourism." *International Journal of Hospitality & Tourism Administration*, vol. 2, no. 3–4, 2001, pp. 1–29. doi: 10.4324/9780203062586.

D'Harlingue, Benjamin. "On the Plantation with Ghosts: Antagonisms of Slavery Tourism." *The South Carolina Review*, Spring 2015.

Di Pietro, Laura, et al. "Heritage and Identity: Technology, Values and Visitor Experiences." *Journal of Heritage Tourism*, vol. 13, no. 2, 2019, pp. 97–103. doi: 10.1080/1743873x.2017.1384478.

Dwyer, Owen, et al. "Commemorative Surrogation and the American South's Changing Heritage Landscape." *Tourism Geographies*, vol. 15, no. 3, 2013, pp. 424–443. doi: 10.1080/14616688.2012.699091.

Evans, Freddi Williams. "Introduction." *Congo Square: African Roots in New Orleans*. U of Louisiana at Lafayette P, 2011.

Gotham, Kevin Fox. "Selling New Orleans to New Orleans: Tourism Authenticity and the Construction of Community Identity." *Tourist Studies*, vol. 7, no. 3, 2007, pp. 317–339. doi: 10.1177/1468797608092515.

Green, Sharony Andrews. *Remember Me to Miss Louisa: Hidden Black-White Intimacies in Antebellum America*. Northern Illinois UP, 2015.

Guerra, Cristela. "Boston Art Commission Votes to Remove Emancipation Memorial from Park Square." WBUR, 30 June 2020.

Hallock, Gardiner. "Mulberry Row: Telling the Story of Slavery at Monticello." *SiteLINES: A Journal of Place*, vol. 14, no. 2, Spring 2019, pp. 3–8.

Hanna, Stephen P., et al. "Following the Story: Narrative Mapping as a Mobile Method for Tracking and Interrogating Spatial Narratives." *Journal of Heritage Tourism*, vol. 14, no. 1, 2019, pp. 49–66. doi: 10.1080/1743873x.2018.1459628.

Heim, Joe. "The Missing Pieces of America's Education." *Washington Post*, 28 Aug. 2019.

Horton, James Oliver, "Slavery in American History: An Uncomfortable National Dialogue." *Slavery and Public History: The Tough Stuff of American Memory*, edited by James Oliver Horton and Lois E. Horton, U of North Carolina P, 2009.

Horton, Lois. "Avoiding History: Thomas Jefferson, Sally Hemings, and the Uncomfortable Public Conversation on Slavery." *Slavery and Public History*, pp. 144–149.

Johnson, Erik. "Slavery, Tourism, and Memory in New Orleans's 'Plantation Country.'" *Africa Today*, vol. 65, no. 4. Summer 2019, pp.100–118. doi: 10.2979/africatoday.65.4.07.

Johnson, Rashauna. *Slavery's Metropolis: Unfree Labor in New Orleans during the Age of Revolutions*. Cambridge UP, 2016. doi: 10.1017/CBO9781316460054.

Keller, Jared. "Inside America's Auschwitz." *Smithsonian Magazine*, 4 Apr. 2016, www.smithsonianmag.com/history/inside-americas-auschwitz-180958647/. Accessed 21 March 2021.

Kelso, William M., and James Deetz. *Archaeology at Monticello: Artifacts of Everyday Life in the Plantation Community*. Thomas Jefferson Memorial Foundation, 1997.

Kytle, Ethan J., and Blain Roberts. "'Is It Okay to Talk about Slaves?': Segregating the Past in Historic Charleston." *Destination Dixie: Tourism and Southern History*, edited by Karen L. Cox, UP of Florida, 2012, pp. 137–153. doi: 10.2307/j.ctvx070hp.

Landrieu, Mitch. "What I Learned from My Fight to Remove Confederate Monuments." *The Guardian*, 24 Mar. 2018.

Litten, Kevin. "Liberty Place Monument Removed on Confederate Memorial Day." *The Times-Picayune*, 25 Apr. 2017.

Mandala Research, "African American Travel Represents $63 Billion Opportunity." *Globe News Wire*, 20 Dec. 2018.

Miles, Tiya. *Tales from the Haunted South: Dark Tourism and Memories of Slavery from the Civil War Era*. U of North Carolina P, 2015, 70–77. doi: 10.5149/9781469626345_miles.

"Monticello Launches New 'Slavery at Monticello' App." Press Release, Monticello, 2 May 2015, www.monticello.org/site/press/new-app. Accessed 21 March 2021.

Natanson, Hannah. "Isaac Franklin and John Armfield Committed Atrocities They Appeared to Relish." *The Washington Post*, 14 Sept. 2019.

Nelson, Velvet. "Liminality and Difficult Heritage in Tourism." *Tourism Geographies*, vol. 22, no. 2, 2020, pp. 298–318. doi: 10.1080/14616688.2019.1666161.

New Orleans Attractions. Tripadvisor, www.tripadvisor.com/Attractions-g60864-Activities-a_allAttractions.true-New:Orleans_Louisiana.html. Accessed 12 July 2020.

New Orleans Slave Trade Marker Tour and Audio Guide. www.neworleansslavetrade.org/. Accessed 1 July 2020.

Nystrom, Justin A. "The Battle of Liberty Place." 64 Parishes, 64parishes.org/entry/the-battle-of-liberty-place. Accessed 21 March 2021.

Ortiz, Aimee. "Richmond Removes Confederate Statues from Monument Avenue." *New York Times*, 2 July 2020.

Raymen, Thomas. "Slavery, Dark Tourism and Deviant Leisure at the American Society of Criminology in New Orleans." *Plymouth Law and Criminal Justice Review*, 2017, pp. 15–26.

Rosenfeld, Paul. "Why America Needs a Slavery Museum." *The Atlantic Magazine*, 25 Aug. 2015, www.theatlantic.com/video/index/402172/the-only-american-museum-about-slavery/. Accessed 21 March 2021.

Savage, Kirk. *Standing Soldiers, Kneeling Slaves: Race, War and Monument in 19th-Century America*. Princeton UP, 1997.

Small, Stephen. "Still Back of the Big House: Slave Cabins and Slavery in Southern Heritage Tourism." *Tourism Geographies*, vol. 15, no. 3, 2013, pp. 405–423. doi: 10.1080/14616688.2012.723042.

Souther, Jonathan Mark. *New Orleans on Parade: Tourism and the Transformation of the Crescent City*. Louisiana State UP, 2013.

Stanonis, Anthony J. *Creating the Big Easy: New Orleans and the Emergence of Modern Tourism, 1918–1945*. U of Georgia P, 2006.

Thomas, Lynnell L. *Desire and Disaster in New Orleans: Tourism, Race, and Historical Memory*. Duke UP, 2014. doi: 10.1215/9780822376354.

United Nations Educational, Scientific, and Cultural Organization (UNESCO). "Annex 3. The UNESCO Recommendation on the Historic Urban Landscape." *The Historic Urban Landscape*, 2011, pp. 209–216. doi: 10.1002/9781119968115.app3.

Ward, Marguerite. "The New York Times bestseller list this week is almost entirely comprised of books about race and white privilege in America." *Business Insider*, 11 June 2020.

Wendland, Tegan. "With Lee Statue's Removal, Another Battle of New Orleans Comes to a Close." NPR, 20 May 2017, www.npr.org/2017/05/20/529232823/with-lee-statues-removal-another-battle-of-new-orleans-comes-to-a-close. Accessed 21 March 2021.

"Whitney Plantation Museum Confronts Painful History of Slavery." *CBS News*, 8 Apr. 2015, www.cbsnews.com/news/whitney-plantation-museum-confronts-painful-history-american-slavery/. Accessed 21 March 2021.

Whitney Plantation review. Tripadvisor, www.tripadvisor.com/Attraction_Review-g1 4166006-d7276731-Reviews-Whitney_Plantation-Wallace_Louisiana.html. Accessed 15 Oct. 2019.

Van Winkle, Christine M., and Ken Backman. "Designing Interpretive Audio Tours to Enhance Meaningful Learning Transfer at a Historic Site." *Journal of Heritage Tourism*, vol. 6, no. 1, 2011, pp. 29–43. doi: 10.1080/1743873X.2010.518761.

Yankholmes, Aaron, and Bob McKercher. "Rethinking Slavery Heritage Tourism." *Journal of Heritage Tourism*, vol. 10, no. 3, 2015, pp. 233–247. doi: 10.1080/1743873X.2014.988159.

Yuhl, Stephanie. "Hidden in Plain Sight: Centering the Domestic Slave Trade in American Public History." *The Journal of Southern History*, vol. LXXIX, no. 3, August 2013, pp. 593–624.

6 Don't mess with (Anglo) Texas

Dominant cultural values in heritage sites of the Texas Revolution

Mark Ward Sr.

Texas is known for an outsized ethos encapsulated in the slogan, "Don't Mess with Texas." Having been raised in Virginia at a time when the dominant culture was constructed on the War That Was Lost, a midlife relocation to Texas gave me fresh eyes to see how the dominant culture of the Lone Star State remains built on the War That Was Won. That war is the Texas Revolution of 1835–6. While the Alamo is the war's best-known heritage site, across the officially designated Texas Independence Trail Region (whose logo is a raised fist clenching a musket) are at least ten heritage tourism sites. These sites collectively collapse a complex history that involves Anglo–Hispanic relations and Black slavery, reducing it to a simplified narrative of Texan pioneer freedom fighters righteously and heroically resisting cruel and unjust Mexican tyranny. In this way, "tropes of honor, pride, and liberty ... [form] the basis for Texan identity" and set aside "the fact that race had everything to do with Texas independence" (Peña). In addition, each Texas Revolution heritage site has its analog in the mythic events of the American Revolution—from the sites of the first shots fired and the Declaration of Independence, to the commanding general's desperate river crossing and the final decisive battle. Thus, the Texas creation myth evokes the larger American creation myth.

This interpretation and my standing to see it are inextricably interwoven with my own story. I am an inveterate heritage tourist, a daytripper with a passion for local and regional history. Professionally, I am also an ethnographer. Putting the two together affords the unique perspective of a tourist-cum-ethnographer who can observe "contemporary uses of the past" (Ashworth 80) and see how culture intersects with "tourism [as] a complex system of supply and demand wherein destinations provide different products and the traveling public desires diverse experiences" (Timothy and Boyd 1). Pairing the stances of tourist and ethnographer can reveal how "Heritage museums have become a pervasive feature of the cultural landscapes of contemporary Western societies" and "important arenas for cultural production and ideological assertion" (Katriel, "Sites of Memory" 1). For that reason, "museums and historic sites have, indeed, become major participants in contemporary efforts to construct culturally shared, historically anchored representations of 'self' and 'other'" (Katriel, "Our Future" 70).

DOI: 10.4324/9781003102830-7

In decoding the "self" and "other" that are constructed by these heritage sites, being a tourist-cum-ethnographer again has advantages. Heritage tourism was a formative experience of my Virginia youth. My grandmother thrilled me with heroic tales of Confederate victories on our many daytrips to the battlefields of Manassas, Fredericksburg, Chancellorsville, the Wilderness, and the Shenandoah Valley. As a child, I attended Stonewall Jackson Elementary School and Washington-Lee High School (our colors, blue and gray; our mascot, the Generals). My county, Arlington, was named for the great General Lee's estate. Our main thoroughfares were Lee Highway, Arlington Boulevard, and Jefferson Davis Highway. For my part, I am the fourth-generation firstborn male of my family to bear the middle name Lee. Today as an ethnographer, though, I can grasp how the dominant culture of my native state was rooted in the War That Was Lost. Selective historical memory, reified from battlefield parks to town squares, constructed a "self" for white Virginians that ignored slavery, marginalized the Black "other," and built an identity on the trope that, although defeated by a materially superior foe, Southerners were the morally and spiritually superior people.

Though being a cultural insider has benefits for an ethnographer, so does being an outsider. This was never truer than when a midlife career change and entry into the academic life transplanted me from Virginia to Texas. A faculty position in Victoria put me in the geographic center of the Texas Independence Trail Region, which stretches roughly from San Antonio to Houston. As a stranger in a strange land, I instinctively slipped into the role of tourist-cum-ethnographer. Soon, as I toured historic sites of the Texas Revolution, I began making sense of my new home by fitting the Texas narrative into a pattern long familiar to me. From my childhood in Virginia, I was nurtured on stories not only of the Civil War but of the American Revolution. Its proud shrines—all of them open to tourists—were all around me: Washington's Mount Vernon, Jefferson's Monticello, the homes of James Madison, James Monroe, George Mason, and other Virginia luminaries, plus the sacred monuments of the nation's capital just a few minutes' drive from my home. Every Virginia child of my generation learned in school how the great General Washington led the new nation from trial to triumph, how the brilliant Thomas Jefferson penned the immortal words of the Declaration of Independence, how the decisive final battle of the American Revolution was won on Virginia soil. With this past as prologue, the analogs of Texas Revolutionary history became evident to me (Table 6.1).

That the Texas myth can recapitulate the American myth is due to the fact that, unlike the defeated Confederacy, Texas won its defining war. In this way, Texas Revolution heritage sites can not only construct a dominant Texan identity built on tropes of honor, pride, and liberty, but can also project Texas exceptionalism as an analog to American exceptionalism. Texas is the "Lone Star," the republic that was once an independent nation and voluntarily joined the United States of America. The unarticulated assumption of such "heritage politics" (Timothy and Boyd 2) is to induct heritage tourists into a "rhetoric of beginnings [that] is designed to establish an authoritative version of the past, to capitalize on the revolutionary phase of national coming-into-being, and mobilize audiences'

106 *Mark Ward Sr.*

Table 6.1 American and Texas Revolution analogs

Event	American Revolution	Texas Revolution
War aims	War of independence	War of independence
First uprising	Boston Tea Party	Turtle Bayou
First shots	Concord	Gonzales
National birth	Declaration of Independence	Washington-on-the-Brazos
Enemy cruelty	Boston Massacre	Goliad Massacre
Existential peril	Valley Forge	Runaway Scrape
Sacrificial resistance	Fort Washington	The Alamo
Desperate crossing	Crossing the Delaware	Lynchburg Ferry
Final victory	Yorktown	San Jacinto
Heroic commander	General George Washington	General Sam Houston
First president	President George Washington	President Stephen F. Austin
First capital	Philadelphia	San Felipe de Austin

commitment to the values of the pioneering era." As such, "the museum tour becomes a ritualized enactment of commonly held understandings and valuations of past events and shared origins" (Katriel, "Our Future" 71–2).

This raises two questions: which values are "commonly held" and which values are thereby marginalized? And in so doing, what "self" and "other" are constructed? As heuristic aids to explore such problems, typologies of cultural values have long been staples of cross-cultural research. Hofstede's Cultural Value Dimensions, a leading typology in the field, holds that the values of a given culture can be plotted along six dimensions: individualism versus collectivism, power distance, uncertainty avoidance, masculinity versus femininity, long- versus short-term orientation, and indulgence versus restraint. This chapter argues that, because all histories are selective reconstructions from incomplete facts, representations at heritage tourism sites fill in the gaps with historical narratives that tacitly reflect the values which "make sense" to the surrounding majority culture. As such, the narratives implicate an idealized cultural self that simultaneously marginalizes cultural others who do not share the "commonly held" values. For a case in point, the present study offers the narratives at historic sites and heritage museums that celebrate the Texas Revolution.

A brief history of the Texas Revolution

The weather of South Texas, where the Revolution was fought, is warm and sunny most of the year. Drawn by the irresistible lure of the open road, once I settled into Victoria then I was soon off on weekends as a tourist to the historic sites of my adopted state. The mystique of Texas looms large in American popular culture. As a boy in Virginia, I thrilled to Saturday morning T.V. reruns of old B-movie Westerns and of *The Cisco Kid* and *The Rifleman* television serials, all set in the romanticized open range of the Old Southwest. Nothing could be more exotic to a boy whose world was concrete canyons and suburban streets. Yet now, as an adult transplanted to the Lone Star State, I found the actual history of Texas engrossing in its complexity. By visiting the state's heritage sites and museums (and, to the everlasting annoyance of my spouse, reading *all* the placards and signs) and then checking my fieldnotes against Texas historical scholarship (e.g., Brands; Hardin; Lack), I gradually pieced together a history.

Inspired by the American and French Revolutions, Mexicans rose up in 1810 against their Spanish colonial rulers and in 1821 established the independent United States of Mexico. Because its vast northern territories were sparsely populated and difficult to defend, Mexico gave Texas land grants to Anglo settlers from the United States of America. Many of these settlers owned Black slaves and were outraged when Mexico banned slavery in 1829. By then, some 30,000 Anglos lived in Texas compared to fewer than 8,000 Mexicans. Alarmed, the Mexican government in 1830 barred further Anglo immigration, authorized military intervention to enforce the emancipation of slaves, rescinded property tax exemptions for Texas immigrants, raised tariffs on goods imported from the United States, and established military border garrisons.

Anglo settlers pushed for Texas statehood within Mexico but were rebuffed when General Antonio Lopez de Santa Anna was elected national president in 1833. Part of the faction that had advocated a strong central government rather than a federal system, he rescinded the Mexican Constitution of 1824. After several Mexican states rebelled against central rule, Santa Anna abolished all state legislatures. In response, Texas militias attacked Mexican army garrisons and expelled Mexican soldiers. When Santa Anna attempted to reestablish a military presence, war broke out and the first shots were fired on October 2, 1835. The next month, delegates to a Texas convention asserted a right to form an independent state as long as the 1824 Constitution remained suspended. Delegates then named Sam Houston commander of a new Texas army. By December, when Texan forces captured the army garrison at the Alamo mission in San Antonio, no Mexican troops remained on Texas soil.

In February 1836, Santa Anna personally led his Mexican army across the Rio Grande River into Texas and besieged the Alamo. Texan delegates issued a declaration of independence and adopted a new constitution—that gave Texas citizenship to white men only and forbade the emancipation of slaves. Yet as the delegates met, the Alamo fell to Santa Anna on March 6. The two opposing armies shadowed each other's movements over the next month and met in open battle at San Jacinto on April 21. With surprise on the Texan side, the final conflict was over in 18 minutes and Santa Anna captured. The generalissimo was forced to sign a treaty that recognized the new Republic of Texas. Yet the defeat led to his removal from power, putting the treaty in doubt. Later, Santa Anna regained the presidency and attempted in 1842 to reconquer Texas but was again rebuffed. The threat of invasion, however, prompted Texas to join the United States in 1845. Mexico maintained its claims and only ceded Texas, along with parts of what would become six other states, when beaten in the Mexican–American War of 1846–7.

The annexation of vast new lands by the United States exacerbated conflicts over the expansion of slavery and led to the Civil War of 1861–5. (Meanwhile, a weakened Mexico was invaded and occupied by France in 1862–7. Today, the Cinco de Mayo holiday commemorates Mexicans' first military victory against the French on May 5, 1862.) Texas seceded from the United States in 1861, joined the Confederacy, and was the site of the Civil War's final battle in May 1865. But though the Confederacy was defeated, Texans could still celebrate the War That Was Won. Memorializing the Texas Revolution went into high gear for its centennial in 1936. With $6 million in state and federal funds (Ragsdale)—equivalent to $112 million today—major monuments in the popular Art Deco style were erected across the Lone Star State and remain actively promoted sites for Texas heritage tourism.

The value of a single word

Today these monuments have become flashpoints for social justice advocates as the nation reappraises its history. That the controversy implicates not just facts but cultural values is illustrated by how the Alamo is remembered. In 2018, a firestorm erupted over the state's standard for seventh-grade history instruction which stipulates that teachers "explain the issues surrounding significant events of the Texas Revolution, including … the siege of the Alamo and all the heroic defenders who gave their lives there" (Sanchez). An advisory panel of the State Board of Education, however, recommended that Texas social studies curricula no longer describe the Alamo defenders as "heroic" because it "is a value-charged word."

Reaction to the proposed change was swift. Governor Greg Abbott tweeted, "Stop political correctness in our schools. Of course Texas schoolchildren should be taught that Alamo defenders were 'Heroic'!" His view was echoed by Texas Land Commissioner George P. Bush who tweeted, "This politically correct nonsense is why I'll always fight to honor the Alamo defenders' sacrifice … [T]he defenders' actions must remain at the very core of TX history teaching. This is not debatable to me." At the Texas Public Policy Foundation, an influential voice for neoliberal reform of the state's higher education system, director Thomas Lindsay of the group's Center for Innovation in Education, opined,

> To intentionally deprive our students of such powerful lessons about human dignity and principled courage is the moral equivalent of child psychological abuse. This twisting of history deprives our students of the truth. If courage in the defense of liberty and equality is not heroic, what, precisely, is?
>
> (Allen)

For her part, State Board of Education chair Donna Bahorich, a Republican appointee, told the press, "The sacrifice they're [the Alamo defenders] willing to make is pretty heroic and I think there's some value in pointing that out" (Armus).

On the national level, these themes were amplified in a best-selling 2019 book, *Sam Houston and the Alamo Avengers*, by television's *Fox & Friends* co-host Brian Kilmeade. Along with the book's subtitle, *The Texas Victory that Changed American History*, the dustjacket copy breathlessly related how "Americans who had moved to Texas looking for a fresh start" at last "secured their freedom and paved the way for America's growth." Led by "war heroes" who demonstrated consummate "courage and calculation," the Texans "won the independence for which so many had died."

By contrast, the Texas Democracy Foundation saw in the Alamo monuments a shrine to white supremacy. "The Alamo is, after all, dedicated to the American fear of the Mexican body, of Mexican invasion, of Mexican agency that firmly and directly contested agendas of white supremacy in early 19th-century Texas" (Peña). The Texas Revolution, the Foundation noted, occurred within a larger context of multiple attempts during the first half of the nineteenth century to extend the "manifest destiny" of white American rule across not only Mexico but all of Central America. Thus, "race had everything to do with Texas independence and with how we remember the Alamo."

If race had everything to do with Texas independence, the contest over how the Alamo and the Revolution are remembered also has to do with whose values are memorialized as the heritage of all Texans. The controversy over the single word "heroic" demonstrated that any attempt to denaturalize the values embedded in the dominant Anglo narrative and expose those values to questioning by other voices would be immediately dismissed as irrational: "This [is] politically correct nonsense … This is not debatable." "Of course … Alamo defenders were 'Heroic'!" To teach youth otherwise "is the moral equivalent of child psychological abuse."

Cultural values, websites, and tourism

In terms of Hofstede's typology, the dominant assumption that the Texas revolutionaries were heroic implicates multiple Cultural Value Dimensions. To see the connection, consider how each of the six dimensions is defined. Individualism versus collectivism is the extent to which members of a culture feel their choices and their places in society are independent from, or interdependent with, larger groups. Uncertainty avoidance is a culture's tolerance for the unknown and ambiguous as compared to fixed customs and rituals. Power distance is the extent to which less powerful culture members expect and accept unequal distributions of power. Masculinity versus femininity addresses expectations for emotional gender roles and the extent to which a culture values competing versus caring and accepts or rejects the use of force. Long- versus short-term orientation assesses a culture's attitude toward change and is manifested, for example, in whether ethics are seen as fluid or absolute. Indulgence versus restraint is the extent to which a culture values acting on feelings and whether duty or freedom is seen as normative. In this light, the way that "heroic" is used in the context of Texas Revolution

110 *Mark Ward Sr.*

heritage sites carries connotations that may be interpreted through the lens of Hofstede's six categories (Table 6.2).

To support this interpretation of dominant cultural values implicit in Texas Revolution heritage sites, I've taken my students on their own tour of the Lone Star State—through a virtual ethnography (Hine) of websites associated with ten heritage sites (Table 6.3). There is considerable warrant in the literature for employing Hofstede's typology of Cultural Value Dimensions as a framework for analyzing websites and tourism. With regard to websites, Avery, Baradwaj, and Singer examined retail banking and found, "Citibank's online banking sites in different countries appear to be adapted to local cultural attributes; each of Hofstede's cultural dimensions is found to have an impact on understanding and explaining the attributes of the various banking websites" (73). Similarly, Wu's study of U.S. and Taiwanese shoppers concluded that "Hofstede's cultural dimensions are predictors for consumers' on-line shopping preferences" (42). Zahedi

Table 6.2 Dominant values celebrated in Texas Revolution heritage sites

The value of ...	is naturalized as heritage sites and museums celebrate the Texans' ...
Individualism	Desire to own their own land and willingness to fight for their individual rights and freedoms.
Low uncertainty avoidance	Willingness to pioneer an unsettled land and risk war for their lives and properties.
Low power distance	Desire to govern themselves.
Masculinity	Assertiveness, toughness, and acquisition of land and wealth through their work.
Short-term orientation	Desires for personal freedom and advancement through individual merit, their pioneer mobility, and their devotion to the ethical absolutes of individual liberty.
Indulgence	Work-hard/play-hard cowboy persona and rejection of strict social norms in favor of rugged individuality.

Table 6.3 Texas Revolution heritage sites and museums

Commemoration	Heritage site or museum
Texas settlement	George Ranch Historical Park/Star of the Republic Museum
First shots	Gonzales Memorial Museum
National birth	Washington-on-the-Brazos State Historic Site
Enemy cruelty	Fannin Battleground State Historic Site/Fannin Memorial Monument
Sacrificial resistance	The Alamo National Historic Site and Shrine
Final victory	San Jacinto Museum of History
First president/first capital	San Felipe de Austin State Historic Site
Honored war dead	Monument Hill State Historic Site

and Bansal analyzed 900 images in 728 websites originating in 39 countries and demonstrated a correlation between cultural values, as defined by Hofstede's typology, and the interpretations that users gave to color schemes and to images of people, buildings, and landscapes. "Culturally appealing Web sites lead to increased online satisfaction and trust," they observed. "Pictures are easier to process than text, and pictures that match Web users' culture may lead to increased stickiness of the Web site" (192). Similarly, Tang discovered that the cultural value dimension of collectivism versus individualism governed images displayed on university websites as "buildings, campus views, and university gates were the predominant visual elements on university websites in China, while single people and small groups of people were the most frequently used visuals on US sites" (417). Other studies have found, for example, that online political advertisements "with cultural appeals produce more favorable attitudes than those with neutral or culturally incongruent appeals" (Gevorgyan 91), that a correlation exists "between a user's cultural dimension scores and their behavior when faced with a webform" to fill out (Recabaren and Nussbaum 87), and that "cultural value dimensions do play a role in parental mediation strategies" for monitoring children's internet usage (Mertens and d'Haenens 411).

The influence of cultural values on tourist behaviors has likewise been studied at length with Hofstede's typology as an analytical framework. Money and Crotts, for example, surveyed a matched sample of 1,042 German and Japanese tourists in the U.S. and demonstrated a "relationship between the cultural dimension of uncertainty (or risk) avoidance with information search, trip planning time horizons, travel party characteristics (e.g. size of group) and trip characteristics (e.g. length of stay)" (191). A follow-up study of the sample confirmed that "low uncertainty avoidance German and high uncertainty avoidance Japanese tourists ... [exhibited] behaviors consistent with those behaviors predicted by Hofstede" (Litvin, Crotts, and Hefner 29). Woodside, Hsu, and Marshall surveyed visitors to Australia from 14 countries. They found that "product marketing for gifts for loved ones and friends at home relates more closely to Eastern cultures while experience marketing during longer visits relates more closely to Western cultures" (798). In a study of 1,544 hotel customers visiting Crete from ten countries, Pantouvakis confirmed that "national cultural differences affect perceived satisfaction and loyalty" (1174). More broadly, Manrai and Manrai surveyed 17 studies and affirmed that cultural values, as typed by Hofstede, influenced how tourists behaved before travel in their formation of destinated preferences, during travel in their consumption of travel-related products, and after travel in their intentions for return visits.

Apropos of the present study, Kang and Mastin analyzed tourism websites for 44 countries and concluded, "Hofstede's cultural dimensions [work] as a frame to identify valid explanatory factors that account for differences in countries' tourism websites" (54). In countries whose cultures valued higher power distance, tourism websites featured complex layouts and "appeared to believe that tourism is for special groups who have neither need for nor interest in promotional [giveaways]," whereas websites for countries with lower power distance "feature casual narratives … [with] the feel of a more personal relationships with website visitors" (55). Tourism websites for collectivistic countries tended to emphasize factual information and group photos, while those for individualistic countries posted photos of individual faces and young couples together with eye-catching graphics, animation, humor, interactive games, and features that allowed visitors to construct tailored travel plans.

A virtual ethnography of heritage tourism

The cultural values that collectively dominated the ten websites for Texas Revolution heritage sites which my students surveyed were not subtle and were easily grasped when employing Hofstede's typology for a framework. The websites' textual narratives, together with their large bold type fonts, colorful images, and site architecture and navigation, quickly called attention either to military triumphs or to persevering pioneers, rugged cowboys, brave war heroes, and visionary statesmen. Visitors to the websites might occasionally find the historical complexities but only with the patience to click through multiple pages and read dense blocs of smaller text.

To illustrate how virtual ethnography can unpack the cultural values embedded in historical narratives, the website for the San Jacinto Museum of History is typical. Located on the site of the Revolution's final victorious battle, the museum is housed in the base of the San Jacinto Memorial Monument. Built between 1936 and 1939 for the Texas Centennial, the Art Deco obelisk rises 567.31 feet, is proudly "taller than the Washington Monument," and is surmounted by a 220-ton Lone Star of Texas. In visiting the homepage of the website, users' eyes are immediately drawn to a color photo, set in an early nineteenth-century picture frame, of a (re-enacted) white male Texan soldier. His face is close up as he looks directly at the viewer with a steely and determined gaze. He holds a musket on his shoulder and in the background are other foot soldiers, one holding a military standard, and a horse-mounted officer. Just below the photo is a collage of artifacts: a sword, a pistol, a captured Mexican eagle standard, a cannon ball, musket balls, uniform coat buttons, a simple daguerreotype of General Sam Houston laid ironically atop a glorified painting of the defeated Santa Anna, a map of the territories that the United States would annex following victory in the Mexican–American War. The Lone Star and a frieze of Texan settlers that crowns the San Jacinto Monument is shown. A framed inset image displays a detail from a painting of victorious Texan soldiers, fists upraised, as one holds the "Come and Take It" flag that flew over the Revolution's first battle in October 1835. This ensemble of photos and artifacts is set against a banner background of a marble slab, matching the stone of the monument, into which are carved in capital letters 18 MINUTES THAT CHANGED THE WORLD. Below that legend, website visitors are invited to "Relive the epic battle that shaped a free Texas, opened the West, and crafted one of the most vital chapters in American history."

By scrolling down the San Jacinto Museum of History homepage, web visitors are invited to learn about THE BIRTH OF A REPUBLIC and "Discover how a decisive 18-minute battle for independence empowered a young nation and forever altered the course of world history. The story of America is infused with the legacy of Texan valor." Underneath this text, visitors can click a thumbnail—depicting a heroically charging soldier—of a short YouTube video entitled A FREE TEXAS. Accompanied by heroic music and a montage of recreated tintypes of battle scenes, the video narrates "A dedicated soldier's letter to his family [that] tells of the tragedy and triumph as the battle draws close—and freedom even closer." As the soldier's letter concludes with the emphatic words "Texas will be free!" a cannon shot is heard, a photo appears of the San Jacinto Monument framed by a sunburst, and the Museum's logo of the Lone Star set inside a starburst comes on screen with the legend COME CELEBRATE THE FREEDOM. Toward the bottom of the homepage are links to photo galleries, most prominently scenes from an annual battle re-enactment. Visitors can also click to an online museum exhibit about the construction of the San Jacinto obelisk to get "A look at the people, technology, and artistic design that contributed to the awe-inspiring Memorial Monument that commemorates the fight for Texas' freedom." Finally, the bottom of the homepage lists corporate sponsors including major petrochemical corporations such as Shell, Dow, Hexion, and LyondellBasell.

Beneath the 18 MINUTES THAT CHANGED THE WORLD and THE BIRTH OF A REPUBLIC legends, website visitors are invited to click an EXPERIENCE IT NOW! link to a page of interactive battle highlights. Here page visitors' eyes are drawn to a photo of (re-enacted) Texan soldiers charging in a line with pointed muskets, plus the legend CONQUER OR PERISH! COME EXPERIENCE SAM HOUSTON'S DEFIANCE IN THE MOMENTS BEFORE A REPUBLIC IS BORN. Then, by clicking each of the eight animated hyperlinks, visitors can variously learn how Sam Houston turned "certain defeat into sudden victory," how the battleground is the "most significant piece of Texas real estate," and "how one small battle in Texas spilled over its borders to leave a mark not only on a young nation, but the world as well." In addition, web visitors can "Take a close-up look at the weaponry used on both sides—when war was generally more up close and personal." Another link allows visitors to focus on the Texan and Mexican commanders and "Experience the wisdom, caution and courage, brilliant maneuvers and costly mistakes that changed history." Or visitors can "Explore maps of the battlefield and the resulting westward expansion to see the true impact of the victory at San Jacinto."

A virtual ethnographic tour of the San Jacinto Museum of History website can end appropriately at its interactive page which details the construction and architectural features of the San Jacinto Memorial Monument. The base of the obelisk is octagonal. A series of inscriptions on the eight sides, photographically reproduced on the website, read in part:

114 *Mark Ward Sr.*

UNSCRUPULOUS RULERS SUCCESSFULLY SEIZED POWER IN MEXICO.
THEIR UNJUST ACTS AND DESPOTIC DECREES LED TO THE REVOLUTION IN TEXAS.
...
WITH THE BATTLE CRY "REMEMBER THE ALAMO! REMEMBER GOLIAD!"
THE TEXANS CHARGED ... VICTORY [WAS] COMPLETE, AND TEXAS FREE! ...
SANTA ANNA, SELF-STYLED "NAPOLEON OF THE WEST," RECEIVED FROM A GENEROUS FOE
THE MERCY HE HAD DENIED TRAVIS AT THE ALAMO AND FANNIN AT GOLIAD.
...
THE FREEDOM OF TEXAS FROM MEXICO LED TO ...
ALMOST ONE-THIRD OF THE PRESENT AREA OF THE AMERICAN NATION (Figures 6.1 and 6.2).

Figure 6.1 San Jacinto Memorial Monument and Battle Reenactment. Credit: The Lyda Hill Texas Collection of Photographs in Carol M. Highsmith's America Project, Library of Congress, Prints and Photographs Division.

Figure 6.2 San Jacinto Memorial Monument and Battle Reenactment. Credit: The Lyda Hill Texas Collection of Photographs in Carol M. Highsmith's America Project, Library of Congress, Prints and Photographs Division.

Conclusions

Which cultural values were implied as normative, and which were thus marginalized, was not too difficult to observe in the San Jacinto Museum of History website—nor in the other nine Texas Revolution websites that my students analyzed. Individualism predominated in an emphasis on individual rights and individual actors. Low uncertainty avoidance was implicit in a glorification of risk. Low power distance was seen in the narrative of self-governance. Masculine values of assertiveness and toughness were idealized, along with the acquisition of territory. A short-term orientation was evident in the assumption that freedom is an unchanging ethical and moral absolute. The indulgence of acting on impulses of defiance was celebrated, as was the assumption that freedom is the normal state of being. As in Kang and Mastin's study of national tourism websites, the San Jacinto site implied low power distance in its simple layout and casual wording, and evoked individualism as dense blocs of facts were absent in favor of close-ups of individual faces, striking graphics, animation, interactivity, and links that allowed users to tailor their virtual visits. As Zahedi and Bansal predicted, the images fit majority cultural values. And as suggested in the findings of Woodside et al., the San Jacinto website reflected individualistic values in its marketing of the experiences available to tourists.

116 *Mark Ward Sr.*

In Hofstede's schema, however, the values of a culture are not typed as either/or. Instead, cultural values are plotted along the six dimensions as tending more toward one pole or the other. Thus, for example, the San Jacinto Museum of History website and its counterparts for other Texas Revolution heritage sites may implicate the indulgent value that freedom is natural, but a somewhat moderating sense of collective duty is not excluded. That cultural values are plotted along latitudes of variability then guides how Hofstede's own research should be interpreted—in this case, his findings on the respective values of U.S. and Mexican culture (Figure 6.3).

With these variations in mind, consider again the historical narrative constructed by the San Jacinto Museum of History website. A Mexican or Mexican-American visitor could make sense of the website's implied masculine values (U.S., 64; Mexico, 62) and short-term orientation (U.S., 26; Mexico, 24) but would struggle to make sense of a creation myth that assumes values of individualism (U.S., 91) versus collectivism (Mexico, 30), low uncertainty avoidance (U.S., 40) versus high (Mexico, 81), low power distance (U.S., 40) versus high (Mexico, 81), and, to a lesser extent, indulgence (U.S., 68; Mexico, 97). Put another way, heritage sites of the Texas Revolution marginalize Mexican cultural values of collectivism and group identity, high uncertainty avoidance and a regard for traditions and rituals, high power distance and the acceptance of authority, and the indulgence to simply enjoy life in the moment.

Heritage sites and museums are, as noted earlier, major arenas in Western societies for constructions of a cultural "self" and "other" based on values implicit in an origin story. As such, these sites proffer a "consensual dialogue" that is "designed to establish an authoritative version of past" so that visitors will "assume a shared adherence to the basic master-narrative." In so doing, the sites delegitimize any "oppositional dialogue" that might question the narrative and have "the effect of relativizing and opening up the museum text, thus challenging its claims to

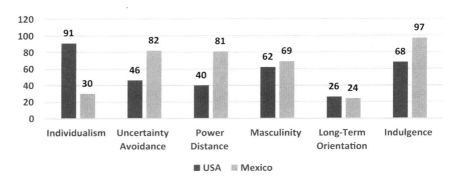

Figure 6.3 Cultural Value Dimensions of the U.S.A. and Mexico compared. Source: Hofstede Insights.

cultural authority" (Katriel, "Our Future" 71–2). The websites of the San Jacinto Museum of History and other Texas Revolution heritage sites, by assuming a consensus on taken-for-granted Anglo cultural values, seek to naturalize a master narrative. In contrast, the recent controversy over the "heroic" defenders of the Alamo suggests an emerging Hispanic oppositional dialogue that seeks to denaturalize the narrative. At the same time, the shocked reaction of threatened Anglos, who immediately branded such a dialogue irrational, illustrates the fundamental challenge of renegotiating collective memory.

As an ethnographer, however, I look for the telling cultural details. Because the act of observing necessarily intersects with my standing in relation to the observed, these details are often encountered in personal ways—as when I became a heritage tourist in my adopted state of Texas, I began to notice the cultural importance of the War That Was Won, and contrasted it with my upbringing in a Virginia culture built on the War That Was Lost. Ethnography starts when "a mundane term, or a mundane social practice ... inexplicably shed their accustomed air of 'naturalness' and become interpretive sites for the exploration of cultural sense" (Katriel, "Communal Webs" 2). Thus, as the Texas myth and its implicit cultural values shed their "naturalness" for me, other realizations opened up. Being transplanted from Virginia to Texas gave me pause to see what I had taken for granted: that my decisions to earn a doctorate, change careers, and relocate for greater self-determination were driven by previously unquestioned values of individualism, low uncertainty avoidance, and low power distance.

That same drive also finds expression in my daily workouts at Victoria's Riverside Park, whose 660 acres meander along the historic Guadalupe River. The park's flat terrain and open spaces are far different than the thickly wooded rolling hills of Virginia. Over time, as I worked out it dawned on me that I did so alone. Many days, though, I would run past groups of Mexican-American extended families, often a dozen or more individuals, celebrating a birthday or holiday or just getting together. Children are laughing, adults are chatting, the grill is smoking, a radio is softly playing Tejano or mariachi music. By Hofstede's typology, they are placing the kinship group before the individual, finding satisfaction in the certainty and tradition of family ties, tacitly ceding power distance to respected elders, and enjoying the indulgence of living in the moment—and unlike me, they are not alone.

Suddenly, I understood in a personal way why the version of heroism celebrated at the Alamo and the narrative constructed at heritage sites of the Texas Revolution had become contested. The values of individualism, low uncertainty avoidance, and low power distance, celebrated and naturalized through Texas heritage tourism, exclude and marginalize other values. The mythic Texas "self" is highly individualistic, a risk taker, one who challenges authority—in other words, an Anglo self. The excluded "other" is culturally group-oriented, prizes tradition and custom, and gives honor to respected authorities. And in the context of the Lone Star State, it so happens that the approved "self" is white and the "other" is brown.

References

Allen, Rebekah. "Don't call the Alamo's defenders 'heroic,' Texas school curriculum panel urges." *The Dallas Morning News*, https://www.dallasnews.com/news/politics/2018/09/07/don-t-call-the-alamo-s-defenders-heroic-texas-school-curriculum-panel-urges. Accessed 26 Nov. 2019, 7 Sep. 2018.

Armus, Teo. "Gov. Greg Abbott warns Texas Education Board of 'political correctness' over Alamo history standards." *The Texas Tribune*, https://www.texastribune.org/2018/09/07/greg-abbott-texas-board-education-alamo-curriculum. Accessed 26 Nov. 2019, 7 Sep. 2018.

Ashworth, Gregory J. "Heritage, identity, and places: for tourists and host communities." *In*: *Tourism in Destination Communities*, edited by Shalina Singh, Dallen J. Timothy, and Ross K. Dowling. CABI Publishing, 2003, pp. 79–97.

Avery, Albert E., Babu G. Baradwaj, and Daniel D. Singer. "An examination of Hofstede's cultural factors in explanation of differences in citibank international retail banking web sites." *Journal of Business and Economic Studies*, vol. 14, no. 2, 2008, pp. 73–90, 117–118.

Brands, Henry W. Lone star nation: the epic story of the battle for texas independence. *Anchor*, 2004.

Gevorgyan, Gennadi. "Does culture matter? Using accommodation, framing, and Hofstede theories to predict chinese Voters' perceptions and attitudes toward culturally oriented online political advertising." *China Media Research*, vol. 6, no. 1, 2010, pp. 91–102.

Hardin, Stephen L. *Texian Iliad: A Military History of the Texas Revolution, 1835–1836*. University of Texas Press, 1994.

Highsmith, Carol M. "The San Jacinto monument," 26 Apr. 2014. *The Lyda Hill Texas Collection of Photographs in Carol M. Highsmith's America Project*. Library of Congress, Prints and Photographs Division. https://www.loc.gov/pictures/collection/highsm/item/2014633452/.

———. "Scene from the Mexican encampment," 26 Apr. 2014. *The Lyda Hill Texas Collection of Photographs in Carol M. Highsmith's America Project*. Library of Congress, Prints and Photographs Division. https://www.loc.gov/pictures/collection/highsm/item/2014633433/.

Hine, Christine. "Virtual ethnography: modes, varieties, affordances." *In*: *The SAGE Handbook of Online Research Methods*, edited by Nigel Fielding, Raymond M. Lee, and Sage Grant Blank. Sage, 2008, pp. 257–270.

Hofstede, Geert. "Dimensionalizing cultures: the Hofstede model in context." *Online Readings in Psychology and Culture*, vol. 2, no. 1, 2011, Article 8. http://scholarworks.gvsu.edu/orpc/vol2/iss1/8 Accessed 21 March 2021.

"Hofstede insights: country comparison tool" *Hofstede Insights*, 2019, https://www.hofstede-insights.com. Accessed 26 Nov. 2019.

Kang, Doo Syen, and Teresa Mastin. "How cultural difference affects international tourism public relations websites: a comparative analysis using Hofstede's cultural dimensions." *Public Relations Review*, vol 34, no. 1, 2008, pp. 54–56. doi: 10.1016/j.pubrev.2007.11.002.

Katriel, Tamar *Communal Webs: Communication and Culture in Contemporary Israel*. Albany, New York: State University of New York P, 1991.

———. "'Our future is where our past is': studying heritage museums as ideological and performative arenas." *Communication Monographs*, vol. 60, no. 1, 1993, pp. 69–75. doi: 10.1080/03637759309376296.

———. "Sites of memory: discourses of the past in israeli pioneering settlement museums." *Quarterly Journal of Speech*, vol. 80, no. 1, 1994, pp. 1–20. doi: 10.1080/00335639409384052.
Kilmeade, Brian. *Sam Houston and the Alamo avengers: the Texas victory that changed american history*. Sentinel, 2019.
Lack, Paul D. *The Texas revolutionary experience: A political and social history, 1835–1836*. Texas A & M UP, 1992.
Litvin, Stephen W., John C. Crotts, and Frank L. Hefner. "Cross-cultural tourist behavior: a replication and extension involving Hofstede's uncertainty avoidance dimension." *International Journal of Tourism Research*, vol. 6, no. 1, 2004, pp. 29–37. doi: 10.1002/jtr.468.
Manrai, Lalita A., and Ajay Manrai. "Hofstede's cultural dimensions and tourist behaviors: a review and conceptual framework." *Journal of Economics, Finance, and Administrative Science*, vol. 16, no. 31, 2011, pp. 23–48. ssrn.com/abstract=1962711.
Mertens, Stefan, and Leen d'Haenens. "Parental mediation of internet use and cultural values across europe: investigating the predictive power of the Hofstedian Paradigm." *European Journal of Communication Research*, vol. 39, no. 4, 2014, pp. 389–414. doi: 10.1515/commun-2014-0018
Money, R. Bruce, and John C. Crotts. "The effect of uncertainty avoidance on information search, planning, and purchases of international travel vacations." *Tourism Management*, vol. 24, no. 2, 2003, pp. 191–202. doi: 10.1016/S0261-5177(02)00057-2.
Pantouvakis, Angelos. "The moderating role of nationality on the satisfaction loyalty link: evidence from the tourism industry." *Total Quality Management and Business Excellence*, vol. 24, nos. 9–10, 2013, pp. 174–1187. doi: 10.1080/14783363.2013.776758.
Peña, Daniel. "Remember the Alamo (differently)." *Texas Observer*, https://www.texasobserver.org/remember-alamo-differently. Accessed 26 Nov. 2019, 22 Aug. 2017.
Ragsdale, Kenneth B. *The Year America discovered Texas: Centennial '36*. Texas A&M UP, 2000.
Recabarren, Matías, and Miguel Nussbaum. "Exploring the feasibility of web form adaptation to users' cultural dimension scores." *User Modeling and User-Adapted Interaction*, vol. 20, no. 1, 2010, pp. 87–108. doi: 10.1007/s11257-010-9071-7.
Sanchez, Carlos. "Should Texas schoolchildren be taught that Alamo defenders were 'heroic'?. " *Texas Monthly*, https://www.texasmonthly.com/news/texas-schoolchildren-taught-alamo-defenders-heroic. Accessed 26 Nov. 2019, 6 Sep. 2018.
San Jacinto Museum of History, 2018, https://www.sanjacinto-museum.org. Accessed 20 Aug. 2020.
Tang, Tang. "Marketing higher education across borders: a cross-cultural analysis of University Websites in the US and China." *Chinese Journal of Communication*, vol. 4, no. 4, 2011, pp. 417–429. doi: 10.1080/17544750.2011.616288.
"Texas independence trail region." Texas Historical Commission, 2019, https://texasindependencetrail.com/public/upload/maps/texasindependencetrail_com/Indep-Trail-Region-Map.pdf. Accessed 26 Nov. 2019.
Timothy, Dallen J., and Stephen W. Boyd. "Heritage tourism in the 21st century: valued traditions and new perspectives." *Journal of Heritage Tourism*, vol. 1, no. 1, 2006, pp. 1–16. doi: 10.1080/17438730608668462.
Woodside, Arch G., Shih-Yun Hsu, and Roger Marshall. "General theory of cultures' consequences on international tourism behavior." *Journal of Business Research*, vol. 64, no. 8, 2011, pp. 785–799. doi: 10.1016/j.jbusres.2010.10.008.

Wu, Ming-Yi. "Cultural influences on consumers' on-line shopping preferences: a cross-cultural study of Taiwan and the United States." *China Media Research*, vol. 9, no. 3, 2013, pp. 42–52.

Zahedi, Fatemeh Mariam, and Gaurav Bansal. "Cultural signifiers of web site images." *Journal of Management Information Systems*, vol. 28, no. 1, 2011, pp. 147–200. doi: 10.2753/MIS0742-1222280106.

7 Bulloch Hall and the movement toward a well-rounded interpretation of antebellum life in Roswell, Georgia

Sara Harwood

Located 20 miles from downtown Atlanta, Roswell, Georgia, is a predominantly white, wealthy, and aging community in northern Fulton County, an economically and racially segregated county that includes much of Atlanta proper. The Roswell Historic District, boasting homes, churches, and cemeteries dating to the 1830s, is listed in the National Register of Historic Places. The City of Roswell operates three antebellum house museums which were all built and sustained by enslaved people.

Bulloch Hall was built by slave labor in 1839 as the family home of James Stephens Bulloch (1793–1849) and Martha Stewart Elliott Bulloch (1799–1864). The couple had three children: Anna, Martha (called Mittie), and Irvine Bulloch, all of whom grew up at Bulloch Hall. Interpretation centers around the early adulthood of Mittie Bulloch, whose son, Theodore Roosevelt, Jr., became the 26th President of the United States. Volunteer docents relate anecdotes about the specific individuals who lived at Bulloch Hall, both enslaved and slaveholding, while signage describes the tasks of enslaved people and exhibits include enslaved individuals' workspaces and living spaces in the interpreted rooms.

Bulloch Hall, managed through a partnership between the City of Roswell and a nonprofit, Friends of Bulloch, Inc., is arguably the most progressive of the three Roswell museums as its interpretation references enslaved individuals. However, the narrative presented by Bulloch Hall falls short of addressing the complicated relationships between enslaved and enslaver. The museum stakes its authenticity in archival research but does not acknowledge the inherent biases in the family letters or the selectivity of the anecdotes included in interpretation.

This chapter draws on my first-hand knowledge as a docent at Bulloch Hall from 2014 through 2020. I utilize the framework laid out by Jennifer Eichstedt and Stephen Small in their exhaustive 2002 survey of Southern plantation museums. Between 1996 and 2001, Eichstedt and Small visited 122 former plantations in order to analyze "the strategic rhetorics that are employed by plantation museums to manage, and in most cases confine to oblivion, the system of slavery and the presence of those enslaved" (2). Eichstedt and Small categorize Bulloch Hall as a plantation because it consisted of a big house surrounded by smaller outbuildings and it was maintained by slave labor that vastly outnumbered the white population (60).

DOI: 10.4324/9781003102830-8

122 *Sara Harwood*

Between 30 and 45 enslaved people labored at Bulloch Hall at any given time, even though the property functioned as a residence rather than a commercial enterprise.

Despite widespread evidence indicating a fraught relationship between the Bulloch family and slavery, the museum utilizes what Eichstedt and Small call the "good owners" narrative to interpret the Bulloch family (201). Geographer E. Arnold Modlin noted in his 2008 survey of North Carolina plantation museums that the managers of those museums have shown increased interest in discussing slavery and that the current state of interpretation must be examined (266). I posit that Bulloch Hall's overt usage of archival material in the guided tour exemplifies Dean MacConnell's 1973 theory of "staged authenticity," the concept that tourist spaces bring previously hidden "back" information to the "front" in order to appear more authentic, while simultaneously and deceptively continuing to obscure the distasteful facts (336). This appearance of accuracy can mislead the tourists who want to learn the truth about the experiences of enslaved persons. Modlin notes that visitors increasingly seek accurate narratives at historic sites, yet they rarely question the authenticity of the stories presented at museums (267). Similarly, geographers Derek Alderman, David Butler, and Stephen Hanna assert in their 2015 study of plantation museums along River Road in southern Louisiana that demand has increased for "unsanitized historical narratives" (210). When Bulloch Hall and other plantation museums present sanitized narratives as the truth, visitors consume this staged authenticity as factual.

The unscripted guided tour of Bulloch Hall, developed by the museum's education coordinator, is based on extensive research on upper-class life in northern Georgia and relies on the Bulloch family letters preserved at Harvard University. Copies of the letters were provided to Bulloch Hall in 2008 and were published in three volumes by Friends of Bulloch, Inc., all edited by the education coordinator in partnership with another historian. Because docents make it clear that they base their tours on primary sources, visitors accept the authenticity of the narrative. Here, the concept of staged authenticity applies not in MacCannell's original spatial sense but to the presentation of a supposedly unknown archive, accessible only to scholars. By positing that Bulloch Hall's guided tour reveals unfiltered history straight from the "back" of the library, docents imply that their information must be accurate. Yet, as MacCannell notes, "The pretentious revelation of supposed back region secrets suggests that what remains actually hidden in postmodern society is so appalling we cannot permit it to appear even behind the scenes" (336). Likewise, at Bulloch Hall, docents present a problematically inaccurate "good master" narrative while omitting more horrific details that belie the tour's main narrative.

Perhaps because of Bulloch's white-columned front piazza and its tree-lined drive, and certainly because of the state of Georgia's self-marketing, visitors associate Bulloch Hall and other frame Greek Revival homes with Tara from *Gone with the Wind*. Eichstedt and Small observe:

> Very, very few Georgia sites incorporated sustained critical discussions of slavery. Perhaps this is related to the dominant *Gone with the Wind* framing

that the state as a whole employs. Such framing is inconsistent with anything but loyal slaves, beautiful white southern women, and a noble life.

(210)

As geographer Perry Carter observes in a study of Tripadvisor ratings in 2015, the *Gone with the Wind* narrative has become so prevalent in some plantation museums that it is effectively "disenabling" other narratives (237). Docents expressly remark that Bulloch Hall did not necessarily serve as the foundation for Tara but they nevertheless claim that Mittie Bulloch may have been an inspiration for Scarlett O'Hara. This legend likely originated in historian David McCullough's seminal biography of Theodore Roosevelt which won the 1981 National Book Award. Prior to the publication of the Bulloch family letters, McCullough's biography, published shortly after the museum's 1978 restoration, was a pivotal source of information on the Bulloch family (Smith 5B). McCullough himself depended on a 1921 biography of Roosevelt written by Theodore's sister, Corinne Roosevelt Robinson (McCullough 53).

Margaret Mitchell claimed that there was no real Scarlett or Tara, McCullough notes, yet "the combination of the beautiful dark-haired Mittie Bulloch with her tiny waist and perfect complexion and the aura of Bulloch Hall is remarkably close to what she created" (47). Docents support this assertion with anecdotes from family letters indicating that, like O'Hara, Bulloch was charming and flirtatious. By positing an actual historic figure as the inspiration for O'Hara, docents reinforce the association of plantation museums with the fictional, idealized novel, problematically implying that Mitchell's depiction of the antebellum South is historically accurate. Ironically, in their 2014 study of Laura Plantation in Louisiana, Perry Carter, David Butler, and Derek Alderman found that while three of the nine visitors interviewed mentioned *Gone with the Wind*, the majority of them recognized that the image presented by that novel is a "farce" (555). Bulloch Hall, on the other hand, maintains this mirage.

Docents learn the tour and new information about Bulloch Hall from the education coordinator and from each other. They receive initial training by observing tours and studying a binder of information prepared by the education coordinator. Once they complete the training and begin giving tours, most docents attend optional monthly meetings, where the education coordinator shares updates about the museum, such as news about upcoming events, then concludes with anecdotes from research that she has completed. Some docents choose to read the still-in-print books recommended by the education coordinator, such as McCullough's biography and the published volumes of Bulloch letters. Because her research focuses on Mittie Bulloch, the information shared by the education coordinator centers on the Bulloch family's perspective and encourages docents to admire Mittie for her intelligence, wit, and charm. Although Mittie did have those praiseworthy traits and was a remarkable, accomplished woman, this centralization of Mittie effectively excludes other perspectives and minimizes, almost to the point of annihilation, non-white interpretations of Bulloch Hall, however unintentionally.

One source of anecdotes shared with docents, Corinne Robinson's out-of-print biography of Roosevelt, demonstrates at best shallow consideration of the enslaved individuals' viewpoints. Robinson claims that "slaves were treated as friends of the family" and enslaved children "were actually considered as foster brother or sister" (10, 11). She describes Irvine Bulloch and his personal slave, Sarah, as "inseparable companions" (11). Although the children, while young, might have viewed the relationship that way, they learned early that any intimacy between enslaver and enslaved had very clear limitations. Robinson remarks that Irvine's "brilliant" older half-brother, Daniel Elliott, went out to the back porch one night and was "much disgusted" to find the two children sitting together (11). Robinson seems to have felt amused that Elliott "demanded that they should be forbidden the back porch on moonlight nights from that time forth!" (11). She presents his reaction as a humorous anecdote and indicates that Mittie Bulloch told her children stories of the enslaved as sources of entertainment. As Robinson states, "we never tired of hearing the stories" of the enslaved from her mother (10). Instead of analyzing the story objectively, docents, identifying with Mittie, retain the narrative's master perspective and encourage visitors to do the same. When they relate this story, docents frame it as a heart-warming example of the companionship between the enslaved and the enslaver.

This interpretation of Robinson's anecdote exemplifies the "production myths" described by Modlin. He observes that interpretation leans toward a one-sided conversation that often hides as much as it presents (268). Production myths are localized stories that, compiled together, create larger meta-myths, misrepresentations of national or regional history (281). Modlin describes the "good master" narrative as an example of a production myth (277). Other production myths include what Hamilton, Hodgson, and Quirk call "self-congratulation by way of comparison" and "self-serving representations of 'benign slavery,' which usually involves actors seeking to excuse or otherwise minimize their involvement in slavery by depicting their own histories as being 'less' oppressive than those of their peers" (8). Bulloch Hall's claim that enslaved children were considered family, implicitly comparing the supposedly tamer domestic slavery at Bulloch to plantation slavery elsewhere, likewise serves as a production myth.

Stories that do not support this production myth are left out of the tour. For example, Robinson explains that Martha Bulloch and her daughter would sometimes visit "the outlying little huts in which the various negroes lived" (12). She explains that one Lucy had "had several children, none of whom had lived but a few hours" (12). Despite that tellingly high infant mortality rate, when Lucy had another baby, the Bulloch family made her deliver and nurse it in the slave quarters (12). After giving birth, Lucy told Bulloch that the baby would be named "Cumsy," short for "Come-see-the-world-and-go" because "I don't 'spec' her to live, dey ain't none of 'em done live" (12). This heartbreaking anecdote—which reveals that newborns did not receive proper care and that the Bulloch family had little sympathy for the bereaved mothers—is not incorporated into the Bulloch Hall tour or discussed at monthly docent meetings. Since Robinson's biography is out of print, most of the docents have not read it and may not know of this story.

Bulloch Hall could develop a more inclusive narrative by sharing these negative stories about slavery with the docents and encouraging an objective evaluation of the Bulloch family.

The study by Eichstedt and Small provides helpful framing for evaluating Bulloch Hall's interpretation. When Eichstedt and Small visited Bulloch Hall, the house tour did not include references to slavery. Of the 29 historic sites the pair visited in Georgia, Bulloch Hall was the only one that they categorized as fitting into their third grouping, "segregation and marginalization of knowledge" (65). Museums using this strategy separate information about slavery from the regular plantation tour, either by offering an optional tour on slavery or, in Bulloch Hall's case, by offering an exhibit on slavery in an outbuilding that is not visited on the regular tour (Eichstedt and Small 10). In the early twentieth century, Bulloch Hall had contracted a master carpenter to rebuild the historic service yard, which included two dogtrot slave quarters and other outbuildings ("Exhibits"). As Small observed in 2013, the presence of slave quarters does not prevent a master-focused narrative from dominating interpretation (in Carter et al. 548). One of the slave quarters is used as a staff office and the other is divided into two interpretive spaces. One side of the dogtrot is interpreted as a period room, reflecting how the slave quarters would have looked while inhabited. The other side is a museum space with interpretive panels and a sign listing the 33 names of known enslaved individuals. Since Eichstedt and Small published their monograph, Bulloch Hall has made minor changes indicating steps toward an inclusive narrative, primarily by addressing slavery in the house tour. Small interpretive signs now describe the tasks of enslaved people, while the new placement of physical objects related to their duties, such as buckets, alludes to the work they did in the house. The education coordinator also directs docents to refer to the enslaved as slaves, not servants.

Most impactfully, the Bulloch children's bedrooms show pallets stuffed with pine needles on the floor to demonstrate where the enslaved children would have slept. This bedding can function as a helpful segue to dialogue about the living conditions of enslaved children in an upper-class urban home, as it visually conveys the physical hardships endured and the inherent inequality of the enslaver–enslaved relationship. Nevertheless, visitors often assume that the white Bulloch children and the enslaved children must have been "friends," a false narrative rarely corrected by docents, but instead reinforced with anecdotes from Robinson's biography and the Bulloch family letters. Carter, Butler, and Alderman argue that marketing throughout the twentieth century has fostered this "happy slave" narrative. Citing consumer goods such as Aunt Jemima pancake syrup and nostalgia-laden Hollywood productions such as *Gone with the Wind*, they assert that "these romanticized metanarratives about the South prime or condition tourist expectations of plantation museums" (549). When Bulloch Hall accurately depicts the living conditions of enslaved children within the physical space but does not provide inclusive context to express the cultural devaluation of those children by the Bulloch family, visitors impose their preconceived biases on the space. By assuming the whiteness of visitors and encouraging them to identify with the enslavers throughout the tour, docents fail to leave room for identification with, let alone empathy for, the enslaved individuals.

In her 2013 study of dark tourism sites, places associated with death and disaster, museum studies scholar Andrea Witcomb proposes a means of inclusion, observed at the Memorial for the Murdered Jews of Europe in Berlin, that brings reality "to the level of what the Holocaust meant for individual people and their families" (165). She reveals that the Memorial describes the experiences of individual victims of the Holocaust (167). The objectivity, she notes, has an especially important effect, as informational panels present excerpts from victims' diaries: "The visitor, then, is not explicitly positioned in relation to either the victims or the perpetrators" (165). Unfortunately, white visitors to plantation museums in the American South are predisposed to identify with the enslavers, so even an objective presentation of archival material can effectively become immersive. Furthermore, as Aaron Yankholmes and Bob McKercher observe in their 2015 paper on slavery and heritage tourism, slavery heritage sites do not neatly fit into the thanatourism category, tourism associated with death, since they do not explicitly represent encounters with violent death as the Holocaust memorial does (234). Slavery sites nevertheless could fulfill the same "desire for redemption, the need to memorialize in order to grieve and the need to demarcate the present from the past while also recognizing the ongoing effects of the past on the present" (Witcomb 153).

Because Bulloch Hall allows docents to assemble their own narratives, the unscripted guided tour provides leeway for docents to depend upon their personal biases when interpreting the house. Kristin Gallas and James DeWolf Perry, scholars writing on behalf of the Tracing Center on Histories and Legacies of Slavery, comment that interpretation hinges on racial identity: "Confronting this history [of slavery] invokes historical narratives at the core of how many Americans understand their identity—whether on the basis of race or ethnicity, or in terms of family, socioeconomic class, or regional affiliation" (30). Bulloch Hall docents who identify with Mittie Bulloch, the focus of the tour, likewise tend to embrace her perspective on the enslaved persons. Except for one white male docent and one female docent of native descent, the staff and docents are all white and female, and their racial identities lead them to establish Mittie's perspective as the norm. Identifying with the slave-owning race, they subconsciously accept the slaveowner's view as the dominant perspective. Since the Friends of Bulloch Hall website markets the museum as "the childhood home of Mittie Bulloch, mother of President Theodore Roosevelt," museum interpretation also centers around encouraging visitors to identify with Mittie Bulloch, thereby creating an upper-class, white-centered lens for viewing the history of slavery ("Welcome").

The master-dominated narrative in the marketing echoes the interpretation at the museum. In her 2011 monograph on Southern literature, Thadious Davis explains that media representations of the South during the last decades of the twentieth century have downplayed the presence of minorities in the South, leading to the "obscuring of a black presence" (28). In turn, the marginalization of minorities in meaning-making has created a definition of the South based on exclusion and robbed Southern Black people of an identity while centering Southern white people (28). Effectively, "in dominant views of the human geography of the South, whites become Southerners" (29). Given that Bulloch Hall is one of the three historic house museums in the City of Roswell's "Southern Trilogy," where, according to the City's promotional website, visitors may "learn about the history of the American south," it should not be surprising that interpretation centers on the white enslavers ("Southern Trilogy"). The erasure of Black lives is evident even on the City's promotional website for Bulloch Hall, which states that "Bulloch Hall was built in the Greek Revival style in 1839 *by* Major James Stephens Bulloch" ("Bulloch Hall," emphasis added). Archival evidence indicates that a white carpenter, Willis Ball, designed Bulloch Hall, and Ball's slaves physically constructed the building. James Bulloch himself did not build the house. The use of the preposition "by" instead of the accurate preposition, "for," erases the role of enslaved people in building Bulloch Hall.

The American South is not the only region to create narratives of exclusion. Cultural historian Emma Waterton's 2013 study of British tourism agencies observes that tourism documents largely present a white elite or middle class as defining British culture (65). She notes that the typical images shown in promotional brochures and websites, such as castles and abbeys, support "one version of heritage" (71). In turn, tourists feel limited in their options, particularly when seeking to explore national heritage (74). As the narratives at these sites encourage visitors to identify with upper-class, white heritage narratives, Waterton finds, minorities and the poor often express discomfort and feeling excluded at these museums, leading to resentment (75). Interestingly, only anecdotally have Roswell Visitors' Bureau staff referred to visitor complaints about "the slave houses." Although no known record exists of visitors experiencing a sense of disconnect at Bulloch Hall, in 2020, an Atlanta journalist pointed to Bulloch Hall as an example of "scrub[bing] painful truths about enslaved people" (Murchison). This article reflects the willingness of one local writer to voice discomfort with Bulloch Hall's white-centered narrative.

The white-dominated narrative hinges on selectivity in relating the full record of the Bullochs as slaveowners, even though docents use anecdotes drawn from primary sources. For example, the introduction to the first volume of Bulloch family letters provides minimal context for the family's move to Roswell. The editors note that Mittie was born during the family's "extended stay" in Hartford, Connecticut; then the narrative skips to 1838, when the family "left Savannah" to move to Roswell (9). However, the actions of the Bulloch family while living in Hartford for two years drew national attention and shed light upon their personalities as enslavers.

When the Bullochs moved to Hartford, Connecticut, in 1835 to enroll their children in local schools, enslaved nurse Nancy Jackson was brought along to care for the couple's newborn daughter, Anna (Wilson 26). In 1837, the Bulloch family planned to return to Georgia, but Jackson decided to stay and sue for her freedom (28). According to local abolitionist Edward Tyler's account, published in William Lloyd Garrison's abolitionist newspaper, *The Liberator*, Jackson "had frequently expressed a strong desire for freedom, and the utmost dread of being carried back to Gorgia [sic]" (1). However, when Jackson told Martha Bulloch about her wishes, Bulloch replied that "it was a foolish notion" and "she must go back where she could be taken care of" (1). James Bulloch threatened to write to the governor of Georgia personally to force her to stay with him (1). Both Tyler and Bulloch hired lawyers and Tyler filed a writ of *habeas corpus* requiring Bulloch to bring Jackson to court (1). The night before they were supposed to appear in court, Jackson overheard Martha Bulloch encouraging James to "never mind the bond and send Nancy south" (Mars 35). In spite of their legal obligation, the Bullochs seemed determined to remove Jackson from the state by force. Before this could happen, Jackson escaped from the house (35). She appeared in court on her own the following morning (35). She later told a friend that she had brought opium pills with her and "had she been sentenced to go back [to slavery] she should have swallowed both of them before she left the court house" (36). Fortunately for her, the judge ruled in her favor, granting her freedom (36). Bulloch bitterly wrote to the Savannah *Georgian* castigating the abolitionists who supported Jackson, calling them "the vilest of these immediate Emancipators, these would-be Philanthropists of the colored race" who, he menacingly claims, "seem to wish to die Martyrs" (2). He promises that "it is a duty I owe to the South to carry it up to the highest Judicial Tribunal," the Supreme Court (2). He must have ultimately realized the futility of doing so, as he does not appear to have ever pursued the case further. Less than two years after the Jackson emancipation case, the Bulloch family moved to Roswell.

Docents only mention this story when describing how Nancy Jackson later reconnected with Mittie Bulloch. When Roosevelt was elected president, Jackson wrote to congratulate him and noted in her letter that while working in New York as a personal maid to another woman, she called upon Bulloch (Jackson 2). They did not meet on equal footing, however; Jackson adds that even though she already had another position that she preferred, "Your Mother wanted me to be housekeeper and I cleaned all her silver" (3). Leaving out this last detail and the challenges Jackson faced while seeking her freedom, docents relate the story of Jackson and Bulloch's reunion to create the production myth that the enslaved people at Bulloch Hall were considered family. Echoing Robinson's paternalistic narrative that the Bulloch family looked upon the enslaved people kindly, docents blatantly encourage identifying with Mittie, rather than with Jackson. Likewise, by overlooking the work that Jackson performed for Bulloch in New York, docents can suggest that the visit—and, by extension, the relationship—was purely social.

The actions of Mittie Bulloch's half-brother, Daniel Stuart Elliott, also belie the "good owner" narrative at Bulloch Hall. McCullough remarks acerbically:

> Half brother Daniel Stuart Elliott once had to be sent abroad for a year of travel, so full of remorse was he. In a fit of rage he had shot and killed his "little shadow," who by then, like Daniel Elliott himself, was no longer very little.
>
> (45)

Elliott evidently did not feel so remorseful; later in life, he killed another man in a duel.

The exhibit area in the reconstructed slave quarters comments on the murder of the enslaved child, albeit with minimal context: "A.R. Cowles tells of young Stewart Bulloch shooting and killing his 'little shadow' in an attack of temper. Stewart's punishment was to be sent abroad for a year of foreign travel" (qtd. in Eichstedt and Small 195). Eichstedt and Small note that the lack of context presents "a mixed message about slavery" particularly because the account about Bulloch does not explicitly identify him (196). Furthermore, the anecdote is surrounded by "examples that seem to operate as signifiers of the goodness of at least some master-enslavers" (196). The scholars indicate that this apparent effort at objectivity overlooks the horrific nature of slavery at the cost of accuracy:

> This [story about Elliott] would be an excellent opportunity for the absolute power of enslavers to be discussed—that is, the text could provide critical commentary highlighting how enslavers could kill enslaved people with impunity and point out the irony of the boy's "punishment" being world travel.
>
> (200)

Indeed, the suicidal nature of Nancy Jackson presents a powerful opening for Bulloch Hall to educate visitors about the cruel reality of slavery. Instead of choosing to incorporate these narratives, interpretation at Bulloch Hall opts to, in the words of Carter, Butler, and Alderman, "promote the merits of appropriation for both colonizer and subjugated other" (550). Rather than encouraging an open conversation about the horrors of slavery, the tour echoes the production myths seen at other historic sites across the South, thus described by Carter et al.: "The principle and thinly veiled message embedded within most plantation museum narratives is that the original white inhabitants of the plantation house were industrious people who lived elegant and honorable lives" (550). Docents praise Mittie Bulloch for meeting with Nancy Jackson instead of questioning James Bulloch's refusal to emancipate his daughter's enslaved nurse.

Signage in the house related to slavery, an addition since Eichstedt and Small's study, utilizes another account published prior to the 2008 acquisition of the Bulloch family letters. Catherine Sever, a cousin of Martha Bulloch, visited the family in Roswell in 1839, when she was around 12 years old. Some four decades later she wrote a description of the visit, ultimately published by a historical society in 1969. Her description of Bulloch Hall, one of the singular available sources for interpretation prior to the publication of the family letters, observes "slave quarters, two nice little houses each divided into two parts" (18). Despite witnessing that the enslaved people lived in those small dogtrot outbuildings, Sever claims that they were "so entirely a part of the family" (18). Sever also mentions "little Bess," who, she notes, slept on a mattress on the floor and whose "only duty" was "just" to attend the dinner table and shoo away flies (19). In fact, Bess was a personal servant to Mittie and Anna (Robinson 12). Sever unfeelingly criticizes Bess, noting sarcastically that this "only service" of shooing flies was "so arduous" for her that she would fall asleep while standing at the table and "the fly brush would descend upon our heads" (19).

At one time, Bulloch Hall chose to incorporate this anecdote into its permanent interpretation. For several years, a recreated "fly brush" made of straw was displayed in the dining room with a sign describing Sever's account. Docents would include this story in the regular tour as an explanation for how upper-class families dealt with insects in the days before window screens. They did not share this anecdote to elicit disgust toward the system of slavery. In fact, visitors would often laugh at the story and say "Cute!" This stunning reaction, which gives no thought to the perspective of the enslaved child, reflects the inherent problems in the "good owners" narrative so often embraced by plantation museums. The image of an exploited child, forced to stand watch while others eat, succumbing to exhaustion and repeatedly falling asleep while standing up, is a poignant example of the terrors of slavery. At Bulloch Hall, even an objective telling of this story can lead visitors to take it as a humorous anecdote without reflection on the suffering of the child, effectively using a horrendous story to confirm the paternalistic narrative. This common reaction exemplifies why museums need to take a leading role in explicitly explaining the negative impact of slavery. Such reactions to white-centric narratives illustrate why Gallas and Perry charge museums to prioritize an inclusive perspective on slavery: "We have an obligation to the public to share a comprehensive and conscientious story of the past, especially as studies show that the public considers museums to be their most trusted source of historical information" (26). When museums fail to present a well-rounded narrative that acknowledges the suffering of the enslaved, visitors mistakenly accept the bias of the enslavers as fact without recognizing the existence of other perspectives. As tourism scholar A.V. Seaton explains, the persistent failure of plantation museums to enlighten audiences exemplifies the problems that can arise when institutions and funders, sympathetic only to the enslavers, "unilaterally" represent subjects (124).

The recreated fly brush fell apart after years of use by the docents, and in 2019 the display was removed. However, Bulloch Hall continues to incorporate imagery from Sever's narrative. Sever explains that Henry, a little enslaved boy, had the task of washing the pine floors every morning: "The way he did it was this: he took corn husks and rubbed them over the floor with his bare feet" (19). In the central hallway, staff have placed a sign describing Henry's task, along with a bucket filled with corn husks. This signage, although placed on the path between rooms where docents rarely pause on the tour, also typically elicits laughter from visitors. This routine response indicates that even when not guided to do so by a smiling docent, visitors chuckle at the concept of enslaved children exhausting themselves for a white family.

This willful indifference to the child's suffering reflects David Butler's observation that tourists seek travel experiences that escape the mundane in favor of "a fantasy of pleasure" (171). Uninterested in confronting or acknowledging the uncomfortable, they deliberately attempt to obfuscate the blatantly negative interpretation they encounter. Similarly, people are drawn to uncomplicated interpretation that makes them feel good about themselves and their heritage. Gallas and Perry remark: "It is no coincidence that that nation's public memory leaves out the connections of most American families to slavery" (36). It is natural, they contend, for people "to prefer ... unambiguous narratives, and to select historical facts promoting positive views of groups with which we identify" (36). As the majority of plantation visitors are white Americans, they tend to identify with the plantation owners and to seek a simple story that idealizes the past (Eichstedt and Small 199). Butler feels that plantation museums are particularly vulnerable to this type of gaze, because even the name "plantation" is often granted to tourist attractions in order to increase visitation, as the concept of a plantation "connotes opulence" (171). Since museums purport to deliver "authenticity," Butler remarks, this self-deception on the part of tourists must be recognized (173). Davis's comment on Southern literature likewise applies to Bulloch Hall:

> I do see the exclusionary representation as a function both of racial blindness and of a discrete discourse that naturalizes the existence of a white racial category and elides the existence of a Black one, and that consequently produces a self-perpetuating discourse that is seemingly racially unmarked but normalized from the perspective of white.
>
> (30)

For white tourists, just like for the white docents, the white-centered, non-inclusive view can, subconsciously, seem natural. Museums therefore must deliberately include other perspectives to decentralize the master narrative.

When museums do not educate visitors about slaveholders' biases, a one-sided interpretation can misleadingly appear complete. Tourism scholars Graham M.S. Dann and A.V. Seaton observe, using MacCannell's theory, that historic sites can create an aura of "staged authenticity" that allows visitors to enjoy their experience without employing critical thought (14). Living history interpretations such as Williamsburg invite visitors to accept what they see as fully accurate (14). Instead of challenging longstanding historical narratives, museums may reinforce nostalgic concepts of the past. Plantation museums, Dann and Seaton note, minimize the impact of slavery in order to focus on the wealthy owners and historic furniture (15). This troubling façade of authenticity consequently permeates sites like Bulloch Hall, where objective information on a sign is interpreted through the lens created by other plantation museums. Encouraged to ignore the horrors of slavery in favor of a paternalistic system, tourists view even clearly troubling history in a positive light. Recognizing the challenges that this situation poses to museums, Dann and Seaton argue that museums must try to correct skewed viewpoints in order to remain true to their mission as educational sites, however great the challenge: "With the bottom line of tourism apparently being profit and that of history seemingly being truth, a delicate course has to be steered through the troubled waters of the authenticity they both purport to share" (16).

Because Bulloch Hall is owned by the City of Roswell, it theoretically falls less subject to pressures to make a profit than might private for-profit museums. Since it does not have the same financial pressures as for-profit sites, it is less likely to focus on providing a pleasurable experience for visitors that overlooks "potentially troubling" topics (Eichstedt and Small 66). However, as Seaton observes, "even the most publicly subsidized attraction comes under fire if it is seen to have too few visitors" (Seaton 124). Fears of driving away business can cause museum staff to avoid discussing controversial topics like slavery (Gallas and Perry 36). Consequently, Carter ponders the possibility of a museum being "both amusement and pedagogic site for coming to terms with a tragic and embarrassing past" (236). This shyness is counter-productive, though, as visitors may feel more frustrated by the misrepresentation of history than elated by self-congratulatory narratives.

Bulloch Hall has unfortunately faced increased pressure from the City of Roswell in the past half-decade to make more money. One City-sponsored study, the Imagine Roswell Arts and Culture 2030 Master Plan, completed in 2015, examined the management structure of all three house museums in Roswell and made a recommendation for "the reconfiguration of the structure and management of historic and cultural programs to improve their effectiveness" ("Charrette"). The Plan recommends making a specific Historic Division run by "a visionary manager" who could "more effectively market their homes" ("Excerpt" 68). The Master Plan also calls for the creation of a nonprofit "to plan for the future development and programming of the homes and *to raise funds to support their operations and programming*" ("Excerpt" 69, italics added). Such thinly veiled threats against job security undoubtedly place stress on the staff at Bulloch Hall. In 2019, the City created a new position, the Historic Assets Manager, to oversee the City's historic properties, including the three historic house museums. The Historic Assets Manager has encouraged staff at the museums to develop more inclusive narratives, particularly after the national galvanizing of the Black Lives Matter movement in 2020. Simultaneously, personnel restructuring led to the sudden resignation of Bulloch Hall's director and education coordinator, much to the dismay of myself and the other docents. This dramatic change in staff, while disruptive and personally challenging for both the former staff and the docents, has created an opportunity to revisit the museum's white-centered interpretation.

Although, as Eichstedt and Small have observed, staff at plantation museums worry that addressing slavery will lead to decreased visitation, well-rounded and inclusive narratives do not necessarily frighten away visitors. Rather, Regina Faden, professor of Museum Studies at St. Mary's College of Maryland, contends that one-sided accounts of slavery run a greater risk of isolating audiences. She explains that museums incorporating a slavery narrative "typically" deny enslaved persons agency (252). The victim role in which museums cast them can make African American visitors uncomfortable and disengaged (252). Nevertheless, she adds, ignoring unpleasant history altogether in favor of a false progressive narrative, as so many museums do, is "cowardice" (256). Even when visitors do not want to discuss slavery, Gallas and Perry note, a visitor can disengage but still "process new historical content" (35). Seaton proposes that the best method for a more inclusive interpretation involves engaging in planning all four stakeholding groups: institutions/funders; subjects, including descendant communities; host communities, including current nearby residents; and audiences (123). While many museum representatives think that visitors do not want to hear about unpleasant topics, Gallas and Perry argue that "it's important to note that visitors come with prior knowledge" and museums have a vital mission "to tangibly demonstrate the connection between the historic experience of slavery and current issues of race, privilege, and human rights" (34).

With the increased interest in the effectiveness of museums in Roswell, an opportunity has arisen for the City to engage broader audiences, including the local African American community and particularly the descendant community. While Bulloch Hall has taken laudable steps in addressing slavery objectively both in a dedicated exhibit and throughout the furnished mansion, permanent interpretation and docent training currently fall short of incorporating what Gallas and Perry call "comprehensive content" that inclusively demonstrates "race and identity awareness" (31). Gallas and Perry charge museums to recognize that the history of slavery "is broader and deeper than our public memory generally acknowledges" (30). As the City reevaluates its historic assets and its cohesive narrative, the moment seems opportune for Roswell to reaffirm its commitment to a more inclusive interpretation of slavery.

References

"Affair of honor." (Macon) *Georgia Telegraph*. February 24, 1857.
Alderman, Derek H., David L. Butler, and Stephen P. Hanna. "Memory, slavery, and plantation museums: the River Road project." *Journal of Heritage Tourism*, vol. 11, no. 3, 2015, pp. 209–218. doi: 10.1080/1743873X.2015.1100629.
Bulloch, James S. "Hartford." *Daily Georgian*. August 19, 1837.
Bulloch Hall. "Exhibits." *Friends of Bulloch, Inc.* www.bullochhall.org/exhibits.html. Accessed 28 October 2019.
———. "Welcome to Bulloch Hall." *Friends of Bulloch, Inc.* www.bullochhall.org/index.html. Accessed 31 October 2019.
Butler, David L. "Whitewashing plantations: the commodification of a slave-free antebellum South." *International Journal of Hospitality and Tourism Administration*, vol. 2, nos. 3–4, 2001, pp. 163–175. doi: 10.1300/J149v02n03_07.
Caroli, Betty Boyd. *The Roosevelt Women*. Basic Books, 1998.
Carter, Perry L. "Where are the enslaved? Trip advisor and the narrative landscapes of southern plantation museums." *Journal of Heritage Tourism*, vol. 11, no. 3, 2015, pp. 235–249. doi: 10.1080/1743873X.2015.1100625
Carter, Perry, David L. Butler, and Derek H. Alderman. "The house that story built: the place of slavery in plantation museum narratives." *Professional Geographer*, vol. 66, no. 4, 2014, pp. 547–557. doi: 10.1080/00330124.2014.921016.
City of Roswell, Georgia. "Agenda. Roswell historic assets summit." *City of Roswell Mayor and City Council Special Called Work Session*. March 7, 2017. http://roswellcityga

.iqm2.com/Citizens/FileOpen.aspx?Type=1&ID=1621&highlightTerms=museums%20profit. Accessed 31 August 2020.

City of Roswell, Georgia. "Agenda item. approval of a text amendment to chapter 9 historic preservation." *Recreation and Parks*. February 11, 2019. http://roswellcityga.iqm2.com/Citizens/Detail_LegiFile.aspx?ID=5190&highlightTerms=%22historic%20assets%20manager%22. Accessed 31 August 2020.

———. "Agenda item. Consideration of a Charrette to gather input regarding Roswell's southern trilogy and other historic assets." *Recreation and Parks*. November 15, 2016. http://roswellcityga.iqm2.com/Citizens/Detail_LegiFile.aspx?ID=3318&highlightTerms=%22historic%20assets%22. Accessed 31 August 2020.

———. "Bulloch Hall." *Recreation and Parks*. www.roswellgov.com/discover-us/southern-trilogy-historic-house-museums/bulloch-hall. Accessed 31 August 2020.

———. "Cultural plan excerpt recommendation 8." *Recreation and Parks*. November 15, 2016. http://roswellcityga.iqm2.com/Citizens/FileOpen.aspx?Type=4&ID=6715&highlightTerms=%22historic%20assets%22. Accessed 31 August 2020.

———. "Roswell Roots." *Roswell Roots*. Roswellgov.com. www.roswellgov.com/government/departments/recreation-and-parks/news-events/roswell-roots. Accessed 26 October 2019.

———. "Southern trilogy summer camps." Roswell, Georgia. www.roswellgov.com/discover-us/southern-trilogy-historic-house-museums/events/southern-trilogy-summer-camps. Accessed 31 August 2020.

Dann, Graham M.S., and A.V. Seaton. "Slavery, contested heritage, and thanatourism." *International Journal of Hospitality and Tourism Administration*, vol. 2, nos. 3–4, 2001, pp. 1–30. doi: 10.1300/J149v02n03_01.

Davis, Thadious M. *Southscapes: Geographies of Race, Region, and Literature*, University of North Carolina P, 2011.

Eichstedt, Jennifer L. and Stephen Small. *Representations of Slavery: Race & Ideology in Southern Plantation Museums*. Smithsonian Institution P, 2002.

Faden, Regina. "Museums and the story of slavery: the challenge of language." *International Journal of Hospitality and Tourism Administration*, vol. 2, no. 3/4, 2001, pp. 252–266, www.taylorfrancis.com/books/e/9780203119075/chapters/10.4324/9780203119075-22. Accessed 31 October 2019.

Gallas, Kristin L., and James DeWolf Perry. "Developing a comprehensive and conscientious interpretation of slavery at historic sites and museums." *Interpreting African American History and Culture at Museums and Historic Sites*, edited by Max van Balgooy. Rowman & Littlefield, 2015, pp. 26–37.

Hamilton, Douglas, Kate Hodgson, and Joel Quirk, editors. Introduction. *Slavery, Memory, and Identity: National Representations and Global Legacies*, Pickering and Chatto, 2012, pp. 1–13.

Huddleston, Connie M. and Gwendolyn I. Koehler. *Mittie & Thee: An 1853 Roosevelt Romance*, Friends of Bulloch, Inc., 2015.

Hulser, Kathleen. "Exhibiting slavery at the New-York Historical Society." *International Journal of Hospitality and Tourism Administration*, vol. 2, nos. 3–4, 2001, pp. 232–257, www.taylorfrancis.com/books/e/9780203119075/chapters/10.4324/9780203119075-21. Accessed 31 October 2019.

Jackson, Nancy. Letter from Nancy Jackson to Theodore Roosevelt, 6 Sept 1902, Letter. Theodore Roosevelt Papers. Library of Congress Manuscript Division. Dickinson State University. www.theodorerooseveltcenter.org/Research/Digital-Library/Record?libID=o38924. Accessed 29 October 2019.

MacCannell, Dean. "Why it never really was about *Authenticity*." *Society*, vol. 45, 2008, pp. 334–337. doi: 10.1007/s12115-008-9110-8.

Mars, James. *Life of James Mars, A Slave Born and Sold in Connecticut*. Hartford: Case, Lockwood & Company, 1865.

McCullough, David. *Mornings on Horseback: The Story of an Extraordinary Family, a Vanished Way of Life, and the Unique Child Who Became Theodore Roosevelt*. First ed. 1981. Simon & Schuster, 2001.

Modlin, Jr., E. Arnold. "Tales told on the tour: mythic representations of slavery by docents in North Carolina plantation museums," *Southeastern Geographer*, vol. 48, no. 3, 2008, pp. 265–287. doi: 10.1353/sgo.0.0025

Murchison, Adrianne. "Roswell works toward a more complete retelling of the city's Black history," *Atlanta Journal-Constitution*, August 17, 2020, www.ajc.com/news/atlanta-news/roswell-works-toward-a-more-complete-retelling-of-the-citys-black-history/NVNQFSYXSJDVPEB252HRB3HBBI/. Accessed 31 August 2020.

Robinson, Corinne Roosevelt. *My Brother Theodore Roosevelt*. Charles Scribner's Sons, 1921.

Seaton, A.V. "Sources of slavery—destinations of slavery. The silences and disclosures of slavery heritage in the UK and US." *International Journal of Hospitality and Tourism Administration*, vol. 2, nos. 3–4, 2001, pp. 107–130. doi: 10.1300/J149v02n03_05.

Sever, Catherine Elliott. "A memory of the south," edited by Monroe F. Cockrell. *The Atlanta Historical Bulletin*, vol. XIV, no. 1, March 1969, pp. 7–25.

Smith, Helen C. "'Antiques showhouse' to aid in Bulloch Hall restoration." *The Atlanta Constitution*. October 12, 1978.

Tyler, Edward R. "Slave case in Connecticut." *The Liberator*. July 7, 1837.

Waterton, Emma. "Heritage tourism and its representations." *Heritage and Tourism: Place, Encounter, Engagement*, edited by Russell Staiff, Robyn Bushell, and Steve Watson. Routledge, 2013, pp. 64–84.

Wilson, Walter E. *The Bulloch Belles: Three First Ladies, a Spy, a President's Mother, and Other Women of a 19th Century Georgia Family*. McFarland, 2015.

Witcomb, Andrea. "Using immersive and interactive approaches to interpreting traumatic experiences for tourists: potentials and limitations." *Heritage and Tourism: Place, Encounter, Engagement*, edited by Russell Staiff, Robyn Bushell, and Steve Watson. Routledge, 2013, pp. 152–170.

Yankholmes, Aaron and Bob McKercher. "Rethinking slavery heritage tourism." *Journal of Heritage Tourism*, vol. 10, no. 3, 2015, pp. 233–247. doi: 10.1080/1743873X.2014.988159

8 Rendezvous with history
Grand Portage National Monument and Minnesota's North Shore

David A. Tschida

Heritage tourism, indigeneity, culture, and the environment converge at Grand Portage National Monument on the Grand Portage Reservation, or Gichi Omingaming as the Anishinaabeg, Indigenous Native Americans, call this place. The current practices of heritage tourism and the cultural legacy of settler colonialism along the 150-mile state highway from Duluth, Minnesota, to the Monument set the stage for this convergence, as do seven state parks, the European American communities with historical remnants of extractive industries, and numerous resorts (Grimwood, Muldoon, and Stevens; Whitson). Tourists cannot avoid encountering these other sites along the only major road to Gichi Omingaming before it passes into Canada. Nor can they bracket each distinct element of their experience which includes narratives by or about the Anishinaabeg (i.e., Ojibwe, Chippewa), a plural form used by the Grand Portage Band to name itself, and the voicing of European fur traders and extractive industries by the National Park Service, Minnesota State Parks, and tourism-centered businesses and communities. Their experience includes tourism memories, re-lived and shared across generations, of Minnesota's "North Shore" of Lake Superior—the so-called "Norwegian American Riviera" (Cochrane).

While Grand Portage National Monument is a distinct place with borders, the tourist experience of it is a diffuse text combining the Monument and a highway filled with places spanning more than 200 years of shared Indigenous and European American history (Brummett; Dickinson, Ott, and Aoki). The tourist memories and experiences become a "dreamscape" (Blair and Michel). Memories of the parks, the decades-old cafes and restaurants, and the historic sites are brought to the forefront of one's thinking. It's not just memories of these places, but also one's education and experiences with popular culture such as films and art that are activated (Dickinson, Ott, and Aoki). The dreamscape becomes a distinct set of norms and expectations for how to act and interact. The tourist sites themselves are experiential landscapes that position the tourist to see, to listen, and to interact in specific ways that appeal to or interpellate something in the tourist (Blair and Michel; Dickinson, Ott, and Aoki).

I contend that Grand Portage National Monument does not stand alone as a text because no tourist arrives at the Monument without experiencing places along the highway first, without drawing some ideas from their education or family story

DOI: 10.4324/9781003102830-9

first, having some desire or hope for the tourist experience first. The Monument's messaging is not designed to have it stand alone. Its location at the furthest point along the highway, and the history of the region, means it cannot stand alone. Whether desired or not, in the current practices of heritage tourism, the Monument and the entire North Shore are always co-experienced. The Monument, for its part, memorializes the fur trade with the voyageurs who came to Gichi Omingaming. The heritage tourist is positioned as a voyageur in a manner that may frame, justify, or reinforce an entire tourist experience of Minnesota's North Shore. Therefore, a method of analysis that can account for this positioning and experience and allow for the greatest intercultural sensitivity and awareness is essential.

Cultural discourse analysis (Cu.D.A.) is a mixed methods approach drawing from a combination of autoethnographic and/or ethnographic approaches and rhetorical analysis. It recognizes communication is shaped by and found in everyday cultural practices. Acts of tourism, experiencing cultural events, and examining displays within a museum are examples of these practices. Cu.D.A. seeks to understand how people, situated in a specific context, engage in what they think is fitting communication, make sense of their communication and that of others, and then explain that sense making. It seeks to understand how people find value and meaning in being self-reflective in this way. Cu.D.A. is a method of explaining the social reality everyday communication constitutes and a meta-cultural commentary where individuals or groups analyze their cultural values, beliefs, or behaviors (Carbaugh, "Cultural discourse analysis"; Carbaugh and Rudnick; Carbaugh and Cerulli; Grimwood, Muldoon, and Stevens).

In Cu.D.A., attention may be given to communication devices about or practices within a setting, such as stories or place names that aid in a person's sense making (Carbaugh and Rudnick). For example, as I experienced tourist sites and materials identified in this essay, variations in spellings were occurring. I found group names such as Anishinaabeg, Anishnabeg, and Anishinaabe. I found Anishinaabeg "voiced" words of naming hyphenated differently by location, such as Gichi Onimgaming or Git-che-O-ni-ga-ming. These variations are linguistic, cultural, and community based and may constitute part of a heritage tourism experience. Some applications of Cu.D.A. highlight sensory experiences, particularly "listening." Listening, as used here, may manifest itself in respect for or a practice of an Indigenous way of knowing or scholarship (Carbaugh, "Just listen"; Whetung). It may be employed as a spirit of Other-directedness and mindfulness while in a culture's former or current environment or dwelling.

Using Indigenous terms or names, in heritage tourism or in scholarship, and employing research methods familiar to or respected by Indigenous cultures are each important to decolonization. I am not Indigenous and cannot fully understand indigeneity or the Indigenous experience by using colonial practices, or any practices, of scholarship. Yet, Indigenous research methods, or those non-Indigenous methods that Indigenous peoples respect, can be used by anyone to improve their understanding (Whetung). For example, autoethnographic methods with rich descriptions of experience are one way greater awareness of Indigenous people and experiences may occur. Indigenous knowledge will not be produced by a non-Indigenous person using Cu.D.A., but the method may decolonize the researcher or their conclusions and that decolonization may aid others in their own perspective taking.

Since one concern of this essay is drawing attention to the types of respect and mindfulness Indigenous people may be asking for as they position themselves within an entire landscape with an Indigenous history and sacredness (such as the North Shore), I must also acknowledge ways in which Indigenous peoples have been communicated about in relation to these landscapes. European Americans historically thought of themselves as cultured. By comparison, nature or wilderness were uncivilized (DeLuca and Demo). This binary placed European Americans in opposition to Indigenous people who were associated with primitiveness and wilderness. An ironic companion argument to this binary has been that civilization is ruining European Americans, especially men; therefore, there has long been a need for tourist places to escape into the "primitiveness" of the environment. Minnesota's North Shore reflects this binary and the irony, and more recently, attempts to move beyond both.

My approach is mindful that for the Anishinaabeg, the entire North Shore is sacred and disputed territory. Settler colonialism and its manifestation in resource extraction and, more recently, tourist practices have challenged and offended that sacredness. Likewise, Indigenous words, names, and myths have been interpreted by some as part of the folklore of the past, charming but irrelevant unless heritage tourism or academic scholarship offers positive explanations and alternatives to past practices (Grimwood, Muldoon, and Stevens; Whitson). In the context of heritage tourism, these alternatives do not happen where one rushes through an attraction, snaps a selfie, and drives away. My approach asks that one deeply experiences a site with a "listening" mindfulness toward the human and the nonhuman Other (Carbaugh, "Just listen"; Carbaugh and Cerulli; Carbaugh and Rudnick; Chronis, "Co-constructing heritage at the Gettysburg landscape"; Galani-Moutafi; Grimwood, Muldoon, and Stevens; Tschida; Whetung; Whitson).

Grand Portage National Monument preserves the late eighteenth- and early nineteenth-century site for and history of the fur trade between the Anishinaabeg and Britain's North West Company near the Pigeon River (Omini zibi), currently constituting part of the border between Minnesota and Ontario. The trading post's fort-like structure's French-derived name, Grand Portage, references the 9-mile carrying of canoes, trade goods, and furs necessary to bypass a 120-foot drop of a waterfall and adjoining rapids near the mouth of Omini zibi where travel into the interior of the continent from Lake Superior (Gichi Gami) would begin.

The system of portages developed by Indigenous peoples in the center of the continent is the reason the North West Company selected this location for its most prominent trading post. Through the economics of trade, Gichi Onimgaming would connect the center of the continent to the Company's headquarters in Montreal, and eventually to Europe, by way of water.

While the National Park Service manages the Monument, it sits within and under the control of Grand Portage Reservation. Few national monuments or parks have this partnership (e.g., Canyon de Chelly National Monument, Badlands

Figure 8.1 View of Grand Portage National Monument, photo by author.

National Park). They have several potential advantages. They may reduce conflicts between the stakeholders by bringing Indigenous voices into the management of the site and they may create shared responsibility for its success (Pinel and Pecos). It took years of working through the injuries and injustices of settler colonialism to make this Monument a success (Figure 8.1).

"Settler colonialism" refers to the European American occupation of lands, taking of resources, and establishment of institutional structures that displaced Indigenous people and cultures within a landscape. Tourism is often a contemporary remnant of this effort, especially where tourism is justified in arguments about remembering the settler past or as justification for current tourism behaviors. Yet, heritage tourism has the potential to challenge settler colonialism narratives and practices. Therefore, attention on settler colonialism within the context of heritage tourism is justified in this chapter as one experiences Grand Portage and the reminders of that colonialism along the state highway.

At the Monument, the National Park Service tells the Eurocentric fur-trade narrative of the voyageurs within the walls of the recreated trading post while the Grand Portage Band tells their cultural narrative, and a variation of the voyageur narrative, within the heritage center and along a path through a "trading village" between the center and trading post. The decade-old center is where tourists typically begin and end their experience. A video ("Rendezvous with History") tells the history of the site. It is an Anishinaabeg story, and it strategically frames Grand Portage to emphasize the Indigenous culture and history. It places the Anishinaabeg not in the third person or as part of a historic past or long since assimilated people, as so many settler colonial narratives do, but in the present as a living, vibrant, and evolving people (Woodstock-Medicine Horse). Adding to the dual-partner management and communication is the nearby waterfall that necessitated the Grand Portage (the highest in Minnesota and its own tourist attraction). In a partnership with Minnesota State Parks, the "High Falls" form Grand Portage State Park. Its cultural center tells brief narratives of the Band, the waterfall, and of tourism in Minnesota.

Indigenous Native American heritage tourism has received some scholarly attention in areas such as museums' incorporation of Indigenous "voice" as a foundational element of the tourist experience and cultural understanding. Attention is given to the authenticity of the myths, legends, and facts that are voiced, the faithful (re)constructions of buildings or sites, and the creation of interculturally respectful maps that will guide a guest as they walk around a museum (Angouri, Paraskevaidi, and Wodak; Brady; Chronis and Hampton; Ewalt; King and Gatchet; Schmitt; Dickinson, Ott, and Aoki). Authenticity is a co-created interpretation, by the museum, an Indigenous people, and guests, of a material experience that transports visitors to a recognizable or believable past and allows them to momentarily live within that past (Carr; Milstein; Schmitt; Senda-Cook; Zagacki and Gallagher).

The narrative frames circulating within the dominant European American culture and available to Indigenous communities for the voicing of their stories have themselves often been colonized and may be inauthentic and negative. David Cuillier and Susan Dente Ross share "the white man's Indian" and "the voiced participant" as examples. Indigenously owned casinos have been constrained by these types of frames used to target non-Indigenous tourists that in words and images suggest Indigenous people define themselves as chiefs with headdresses and maidens in dresses, each near tepees. A fully "voiced" community would not be constrained by the negative or inaccurate frames of a dominant culture when contextualizing their own past, portraying their present, and/or building a future on Indigenous terms. These frames may be the harmful lens tourists use, in the lack of alternatives, when sense making of even non-tourism issues such as environmental justice or treaty rights.

Historically, minoritized people were directly excluded by laws and policies or indirectly excluded by the violence or threats of violence of others from having a physical presence in our national parks and monuments. Too often, even today, minoritized people's own culture, experiences, and history, which some parks and monuments are meant to honor, have not fully been voiced. Sustainable Indigenous heritage tourism practices must speak to the convergence of tourism, indigeneity, and the environment and create awareness that privileges Indigenous people finding their contemporary presence in these sites recognized and their stories heard (Finney; Grimwood, Muldoon, and Stevens; Walker and Moscardo; Woodstock-Medicine Horse).

As a returning North Shore tourist, I strategically choose sites to visit as I drive north. Gooseberry Falls State Park's 1937 founding ensured tourists of all economic classes would have a place for tourism on the North Shore. Its website describes the area's history of human use. The Cree, Dakotah, and Ojibwe once lived here. The river appeared on explorer maps as early as 1670. Commercial fishing began in Gichi Gami in 1870 and logging began in the surrounding Sawtooth Mountains in the 1890s. Tettegouche State Park, with its prominent cliffs and waterfalls, invites tourists to stop. In its visitor center, a wall display notes "Gitchigami, or 'Big Water,' is the Ojibwe word for Lake Superior." Another explains Ojibwe life before the arrival of Euro-American settlers. While this sign recognizes the past and current importance of specific activities such as hunting and rice harvesting, it does not recognize the Ojibwe as still being present along Gitchigami to do these activities.

I briefly hike at Temperance River State Park. Here too are waterfalls, cliffs, and gorges. Outdoor signage at all these parks warn against diving, climbing, or off-trail hiking. Once, these prohibited actions were a part of the typical extractive experience of tourism, but safety and environmental protections have changed. The message on the websites, at visitor centers, or even through generational stories is that Indigenous peoples were once at all these locations, but not "established." The area's "valuable" resources were waiting—and some argue they are still waiting—to be extracted by a culture that sees their usefulness. Extractive industries such as mining, logging, and fishing may be ended, but their modern incarnation comes in tourist practices. The sanctioned or rebellious tourist interactions with the falls, cliffs, and paths are a material rhetoric that along with the wall texts and signs around the park or in the visitor center are each explorable through Cu.D.A. (Dickinson, Ott, and Aoki; Senda-Cook).

With C.u.D.A., we can also reflect upon settler colonialism's role in shaping the heritage tourism experience (Carr; Grimwood, Muldoon, and Stevens; Woodstock-Medicine Horse). The entire northeastern part of Minnesota, including the North Shore, is referred to as the "Arrowhead" due to its shape when seen on a map. The Arrowhead is also the site of the "Iron Range," an area where one of the world's richest deposits of iron ore was once mined to serve the needs of a growing nation and two world wars. The ore would be moved by train to harbor towns along the North Shore, linking their stories. The extractive industry left behind a series of "authentic" heritage tourism attractions including the largest open pit iron mine in the world, the Hull-Rust Mine (i.e., "Grand Canyon of the North"), and the Soudan Underground Mine, both National Historic Landmarks (Whitson). The working-class towns with eastern and northern European roots once owed their livelihood to the mines. Today, the mines are mostly silent except for a struggling tourism industry promoting them as heritage tourism. For many Minnesotans, the perception of the Arrowhead is based in a collective cultural memory of industrial resource extraction by "Iron Rangers" that forgets the removal of Indigenous Native Americans (Whitson). Many of the residents of the Minnesota's biggest cities, Minneapolis and St. Paul, trace family roots and generational stories to the narratives of the Iron Range and these narratives color their heritage tourist experiences of the North Shore.

This will be my fourth visit to G.P.N.M. To get there, I will pass through Grand Marais (Gichi Bitobig), one of several former harbor towns along the lake but currently a resort community known for its shops and restaurants. Naniboujou Lodge and Restaurant, named after a character in Ojibwe and Cree narratives, blends Euro-American interpretations of Indigenous Native American and Art Deco influences into a rustic lodge architecture. In the state's heritage tourism promotion materials, people are encouraged to view this fusion of styles.

As several of the previous paragraphs describing the North Shore suggest, a sense of place is foundational to tourism and to our understanding of and relationship to our environment (Cantrill and Senecah; Carbaugh and Cerulli). My sense of place, further informed by Cu.D.A., reflects a shared experience of heritage tourism and the entire North Shore. Cantrill and Senecah contend, "a sense of place is the perception of what is most salient in a specific location, which may be reflected in value preferences or how that specific place figures in discourse" (187). Places sustain us, ground us, divide or unite us, and captivate us. A captivating North Shore and Grand Portage National Monument experience happens because one is emplaced in this 150-mile landscape's towns, resource-based and shipping legacies, parks, resorts, restaurants, and environments.

At Grand Portage Reservation, my first stop is Grand Portage State Park. Its website promotes its displays and murals created by members of Grand Portage Band. "Git-che-O-ni-ga-ming and Grand Portage are Ojibwe and French words for 'a great carrying place.'" Inside the cultural center, one wall display states the importance of grounding Anishnabeg children in their culture through attention to place, a grounding the Band also communicates to tourists. Elsewhere, the Anishinaabeg "clans" are named and described. They are represented by the area's birds, bears, martens, deer, and fish. Images that reference these clans appear inside and outside the cultural center. The representation of clans by animals speaks to a particular unity with the nonhuman Other in a shared environment.

It is a message about Grandmother Earth and Turtle Island, expressed in a Band member's creation narrative, that is the most significant item in the cultural center. A plaque tells the story of Nanabozho (i.e., Naniboujou in the lodge's name), a great nephew to all Anishnabeg people. His mother was impregnated when a spirit entered her body and he was born to watch over the Earth. His story includes a component about a flood that was so large he needed a log to rescue all the animals. In that flood, the water animals brought him soil, so on the back of a great turtle he created an island—Turtle Island—for all animals. The wall sign claims that the Ojibwe people have spoken of this creation narrative for generations.

I wondered if this creation story inspired any Cu.D.A.-styled comparisons in the primarily Euro-American appearing tourists gathered around the sign. Heritage narratives are built on the imaginaries of the communicators and audiences (Angouri, Paraskevaidi, and Wodak). I can only guess how readers engaging in their own examination of this narrative compare it to others they already understand. Their attitudes, values, and beliefs about this narrative will add to the shape of the intertextual imaginary they form in this moment. Further, I speculated if within this creation story, among other parts of the experiencing of the Monument, is some inspiration for a more mindful interacting with the whole of the North Shore in culturally aware and environmentally respectful ways. Which tourists will listen to the entirety of the North Shore as an Other or series of Others in ways faithful to Cu.D.A. and to Anishinaabeg values?

Scholars argue that heritage discourses are political (Angouri, Paraskevaidi, and Wodak). They represent the worldviews and values of those telling them. They are intertextual, built from myths, ideologies, regionalisms, nostalgia, and marketing. In tourism, they become a commodity to be traded or exchanged. They are rhetorically contested. Neighboring cultures may tell contradicting or competing narratives. Over time, it may be hard to know who owns or should control narratives that are richly layered and intertextual. Further, minoritized communities communicate these discourses in the public sphere of heritage tourism that is only partially of their making and is, in many ways, significantly out of their control.

I arrive at Grand Portage National Monument. "Greetings! Boozhoo! Bonjour!" The first signage welcomes me inside the heritage center as if I too am a voyageur—and in a way, I am. The first set of visual displays I encounter, following the center's layout, includes information on the voyageurs, the beaver of the fur trade, birch trees used to make canoes, and the portaging of rivers. I am presented with a diorama of the trading post as it would have looked in 1797. The second set addresses Gichi Omingaming as the home of the Grand Portage Band and the North Shore as the home of the Anishinaabeg people. Multiple display cases exhibit historic artifacts and artist renderings or photographs of prominent people, places, and events starting in the 1850s. I am struck by how familiar and everyday this part of the display appears. Its strategic design blends the use of display cases common at monuments and historic sites—including other places in the center—with the feeling that what is being displayed are items taken from personal photo albums and scrap books that have been modified for this display. It does not have the feel of an outdated or simplistic museum display. Instead, it makes the people and events displayed personal and relatable, and therefore the entire Reservation community becomes relatable. The cultural center is evidence that the Anishinaabeg people continue a way of life they refer to as anishinaabewin (Figures 8.2 and 8.3).

The most significant interactive display creates a very personal experience on a digital screen seen through the open door of an Anishinaabeg birch bark wigwam. I view Adaawaweikwe, a woman representing the Anishinaabeg, and a single voyageur seated next to her. The scene and the message draw me in as a second voyageur in the shared space. She explains how the original voyageurs were strong and fearless in their endeavors that brought them to Gichi Omingaming, but poorly prepared to survive in the environment and not skilled at being traders. It was women like her that taught the voyageurs how to survive and how to trade. Never is the voyageur's personal character attacked, nor are they ever blamed for the hardships that would happen at Gichi Omingaming. The scene and the narrative position me in the joint role of tourist coming to understand the importance of the fur trade to the Anishinaabeg and as a voyageur who likewise may have found

144 *David A. Tschida*

Figure 8.2 Interior of Grand Portage National Monument museum, photo by author.

Figure 8.3 Re-enactors at Grand Portage National Monument museum, photo by author.

Figure 8.4 Exterior view of Grand Portage National Monument museum, photo by author.

the experience challenging. I find the approach disarming, almost humorous in its playful effort to point out the strengths and weaknesses of the voyageurs without any hint of blame or guilt.

When one leaves the cultural center to follow a path to the Monument, one does not initially see it through the trees. As tourist, I seemingly must walk back in time and into a different world. I am welcomed with a sign that reads:

> Boozhoo, daga Biindigen Anishinaabeg Oódena. Welcome, Please Come in to the Ojibwe Village. The Ojibwe, who call themselves Anishinaabe (the original people), gather each summer, today as in the past, to reconnect with family and friends, to fish and acquire food for the year ahead. Until the 1900s, Ojibwe moved often, following the land's bounty—bark for canoes and houses, fish in rivers and lakes, meat and furs, wild rice and maple sugar to eat and trade. For centuries, at large villages along the Great Lakes … the Ojibwe were middlemen between European traders and tribes farther to the west. From them, Europeans learned how to survive.

In one area, tourists are able to see a tepee and a wigwam and observe the preparing of food; in another, they see a reflection of the voyageurs' camp during Rendezvous. The warehouse just outside the fort's gate recreates a structure that once stood there and currently offers tourists an introduction to the act of canoe making (Figure 8.4).

Inside the trading post's walls, signage describes the purpose of former buildings. Inside the reconstructed Great Hall there are five rooms on the main floor. The central space is a large rectangle with a stone fireplace centered at each end. Three large tables fill the space with three styles of seating and place settings for dinner. The hierarchy is clear by the quality of the seating and dinnerware. Along the walls there are numerous representative artifacts such as clothing and furs that illustrate the cultures and the classes of non-Indigenous people that would have come under this roof. At each end of the hall, on either side of the fireplace, is a smaller room. These would have been the private quarters for the most prominent of the North West Company who had come to Rendezvous. One recreates a typical bedroom and office; the others are for themed displays related to the operation of the trading post. At the back of the hall via a covered porch is the kitchen. Actors prepare historically accurate foods by authentic techniques and talk about feeding the Company and the voyageurs. From a pier extending out into the lake I can walk out over the water and imagine the experience of arriving at Grand Portage. Like the cultural center, the post positions me with the voyageurs in the Company and in the context of a tangible material rhetoric it may be the most important cultural or material discourse of the historic and physical Monument.

The 25-minute video playing in the cultural center is a valuable text for understanding the Indigenous perspective on heritage tourism, indigeneity, culture, and the environment at this early American site. The video opens by grounding the viewer in Gichi Omingaming. There is the call of the common loon. A woman sings in the Anishinaabeg language. Waves are seen and heard sloshing on the shore. There is pipe music. A narrator introduces himself as a member of Band but is himself nameless. He stands on a rocky beach, looking over Gichigami. We see him in profile. He could be almost any member of this community while representing everyone. He begins:

> For generations, my people have been warmed by the sun rising over the lake we call "Gichigami." Gichigami has provided for my people. For us, the Big Lake has a spirit. Its waters are generous and alive. They can also be dangerous and unforgiving. Along these waters, and along these lakes and rivers, is a great story. One that is unknown to most. This is a story about when my people, the Ojibwe, were the most powerful tribe of the Great Lakes. During the 1700s, this land was the center of a great trade. A global trade. In those days, the Europeans needed us more than we needed them. They needed our skills as hunters. Just as important, they needed our knowledge of this vast country.

Grounding the narration in Gichigami is an example of the importance of place as an element of the identity of the Anishinaabeg people. Further, the narration reclaims the Anishinaabeg's significant role in the fur trade. This is not the narrative of other sites along the North Shore or Arrowhead, and this is not the typical "white man's Indian" who was part of the landscape or primitive and uncivilized. Next, I am introduced to the characters, setting, and action of this Anishinaabeg fur-trade heritage narrative. Parts of the narrative, in order of telling in the video and broken by the narrator's style of storytelling and the inclusion of visual images, are represented in the paragraphs that follow.

One element of the narrative deserving attention within the broader context of identity is the contrast between the voyageurs and the Indigenous peoples.

> Today we know them as "voyageurs," a French word for traveler. It is said that the fur trade was built upon their backs ... The voyageurs were human beasts of burden ... Voyageurs bringing furs from the west converged with canoes with trade goods from the East ... It was a time when the world came to and through Grand Portage.

The juxtaposition of the voyageur in this narrative, and to a lesser extent the interactive display noted earlier with the same characters/actors, compared to the physical Monument and even the other narratives of the region is significant. Rarely are voyageurs anything but heroic adventurers and the center of the story. Here, however, their social status is second to that of the Anishinaabeg. In this narrative, the Anishinaabeg are heroic. In this narrative, I am not positioned as the tourist-voyageur as I am elsewhere. I am not positioned as a character at all. I watched this video as one of the final parts of my experience at the Monument. Therefore, how I was positioned in earlier parts of my experience was now in contrast with this current positioning simply as viewer/learner. However, since I was not pushed enough to identify with the voyageurs in the previous points of messaging to now take offense at being excluded, I was able to interpret this narrative as a sort of prequel to the materials found in the second set of displays in the cultural center that were about the Band.

> In other parts of America, stockades were built to keep Indians out. At Grand Portage, the stockade was built to welcome us in ... In the fur trade, the Europeans and the Ojibwe found common ground, born of opportunity and profit.

The Anishinaabeg take center stage and world-wide significance in ways comparable to the colonial powers of Britain or France. The framing of the Anishinaabeg as a powerful people, as a powerful nation, and as a respected community continues throughout the video. They are the protagonists.

In the next section, a specific protagonist is named. Considering the absence of Anishinaabeg women in the written records from the time and considering that in settler colonial narratives it is Indigenous men who often get the majority of attention (with exceptions like Pocahontas or Sacagawea), this narrative presents an alternative (Cochrane).

> My great-grandmother was an important person at Grand Portage. Her name was Adaawaweikwe. In our language that means "Trading Woman" ... In many ways, women like Adaawaweikwe helped create a bond between the Europeans and our people ... During this time, the Ojibwe and Europeans lived in peace ... During the fur trade, the North West Company prospered, and so did we.

This great-grandmother character is present in the video from near its beginning through the entire presence of the North West Company at Gichi Omingaming, a time span of several decades. The prominence of her positioning representing what is certainly multiple women from this time challenges competing "white man's Indian" narratives tourists find in other places like casinos and popular culture. It gives her and all women a respected status within the context of Gichi Omingaming.

The importance of oral traditions in storytelling is recognized in the next section of the video. The narrator speaks of challenges the Anishinaabeg experienced, including alcohol and smallpox. The harm of each was not just the loss of life. "The Ojibwe at Grand Portage, Rainy Lake and Leech Lake were devastated, especially our elders. When they died, so did many of our Ojibwe stories and traditions." Retaining this story of Adaawaweikwe, and keeping this Anishinaabeg experience of Gichi Omingaming alive in contemporary narratives voiced by the Band, is a challenge to the stereotype of the "voiced participant" who has only been given a space to share a narrative consistent with settler colonialism. Retaining oral traditions and their content empowers the Anishinaabeg people.

Next, the narrator juxtaposes Rendezvous, the weeks of trading, camaraderie, and partying in the summer when the Company leadership, the fur traders, and the Anishinaabeg were gathered at Grand Portage with the eventual demise of the trading post when the United States and Britain divided this area into two nations at Omini zibi. After which, the Company would move its trading post 50 miles north, to Fort William in Ontario.

> Our homeland was to be cut in two pieces by strangers. Even our waters were divided. To us, this wasn't English or American land. The creator had made this land for our people ... The partnership and prosperity we shared with the Europeans would never be the same.

This section then introduces what the narrator refers to as "the hungry years," a time when the Anishinaabeg's ability to sustain themselves would be tested. Settlers would establish North Shore towns by the 1850s and the Anishinaabeg would be forced onto reservations.

> Like so many other tribes, the Grand Portage people were now at the mercy of the United States government. They wanted to assimilate us, to be civilized white Americans just like them. There were many hardships, but we endured ... and today we remain ... Gichigami is still here. And so are the Grand Portage people.

This statement is not accusatory. A distant U.S. government is blamed, but not U.S. citizens or tourists. The narrator does not speak of the Anishinaabeg as victims. Here there is only strength and survival in the presence of adversity. It is that spirit that the narrator closes with in his last lines. He notes the Band's sovereignty and their faithfulness to their culture as still tied to this place.

We have our own government and care for our own tribal lands. We are Anishinaabeg. We are also Americans. Today we carry on many of the old traditions ... We are still connected to the land. And through this place, we are connected to our ancestors ... At Grand Portage is a story I am proud to be a part of. A story I will pass along to my children. Hopefully, they'll pass it forward to the generations to come.

The multi-part narrative, setting the context, telling the story of the voyageur, highlighting the role of women, and claiming triumph in the face of adversity, positions the Band in a highly positive light.

I would argue my tourist experience, explained in the pages of this chapter, is similar to those of other tourists and therefore sets the stage for several conclusions about heritage tourism at Grand Portage National Monument and the North Shore. I argue this also recognizing that in writing for academic reasons, my interpretations of my experience may never replicate the typical tourist's interpretive experience.

First, issues of identity (e.g., Indigenous, Minnesotan, tourist), culture and intercultural relationships or experiences, and place or environment each play a role in the heritage tourism of Grand Portage National Monument and tourism along the North Shore. Most importantly, at Gichi Omingaming, tourists are positioned as voyageurs throughout much of their experience at the Monument. This is a type of positioning no other monument, park, or museum can completely replicate. This positioning, with its historic and cultural symbolism attached to the strength and character of the voyageur and with the modern ways the term "voyageur" is synonymous with a traveler and explorer moving across distances and challenges as a learner on a mission of discovery, is useful for the ways that it may disarm tourists, leaving them receptive to alternative messages that challenge historical narratives or stereotypes, settler colonialism practices, and environmental practices, and ultimately leads to the questioning and exploring of their previous understandings of and relationships to Indigenous Native American communities, cultural beliefs, and behaviors. Other sites of heritage tourism may also have historic persons whose label or title is equally useful to the positioning of the tourist and the tourism experience. Identities and emotions, as tourists or as Minnesotans, can be the subject of self-examination. If the heritage narratives of Indigenous peoples are to be fully appreciated, they demand attention to listening. Not just listening to a video's narrator, but to the substance of the message in the tourism sites and in the environmental places. There is a demand that the heritage tourist, who in this case is likely to also be an environmental tourist, listen to the places and dwellings and the Indigenous people who live in the location. Failure to do so means a potential loss in intercultural understanding, appreciation, and respect.

Next, the voice of the Anishinaabeg is a significant element of the Monument and Grand Portage State Park. At one level, it is the empowered and contemporary "voiced participant" and not the "white man's Indian" that is heard. The heritage narratives that are shared are powerful statements of authenticity in a location that could, lacking these partnerships, still cater to old stereotypes and prejudices found in the non-Indigenous tourist and in settler colonialism. The cultural center's attention to the Anishinaabeg today as community members and Americans, parents and providers, and artists reminds tourists that Indigenous people are still alive and thriving in their indigeneity. Further, the "voiced participant" claims their rightful place as leader and partner in the fur trade, not victim of the North West Company or of the United States or of settler colonialism. This "voiced participant" asserts that Anishinaabeg women were (and are) key members of the clans and not maidens in dresses. Finally, the "voiced participant" shares creation heritage narratives similar to those adopted in the practice of a Christian faith. The "voiced participant" shows through art that the people of the Band are civilized and cultured while still wanting and needing a relationship with the environment. They honor generations of family, in Grandmother Earth, the great-grandmother and trading woman Adaawaweikwe, and in the nephew Nanabozho.

At another level, when the heritage narrative of the video notes the problems of alcohol and references the "hungry years," or the cultural center notes the problems of boarding schools and educating the youth of the Band in its second area of display, it is the act of trade itself, the government of a new nation, or the opening of the state of Minnesota to settlement that are made the causes or perpetrators of an offense and an injury. Strategically, this narrative choice reimagines the "white man's Indian" frame to relieve the tourist of any guilt or obligation felt during the visit—perhaps because they are positioned as voyageur and not settler. This framing of the narrative would not seem to offend that portion of the audience who could otherwise interpret other frames or themes as a personal or cultural attack. A similar argument is made about displays at the Plains Indian Museum in Cody, Wyoming, where a discourse of reverence is emphasized (Dickinson, Ott, and Aoki). These framing choices offer an alternative way of seeing and understanding Indigenous Native Americans and their culture where any allegiance to country or culture does not stand in the way of understanding of another community of people. At the same time, it may also lead to questioning of fundamental narratives such as settler colonialism while separating the tourists from the historical legacy of that colonialism. Just as the Band are not victims, tourists need not be villains. Both groups can look at the legacies of the past and find a path forward. Being free of continuous shame or guilt makes accepting that path easier. Settler colonial narratives are hard to challenge. There is a lot of support for those narratives in the route to Grand Portage National Monument, in the Arrowhead region, and in Minnesota. Yet, the tourist experience of the Monument suggests an alternative.

References

Angouri, Jo, Marina Paraskevaidi, and Ruth Wodak. "Discourses of cultural heritage in times of crisis: the case of the parthenon marbles." *Journal of Sociolinguistics*, vol. 21, no. 2, April 2017, pp. 208–237. doi: 10.1111/josl.12232

Blair, Carole, and Neil Michel. "Commemorating in the theme park zone: reading the astronauts memorial." *At the Intersection: Cultural Studies and Rhetorical Studies*, edited by Thomas Rosteck. Guilford Press, 1998, pp. 29–83.

Brady, Miranda J. "Mediating indigenous voice in the land museum: narratives of place, land, and environment in new exhibition practice." *Environmental Communication*, vol. 5, no. 2, 2011, pp. 202–220. doi: 10.1080/17524032.2011.562649

Brummett, Barry. *Rhetoric in Popular Culture*. Sage, 2017.

Cantrill, James G., and Susan L. Senecah. "Using the 'sense of self-in-place' construct in the context of environmental policy-making and landscape planning." *Environmental Science & Policy*, vol. 4, nos. 4–5, 2001, pp.185–203. doi: 10.1016/S1462-9011(01)00023-5

Carbaugh, Donal. "Cultural discourse analysis: communication practices and intercultural encounters." *Journal of Intercultural Communication Research*, 2007, pp. 167–182.

———. "'Just listen': 'listening' and landscape among the blackfeet." *Western Journal of Communication*, vol. 63, no. 3, 1999, pp. 250–270. doi: 10.1080/10570319909374641

Carbaugh, Donal, and Lisa Rudnick. "Which place, what story? Cultural discourses at the border of the Blackfeet Reservation and Glacier National Park." *Great Plains Quarterly*, vol. 26, no. 3, 2006, pp. 167–184. https://www.jstor.org/stable/23533732

Carbaugh, Donal, and Tovar Cerulli. "Cultural discourses of dwelling: investigating environmental communication as a place-based practice." *Environmental Communication*, vol. 7, no. 1, 2013, pp. 4–23. doi: 10.1080/17524032.2012.749296

Carr, Anna. "Indigenous peoples and tourism: the challenges and opportunities for sustainable tourism." *Journal of Sustainable Tourism*, vol. 24, nos. 8–9, 2016, pp. 1067–1079. doi: 10.1080/09669582.2016.1206112

Chronis, Athinodoros. "Co-constructing heritage at the Gettysburg storyscape." *Annals of Tourism Research*, vol. 32, no. 3, 2005, pp. 386–406. doi: 10.1016/j.annals.2004.07.009

Chronis, Athinodoros, and Ronald D. Hampton. "Consuming the authentic gettysburg: how a tourist landscape becomes an authentic experience." *Journal of Consumer Behavior*, vol. 7, no. 2, 2008, pp. 111–126. doi: 10.1002/cb.241

Cochrane, Timothy. *Gichi Bitobog*, Grand Marais. U of Minnesota P, 2018.

Cuillier, David, and Susan Dente Ross. "Gambling with identity: self-representation of american indians on official tribal websites." *The Howard Journal of Communications*, vol. 18, no. 3, 2007, pp. 197–219. doi: 10.1080/10646170701490781

DeLuca, Kevin, and Anne Demo. "Imagining nature and erasing class and race: Carleton Watkins, John Muir, and the construction of wilderness." *Environmental History*, vol. 6, no. 4, October 2001, pp. 541–560. doi: 10.2307/3985254

Dickinson, Greg, Brian L. Ott, and Eric Aoki. "Spaces of remembering and forgetting: the reverent eye/I at the Plains Indian Museum." *Communication and Critical/Cultural Studies*, vol. 3, no. 1, 2006, pp. 27–47. doi: 10.1080/14791420500505619

Ewalt, Joshua. "A colonialist celebration of national (heritage): verbal, visual, and landscape ideographs at Homestead National Monument of America." *Western Journal of Communication*, vol. 75, no. 4, 2011, pp. 367–385. doi: 10.1080/10570314.2011.586970

Finney, Carolyn. *Black Faces, White Spaces: Reimagining the Relationship of African Americans to the Great Outdoors*. U of North Carolina P, 2014.

Galani-Moutafi, Vasiliki. "The self and the other: traveler, ethnographer, tourist." Annals of Tourism Research, vol. 27, no. 1, 2000, pp. 203–224. doi: 10.1016/S0160-7383(99)00066-3

Grimwood, Bryan S. R., Meghan L. Muldoon, and Zachary M. Stevens. "Settler colonialism, indigenous cultures, and the promotional landscape of tourism in Ontario, Canada's 'Near North.'" *Journal of Heritage Tourism*, vol. 14, no. 3, 2019, pp. 233–248. doi: 10.1080/1743873X.2018.1527845

King, Stephen A., and Roger Davis Gatchet. "Making the past: civil rights tourism and the Mississippi freedom trail." *Southern Communication Journal*, vol. 83, no. 2, 2018, pp. 103–118. doi: 10.1080/1041794X.2017.1404124

Milstein, Tema. "Nature Identification: The Power Of Pointing And Naming." *Environmental Communication*, vol. 5, no. 1, 2011, pp. 3–24. doi: 10.1080/17524032.2010.535836

Pinel, Sandra Lee, and Jacob Pecos. "Generating co-management as Kasha Katuwe Tent Rocks National Monument, New Mexico." *Environmental Management*, vol. 49, no. 3, 2012, pp. 593–604. doi: 10.1007/s00267-012-9814-9

Rendezvous with History: A Grand Portage Story. Directed by Hutchinson, Sonny, et al. Great Divide Pictures, 2012.

Schmitt, Casey R. "Mounting tensions: materializing strategies and tactics on national park 'social trails.'" *Environmental Communication*, vol. 10, no. 4, 2016, pp. 418–431. doi: 10.1080/17524032.2015.1018297

Senda-Cook, Samantha. "Materializing tensions: how maps and trails mediate nature." *Environmental Communication*, vol. 7, no. 3, 2013. doi: 10.1080/17524032.2013.792854

Tschida, David A. "The ethics of listening in the wilderness writings of Sigurd F. Olson," *Voice and Environmental Communication*, edited by Jennifer Peeples and Stephen Depoe. Palgrave Macmillan, 2014. 205–227.

Walker, Kaye, and Gianna Moscardo. "Moving beyond sense of place to care of place: the role of indigenous values and interpretation in promoting transformative change in tourists' place images and personal values." *Journal of Sustainable Tourism*, vol. 24, no. 8–9, 2016, pp. 1249–1261. doi: 10.1080/09669582.2016.1177064

Whetung, Madeline. "Nishnaabeg Encounters: Living Indigenous Landscapes." University of Toronto, 2016. MA Thesis. http://hdl.handle.net/1807/76189

Whitson, Joseph. "Monumental mines: mine tourism, settler colonialism, and the creation of extractive landscape on Minnesota's iron range." *The Public Historian*, vol. 41, no. 3, 2019, pp. 49–71. doi: 10.1525/tph.2019.41.3.49

Woodstock-Medicine Horse, Jennifer Néso'ésoif. "Green museums waking up the world: indigenous and mainstream approaches to exploring sustainability." Montana State University, American Studies PhD Public Defense, 2018.

Zagacki, Kenneth S., and Victoria J. Gallagher. "Rhetoric and materiality in the museum park at the North Carolina Museum of Art." *Quarterly Journal of Speech*, vol. 95, no. 2, 2009, pp. 171–191. doi: 10.1080/00335630902842087

Afterword

Memory and heritage in the "era of just redemption"

Shevaun E. Watson

I re-read these essays on the eve of Joseph Biden and Kamala Harris's inaugurations, and the prescient words of Amanda Gorman are ringing in my ears. Her poem for this momentous occasion, entitled "The Hill We Climb," takes up memory, history, heritage, and healing, calling Americans to confront together the many challenges that "stand before us." Gorman understands intuitively, viscerally, that meaningful change, the kind that could reshape America's social fabric and its institutions, does not lie in platitudes about "getting over" the past but rather in reckoning with the many "blunders" in our shared past that have become our collective "burdens."

> It's because being American is more than a pride we inherit,
> it's the past we step into
> and how we repair it.
> …
> But while democracy can be periodically delayed
> it can never be permanently defeated.
> In this truth
> in this faith we trust.
> For while we have our eyes on the future
> history has its eyes on us.
> This is the era of just redemption
> we feared at its inception.
>
> (lines 52–4, 59–66)

Though we are not alone in this predicament, Americans inherit a good deal more than victories and heroes. We are also the progenies of periodic but grave "delays" in the fulfillment of our democratic ideals. From its inception, "American democracy" (whatever images and associations one brings to that topos) had deep inequalities with dire consequences written into its very fabric, necessitating some kind of recompense at some time. American identity is comprised of, perhaps even defined by, an array of its own unique historical tensions and complexities. The great majority of these enduring conflicts revolve around race and racism.

DOI: 10.4324/9781003102830-10

Gorman suggests not only that this flawed and freighted past we hold in common needs repair, but that we must attend to "how we repair it" (line 54). Part of that "how" is public memory. There are undoubtedly other critical components of a larger social justice "toolkit" needed to bring about lasting change, including "rituals of atonement," school curriculum, community development, truth commissions, "sites of conscience," and more (Glisson). But public memory must play a central, not ancillary, role in reckoning and reconciliation. Indeed, memory work is the necessary "starting point of racial justice" (Tell 105). As John Bodnar argues in *Remaking America*, public memory pertains to "fundamental issues about the entire existence of society ... it is an argument about the interpretation of reality" (14). It is about belief. What people believe to be right and true about their cultural inheritances. Put another way, "memory work is about heritage development" (Shackel xiii). And so, the abstract concept of "public memory" and the equally unwieldy construct of "heritage" become fused, concrete, and consequential. We should engage in memory and heritage for healing like our lives depend on it. "Our inaction and inertia," Gorman cautions, "will be the inheritance of the next generation / Our blunders become their burdens" (lines 83–5).

Her poem is remarkable not only for rising to its historic occasion, but also for addressing the palpable anxiety still gripping the nation after the January 6 siege on the U.S. Capitol:

> We did not feel prepared to be the heirs
> of such a terrifying hour.
> But within it found the power
> to author a new chapter.
> ...
> We will not march back to what was
> but move to what shall be.
>
> (lines 67–70, 77–6)

Gorman's references, here and throughout the entire poem, to our shared history of racial struggles and our collective responsibility for authoring a different kind of American heritage to pass on point to the troubling way that heritage has been marshaled by ultra-conservative populists in the U.S. (and across the world), bringing the urgency of attending to public memory and heritage into stark relief. As international heritage expert Laurajane Smith remarks, twenty-first-century "right-wing populism is almost defined by its use of the 'past' in its political rhetoric" (*Emotional Heritage* 304). One could even go so far as to say that Gorman is attempting to wrestle "American heritage" back from extremists by calling on more Americans to participate in the critical memory and political work it takes to redefine a national legacy:

> But one thing is certain:
> If we merge mercy with might,
> And might with right,

Then love becomes our legacy
And change our children's birthright.

(lines 86–90)

Of greatest relevance and concern here is the way that early American heritage in particular grounds ultra-right-wing orthodoxy. Though there is some use of Confederate-era symbols among these groups (mostly to signify their fealty to white supremacy), a good part of their rhetorical strength and righteous conviction derives from the memories they have forged together and circulated publicly about the nation's founding and its "true" meaning.

Exhibit A in this heritage crusade is Trump's 1776 Commission and its report (which came out two days before he left office). The Executive Order forming the group, made up of arch-conservatives and Trump loyalists—not one historian among them—calls for a patriotic return to the "principles of the founding of the United States in 1776" against "the radicalized view of American history … that obscures virtues, twists motives and magnifies flaws" (70951). It goes on to inveigh, "poor scholarship has vilified our Founders and our founding," teaching children to "hate their own country and to believe that the men and women who built it were not heroes, but rather villains" (70951). The resulting *Report* follows suit, leaning hard on tropes of American exceptionalism and "longstanding conservative talking points" (Schuessler) to argue for a "patriotic" education based on the "eternal" and "universal" principles articulated in the Declaration and the Constitution: "It is the sacred duty of every generation of American patriots to defend this priceless inheritance" (*1776 Report* 10). Trump's rallying cry on January 6 employed this kind of hyperbole, activating some inchoate but still powerful memory of this glorious era among his followers. Notably, much of the talk, garb, and symbolism at the Capitol siege referenced the Revolutionary era, though a very narrow slice of it, including chants of "1776!" by self-styled "patriots" in eighteenth-century get-ups, "We the People" patches and tattoos, "Don't Tread on Me" signs and flags, proud affiliations with the "Three Percent," and too many refrains about traitors, tyranny, and armed militias to count (Mogelson).

Although these extremist groups lay claim to a collective memory of this time period that does not square with historical facts, for the *1776 Report* was roundly criticized by academics, progressives have mostly struggled to respond with any fervor matching that of the right about the significance of early America for current-day race work. I worry the left has ceded this large chunk of history to the right because early America either seems to smack of flag-waving, feel-good patriotism or to fall a bit flat in its relevance to today's contexts and struggles. This is one reason why it's so important to have more early Americanists involved in the work of public memory, heritage sites, and racial reconciliation.

We might consider the possibility that early American sites hold more power, not less, in reshaping public understandings of race and racism than destinations associated with later periods of history. For one, the fact that most people are less familiar with the details of colonial and Revolutionary America makes it more possible to offer perspectives that challenge simplified notions of America's city-on-a-hill creation myth. While a lack of deep knowledge can lead to the kind of blind faith in the "Founders" pedaled by right-wing groups, for others willing to "unflinchingly address not just 'difficult knowledge' but also the difficult emotions ... associated with such knowledge" (Smith 308), some level of ignorance, when combined with curiosity about this history, can provide a productive opening for learning something substantially new and different. Perhaps counterintuitively, the less one knows, the less likely one will use a heritage site visit to reinforce what one already thinks is true. Greater familiarity with the issues, people, or events represented at a historic site increases the likelihood of one's existing beliefs and feelings about it to be affirmed or reinforced (similar to the way that confirmation bias works).[1]

Relatedly, early American sites are not nearly as fraught with the regional identities, strong emotions, or politics that course through antebellum, Civil War, Jim Crow, and Civil Rights heritage sites. It can be much more difficult to change minds when visitors feel their own heritage is being attacked for some larger political motive. While some may want to cling to romanticized conceptions of George Washington, their core identity is not staked on the historical representation of him, as it might be for Martin Luther King, Jr., or Stonewall Jackson, who tend to elicit more emotional identifications.[2] The many debates and actions surrounding Confederate statues and other monuments of white supremacy across America, especially over the past five years, point to the way that heightened emotions and deep personal convictions complicate public discourse and decision-making about the commemorative landscape. In these ways, early American heritage sites present a unique opportunity for more fruitful and dispassionate engagements with the country's difficult racial past. The temporal distance of early America surely cuts both ways. The "time depth" can make it seem like we have "evolved" beyond those antiquated ways, which is a common justification for not engaging more deeply with hard truths (Smith, "'Man's Inhumanity'" 209). Yet, the gulf in time between the twenty-first and eighteenth centuries can be leveraged more pointedly for visitors to recognize more commonalities and connections, which have deeply shaped the circumstances we need to confront today. The ties are there; we just need to bind them.

To underscore the inextricable connections between history, heritage, memory, the present day, and the possibility of societal change, I offer Paul Connerton's opening assertions in *How Societies Remember*:

> [W]e may note that our experience of the present very largely depends upon our knowledge of the past. We experience our world in a context which is causally connected with past events and objects, and hence with reference [to them]. And we will experience our present differently in accordance with the different pasts to which we are able to connect that present: not simply because present factors tend to influence—some might want to say distort—our recollections of the past, but also because past factors tend to influence, or distort, our experience of the present. This process, it should be stressed, reaches into the most minute and everyday details of our lives.
>
> (2)

Our present beliefs, attitudes, and actions are profoundly shaped by the past through the collective memories we inherit about historical events and objects. We can only change (our own and others' beliefs, attitudes, actions) by changing what we know about the past.

I cannot help but think of the 2015 church shooting in Charleston, South Carolina, when I read Connerton's characterization of memory. How a young man, his worldview, and his atrocious actions were shaped by deeply shared, though distorted, understandings and memories of the past. Tellingly, this young man did have some sense of causal connections between what he perceived as the Lost Cause of the Civil War and "reverse racism" and "black on white crime" supposedly ravaging modern America.[3] Though grossly, horrifically misguided this sense was, he was acting on collective memories of a powerful through-line drawn clearly for him from the past to the present day. We know this (deeply and tragically skewed) historical sensibility galvanized his thoughts and actions: he sought to meld memory and heritage himself by visiting several plantations outside of Charleston before deciding on the parishioners of the historic "Mother Emanuel" A.M.E. Church to be the victims of his racist, hate-mongering massacre. What we remember together matters. What we believe about our shared heritage matters. Where we visit, what we learn and do there, and what we take away from it matter. Heritage tourism and the cultural memories promulgated at every destination, big or small, matter.

In these ways we can see that public memory is integral to uncovering, interrogating, and changing the implicit ways that racism, prejudice, and structural inequalities are maintained. Because public memory attends to the unofficial, the "commonsensical," and the ordinary ways that people remember and forget together, because it helps explain how collective understandings are shaped and shared through popular and material culture, it can play a crucial role in redirecting the public's attention to the unquestioned assumptions undergirding the country's commemorative landscape, a landscape that all too often authorizes and normalizes oppression. In other words, if bigotry and injustice are effectively sustained by tacit knowledge and unspoken "truths," and if public memory resides in those kinds of cultural practices like an innocuous roadside marker or local museum, then public memory can also be galvanized for counteracting racism with updated and complex historical narratives that foster meaningful change. Always staked in contestation over truth, public memory is uniquely poised to do this race work as memory shapes racial understandings, and racial identities and identifications influence practices of remembrance.

Ours is the era of just redemption. Will we seize it?

Notes

1. See Smith's *Emotional Heritage* (chapters 3, 5, 9) and her article, "Visitor Emotion," on the phenomenon of "reinforcement" among heritage visitors.
2. See Smith on demographic variables and different visitor responses to different kinds of heritage sites, especially in terms of race and ethnicity (chapters 5, 6, 7).
3. In *Algorithms of Oppression*, Safiya Noble examines this man's fateful Google search in June 2015, which seems to have contributed to his radicalization. See Chapter Three.

Briefly, she notes, "According to the manifesto, [he] allegedly typed 'black on White crime' in a Google search to make sense of the news reporting on Trayvon Martin ... What Roof found was information that confirmed a patently false notion that Black violence on White Americans is an American crisis" (111).

References

Connerton, Paul. *How Societies Remember*. Cambridge UP, 1989.

"Establishing the President's Advisory 1776 Commission." Executive Order 13958 as of November 2, 2020. Presidential Documents. *Federal Register*, vol. 85, no. 215, 5 Nov. 2020, pp. 70951–7094. https://www.govinfo.gov/content/pkg/FR-2020-11-05/pdf/2020-24793.pdf Accessed 21 Jan. 2021.

Glisson, Susan. "The sum of its parts: the importance of deconstructing truth commissions." *Race and Justice*, vol. 5, no. 2, 2015, pp. 192–202. doi:10.1177/2153368715572049

Gorman, Amanda. "The hill we climb." *New York Times*, 20 Jan. 2021, https://www.nytimes.com/2021/01/19/books/amanda-gorman-inauguration-hill-we-climb.html. Accessed 21 Jan. 2021.

Mogelson, Luke. "The storm." *The New Yorker*, vol. XCVI, no. 45, 25 Jan. 2021, pp. 32–53.

Noble, Safiya Umoja. *Algorithms of Oppressions: How Search Engines Reinforce Racism*. New York UP, 2018.

Schuessler, Jennifer. "The ideas behind Trump's 1776 Commission Report." *New York Times*, 19 Jan. 2021, https://www.nytimes.com/2021/01/19/arts/1776-commission-claims-trump.html?searchResultPosition=4 Accessed 25 Jan. 2021.

"The 1776 Report." The President's Advisory 1776 Commission. 18 Jan. 2021. https://f.hubspotusercontent10.net/hubfs/397762/The%20President%E2%80%99s%20Advisory%201776%20Commission%20-%20Final%20Report.pdf Accessed 21 Jan. 2021.

Shackel, Paul. Foreword. *Excavating Memory: Sites of Remembering and Forgetting*. edited by Maria Theresia Starzmann and John R. Roby. UP of Florida, 2016. xiii–xv.

"Sites of conscience." *International Coalition of Sites of Conscience*. https://www.sitesofconscience.org/en/home/ Accessed 25 Jan. 2021.

Smith, Laurajane. *Emotional Heritage: Visitor Engagement at Museums and Heritage Sites*. Routledge, 2021.

———. "'Man's inhumanity to man' and other platitudes of avoidance and misrecognition: an analysis of visitor responses to exhibitions marking the 1807 bicentenary." *Museum and Society*, vol. 8, no. 3, 2010, pp. 193–214.

———. "Visitor emotion, affect, and registers of engagement at museums and heritage sites." *Conservation Science in Cultural Heritage*, vo. 14, no. 2, pp. 125–132. doi:10.6092/issn.1973-9494/5447

Tell, Dave. *Remembering Emmett Till*. U of Chicago P, 2019.

Index

1776 Commission, 155
1776 Report 155
2015 Charleston church shooting 157

Abbott, Greg 108
African American heritage sites 100
African migration history: Algiers Point 21; Sullivan's Island *see* Sullivan's Island (South Carolina)
African Passages, Sullivan's Island (South Carolina) 28
A.I.M. (American Indian Movement) 46
The Ajax 94
Alabama: Florence Indian mound *see* Florence Indian mound
Alabama Fever 38
Alamo 108–109
Albrecht, Julia N. 28
Alderman, Derek 122–123, 129
Algiers Point (Louisiana) 21, 29
Allen, Michael 29
American democracy 153
American heritage 154–156
American identity 153
American Indian Movement (A.I.M.) 46
American Revolution 105–106
Americans 57
Angel Island (San Francisco Bay) 18, 20–21, 25, 30
Angel Island Immigration Station Foundation 30
Anglo-European settlers 3
Anishinaabeg *see* Grand Portage National Monument
apps: as intervention in urban landscape 91–94; New Orleans Slave Trade app 93–99; Slavery at Monticello: Life and Work on Mulberry Row 92
Araujo, Ana L. 19, 29

Archaeological Resources Protection Act (A.R.P.A.) 46
Armfield, John 96
A.R.P.A. (Archaeological Resources Protection Act) 46
Arrowhead, North Shore (Minnesota) 141
arrowhead hunting 46
artifacts, Florence Indian mound 44–47
Atchatchakangouen 70
Atlantic World 3–4
Atwater, Caleb 38
audio tours 95–96
authenticity 75, 131, 140; staged authenticity 122; tourism authenticity 87
autoethnographic methods 137
Avery, Albert E. 110

Bacon, Delos H. 40
Bahorich, Donna 108
Bailyn, Bernard 3
Ball, Willis 127
Banks, Thomas 98
Banks' Arcade 98
ban on international slave trade 94
Bansal, Gaurav 111, 115
Baradwaj, Babu G. 110
Barrett, Hersey 66n14
Barrett, Richard 58
Bayor, Ronald H. 25
Betton, Anne 58
Betton, Bob 58
Biser, Margaret 90
Black Lives Matter movement 86, 89, 100
Blair, Carole 8
Block, Sharon 5
Bodnar, John 7, 20, 154
Bottiger, Patrick 69
Boyd, Stephen W. 73, 75
British tourism 127

160 Index

Brown, John 96
Brown, William Wells 96
Browne, Stephen 8
Browning, Elizabeth Barrett 59
Bryant, William Cullen 39
Bulloch, Irvine 124
Bulloch, James Stephens 121, 128
Bulloch, Martha (Mittie) 121, 123–124, 126–127
Bulloch, Martha Stewart Elliott 121, 124, 128
Bulloch Hall 121, 132; docents, training 123; good owners narrative 128–130; interpretation 127–130; production myths 124; slavery 124–125, 128–129; white-dominated narratives 127
Burchell, Thomas 60
Bureau of American Ethnology mound survey (1894) 40
Bush, George P. 108
Bushell, Robyn 2, 11
Butler, David 122–123, 129–130
Butler, Nic 25
Butler, Richard 80

Cabildo 94–95
Cantrill, James G. 142
Carter, Perry 123, 129
Cash, Johnny 56, 66n13
Chambers, Douglas B. 21
changes in interpretation of slavery 88–90
Charleston, SC 19; Old Slave Mart Museum 87; Sullivan's Island *see* Sullivan's Island (South Carolina)
Charleston church shooting (2015) 89
Charleston Harbor 26
Chase, Judith Wragg 87
chattel slavery *see* slavery
Cherokee 42, 47, 50n7
Chickamauga Cherokee 47
Chickasaw 37, 43
Chickasaw Explorers Program 48
Chickasaw Nation 48
Chiles, Katy 5
Choctaw 43
Christmas Rebellion (Jamaica) 54, 58, 65n8
Chronis, Athinodoros 19, 29, 53
Cinco de Mayo 108
Citibank 110
City of New Orleans Tricentennial Commission 86
City of Roswell, GA: Bulloch Hall *see* Bulloch Hall; Imagine Roswell Arts and Culture 2030 Master Plan 132

civility 6
Civil War, monuments 88–89
The Clio 91
Cockrum, William Monroe 69
collective memory *see* public memory
collectivism 111
colonial America *see* early America
colonialism, Feast of the Hunters' Moon 76–80
Colonial Williamsburg: historic site 13–14; slave auction 87
complexion 5–6
Confederate monuments, removal of 89
Congo Square, New Orleans 98
Connerton, Paul 156
Cowles, A.R. 129
Cox, Karen 89
creation stories, Ojibwe people 142
Cree 141
Creek 43
critical reflexivity 68–69
Crotts, John C. 111
Cu.D.A. (cultural discourse analysis) 137, 141
Cuillier, David 140
cultural discourse analysis (Cu.D.A.) 137, 141
cultural memory *see* public memory
cultural values: Mexico 116; Texas 109–112, 116
Cummings, John 89
Curatescape 91

Dabney, R.S. 42
Dakotah 141
Dann, Graham M.S. 131
dark tourism 90, 126
Davis, Edwin H. 40
Davis, Thadious 126, 131
De Groot, Jerome 11, 69–70, 75
Delaware 71
Deloria, Phil 46
Desmeloises, Nicolas-Marie Renaud (d'Arnaud) Davenne de 76
Dickinson, Greg 8
digital exhibits 91
digital tools, apps *see* apps
Dillard, Brandon 92

early America 2–4; race 4–7
Egerton, Douglas 3
Eichstedt, Jennifer 121–122, 125, 129, 132
Elliott, Daniel Stuart 124, 128–129
Ellis Island (New York Harbor) 18, 20–21, 25, 30

escapism, Rose Hall Great House (Jamaica) 57
Esfehani, Minoo H. 28
ethnography 117
Euchee tribe 43
Euro-Americans 138
European settlers 3
exclusionary representation 131
exclusion narratives 127

Feast of the Hunters' Moon 68–69, 73–76, 81–82; colonialism 76–80; representation 80–81
F.I.M.M. (Florence Indian Mound Museum) 36–37, 43–49; myths 37–41
Finegan, Chance 77
Florence Indian mound (Alabama) 37–41, 44–45; artifacts 44–47; preservation of 41–47; self-determination 42–47
Florence Indian Mound Museum (F.I.M.M.) 36–37, 43–49; myths 37–41
Floyd, George 89
Fort Johnson 22
Fort Moultrie 24, 26, 29
Fort Ouiatenon 68, 71, 72; Feast of the Hunters' Moon *see* Feast of the Hunters' Moon
Fort Sumter National Monument 27–28
Fox 71
Franklin, Isaac 96
Friends of Bulloch, Inc. 121, 126

Gadsden's Wharf (South Carolina) 29
Gallas, Kristin 126, 130–133
Games, Alison 3, 4
gender roles 109
Georgia, Bulloch Hall *see* Bulloch Hall
Gichi Gami 141
Gichigami 146
Gichi Omingaming *see* Grand Portage National Monument
gift shops, F.I.M.M. (Florence Indian Mound Museum) 48
Gilroy, Paul 3
Gone with the Wind 122–123
good owners narrative 122, 124, 128–130
Gooseberry Falls State Park 141
Gordon, Nickesia 64
Gorman, Amanda 153–154
Gotham, Kevin Fox 87
Grandmother Earth 142
Grand Portage Band 136, 142

Grand Portage National Monument (Minnesota) 136, 138–139, 143–150
Grand Portage Reservation 138–139, 142
Grand Portage State Park 140, 142
Graves, Louise Alston Wragg 87
great houses (Jamaica) 52; Greenwood Great House 53, 58–64; Rose Hall Great House 53–58
Green, Nichole 87
Greenwood Great House (Jamaica) 53, 58–64
Grimwood, Bryan 77, 80
gumbo pot history 88

Halbwachs, Maurice 7
Hallock, Gardiner 91
Hamilton, Douglas 124
Hampton, Ronald D. 19
Hanna, Stephen 122
happy slave narrative 125
Harvey, Sean 6
haunted tours 90
Heath, William 78
Heinrich, Horst-Alfred 24, 57
Hemings, John 92
Hemings, Madison 92
Hemings, Priscilla 92
Hemings, Sally 91–92
Hendrix, Tom 43
Henry, Bulloch Hall 130
heritage 10–11, 69, 76, 154
heritage narratives 142–143, 150
heritage sites 76
heritage tourism 2, 9–11, 73, 80, 139; slavery 87–88; virtual ethnography 112–115; websites, Texas Revolution 112–115
heritage travel 1–2
heroic, in context of Texas Revolution 108–109
Hewlett, John 96
Hewlett's Exchange, New Orleans 96
"The Hill We Climb" (Gorman) 153–154
Hinch, Thomas 80
hiraeth 77
historic sites, traditional presentations of slavery in tourist sites 86–87
history 69–70
Hodgson, Kate 124
Hofstede's Cultural Value Dimensions 106, 109–110, 116
Holmes, Ekua 89
Horton, James Oliver 91, 95
Horton, Lois 91

Houdek, Matthew 7
Houston, Sam 107, 112
Howey, Meghan C.L. 39
Hsu, Shih-Yun 111
Hubbard, David 39–40
Hull-Rust Mine 141
human remains, F.I.M.M. (Florence Indian Mound Museum) 48
hungry years, Anishinaabeg 148, 150

identity 126; American identity 153; Grand Portage National Monument 149
idolatry 40
Imagine Roswell Arts and Culture 2030 Master Plan 132
inauthentic heritage 76–77
Indiana 68, 70–72; Feast of the Hunters' Moon *see* Feast of the Hunters' Moon; power 73; middle ground 72–73; race 71, 79
Indian burial mounds 35–36; Florence Indian mound *see* Florence Indian mound; myths 37–41
"Indian Grave" (Ridge) 35–36
Indian Removal Act (1830) 39
Indigenous people 137–138
Indigenous research methods 137–138
Indigenous stakeholders 81
Indigenous tourism 80–81, 140; culture disposed tourism 80
individualism *versus* collectivism 109, 111, 117
indulgence *versus* restraint 109
intercultural relations, Grand Portage National Monument 149
International African American Museum 26
interpretation, Bulloch Hall 127–130
interracial harmony, New Orleans 88
Iron Range, Arrowhead (Minnesota) 141

Jackson, Andrew 39, 49n4
Jackson, Nancy 127–129
Jackson Square, New Orleans 95
Jamaica: Christmas Rebellion 58; great houses 52; Greenwood Great House 58–64; Rose Hall Great House 53–58, 63–64; slavery 53; tourism 52–53
Jamaican National Heritage Trust 52
Jamaica Tourist Board 52–53
James Island 25–26; Point Comfort 24–25, 29

Janiskee, Bob 30
January 6, 2021 155
Jefferson, Thomas 91–92
Johnson, Rashuana 88, 99

Kachelman, John 41
Kammen, Michael 7
Kang, Doo Syen 111, 115
Kaufman, Ned 30
Kickapoo 71
Kilmeade, Brian 109
Kim, Soojung 75
Knibb, William 60
Kytle, Ethan J. 19

Lafayette, Indiana 71; *see also* Feast of the Hunters' Moon
Lake Superior 141
Lalaurie, Delphine 90
Lamanites 39
Landers, Jane G. 3
Landrieu, Mitch 89
Lane, Kris 3
Laura Plantation (Louisiana) 123
Laveau, Marie 86
Lee, Erika 25
Lenape (Delaware) 70
"The Level Crossing" 60–61
Lilly, Gabriel 92
Lincoln, Abraham 96
Lindsay, Thomas 108
listening 137–138, 149
"little Bess," Bulloch Hall 129–130
long- *versus* short-term orientation 109
Louisiana: Laura Plantation 123; New Orleans *see* New Orleans; Whitney Plantation 89–90
Lowenthal, David 10, 70

MacCannell, Dean, 9, 122, 131
Mack, Katherine 8
Mallouf, Robert 47
Manrai, Ajay 111
Manrai, Lalita A. 111
Marshall, Roger 111
Mascouten 71
masculinity *versus* femininity 109
Maspero, Pierre 96
Maspero's Exchange, New Orleans 96
Mastin, Teresa 111, 115
May, Daniel E. 30
McCullough, David 123

Index

McDonnell, Michael 71
McKercher, Bob 126
media representations of the South 126–127
Memorial for the Murdered Jews of Europe (Berlin) 126
memory: collective memory 90; public memory 7–9, 154, 157
memory work 11, 154
Merieult, Jean Francois 94
Merieult House, New Orleans 94
Mexico 107–108; cultural values 116
Miami 71, 73, 78
Middle Passage 21–24, 26, 93
Miles, Suzannah S. 19
Miles, Tiya 90
Minnesota: Grand Portage National Monument *see* Grand Portage National Monument; North Shore 136–138, 141
Minnesota State Parks 140
Mitchell, Margaret 123
Miyaamiaa (Miami) Nations 70–73
mobile apps as intervention in urban landscape 91–94
mobilities 9
Modlin, Arnold 122, 124
Money, R. Bruce 111
monogenesis 5
Monticello (Virginia) 91–92
monuments: to Civil War era 88–89; Texas 108–109
The Moonwalk 95
morality 24
moral responsibility 57
Morris Island 25
Morrison, Toni 18
"Mother Emanuel" A.M.E. Church 157
Moultrieville 25
mound-builder myths 37–41
Mound Garden 41
multicultural tours 88
Muscle Shoals 37, 49n3
Myers, Kelsey Noack 69
myths, mound-builder myths 37–41

Nanabozho 142
narratives of exclusion 127; Bulloch Hall *see* Bulloch Hall
national identity, Indiana 71
national legacy 154–155

National Park Service; Ellis Island (New York Harbor) 30; Grand Portage National Monument 138–139
Native Americans 39
Native inferiority 6
Nephites 39
Neshnabe (Potawatomi) 70
New Orleans 86, 88; haunted tours 90; interracial harmony 88; New Orleans Slave Trade app 86, 93–99; New Orleans Slave Trade Project 86
New Orleans Slave Trade app 86, 93–99
New Orleans Slave Trade Project 86
Nichols, Elaine 19
Nielsen, Noah 68, 80
Nora, Pierre 7
Northrup, Solomon 98
North Shore (Minnesota) 136–138, 141
North West Company 138

Ohio River Valley 69, 71–72
Ojibwe 141; Grand Portage National Monument 145
Old Slave Mart Museum (Charleston, SC) 87
online political advertisements 111
other 104–105, 117, 138
othering 79
otherness of history, re-enactment 75
Ott, Brian 8
Ouiatenons 71

Palmer, Annee 53, 55–58, 63–64
Palmer, John 54
Peoria Tribe 78
Perry, James De Wolf 126, 130–133
pesthouses 19; Sullivan's Island (South Carolina) (1707-99) 22–24
Phillips, Kendall 7
Piankashaw 70–71
plantation museums 121; Bulloch Hall *see* Bulloch Hall; *Gone with the Wind* 122–123; slavery 131–132
plantation tourism 87
Point Comfort 25, 29
polygenesis 5–6
positioning, Grand Portage National Monument 149
post-removal romanticization, Shoals Native American heritage tourism 43
Potawatomi 71

power distance 109
production myths 124
public memory 7–9, 154, 157

quarantine, Sullivan's Island (South Carolina) 22–23
Quirk, Joel 124

race: in early America 4–7, 63, 155–157; Indiana 71, 79; mound building 39; public memory 154–157; Texas 104, 109; tourism 6–7, 18–19, 64, 70–71, 88–90
racial identity 126
racial justice, reconciliation 31, 63–64, 80, 153–155, 157
Raden, Regina 132
Ray, Celeste 10–11
re-enactment, otherness of history 75
removal of monuments 89
representation: exclusionary representation 131; Feast of the Hunters' Moon 80–81; of the South 126–127
Revolutionary War, Sullivan's Island (South Carolina) 24–25
Ridge, John Rollin 35–36
Rifkin, Mark 42
River, Charles 20
Roberts, Blain 19
Robinson, Corinne Roosevelt 123, 124
Rollins, John 55
Rollins, Michelle 55
Roosevelt, Jr. Theodore 121, 123
Rose Hall Great House (Jamaica) 53–58, 63–64
Ross, Susan Dente 140
Rothman, Joshua 96
Royce, Charles C. 69

Saint Charles Hotel, New Orleans 96
San Jacinto Memorial Monument 112–115
San Jacinto Museum of History 112–116; websites 117
Santa Anna, Antonio Lopez de 107
Sauk 71
savage heathens 6
Save Ellis Island 30
Schwartz, Barry 24, 57
Sea Islands 21
Seaton, A. V. 130–131, 133
self 104–105, 117
self-determination, Florence Indian mound 41–47

self-serving representations of benign slavery 124
Seminole 43
Senecah, Susan L. 142
Senecca 71
settler colonialism 12, 81, 136, 138–139, 141, 148–150
Sever, Catherine 129–130
Shackel, Paul 11
Sharpe, Samuel 54, 60
Shawnee (Sewanee) 70–71
Shoals 49n3; Native American heritage tourism 43
Singer, Daniel D. 110
'singing river' 43
skin color 5–6
slave auction, New Orleans 96
Slave Depot on Common Street, New Orleans 98
slavery: ban on international slave trade 94; Bulloch Hall 124–125, 127–130; changes in interpretation of 88–90; Greenwood Great House (Jamaica) 59–63; heritage tourism 87–88; Jamaica 53; New Orleans 86; New Orleans Slave Trade app 93–99; plantation museums 131–132; Rose Hall great house (Jamaica) 54–58; self-serving representations of benign slavery 124; Sullivan's Island (South Carolina) 18–24; traditional presentations of 86–88
"Slavery at Monticello: Life and Work on Mulberry Row" app 92
slavery heritage sites 18–31, 52–64, 86–100, 121–133
Small, Stephen 121–122, 125, 129, 132
smallpox, Sullivan's Island (South Carolina) 22, 24
Smith, Joseph 39
Smith, Laurajane 1–2, 11, 154
Smith, Susan Sleeper 69
Smithers, Gregory D. 47
Smithsonian Fieldwork report (1924), Florence Indian mound 41
social memory *see* public memory
Soudan Underground Mine 141
South Carolina: Gadsden's Wharf 29; Sullivan's Island *see* Sullivan's Island
Souther, J. Mark 86
"Southern Trilogy" 127
space, unsettling settler colonialism 81
Squier, Epraim G. 40
staged authenticity 122

Staiff, Russell 2, 11
Stanton, Lucia 92
Stantonis, Anthony 86
Statue of Liberty-Ellis Island Foundation 30
St. Louis Hotel 96
stories, Feast of the Hunters' Moon 80
Sullivan's Island (South Carolina) 18–22, 26–31; African migration history 28; contrasting interpretation of arrival with other locations 25–31; erosion of pesthouse 24–25; Fort Moultrie 26; pesthouse (1707-99) 22–24
sun-fire temple, Florence Indian mound 41
sustainable Indigenous heritage tourism 140

Tang, Tang 111
Tawil, Ezra 5
T.C.H.A. (Tippecanoe County Historical Association), Feast of the Hunters' Moon *see* Feast of the Hunters' Moon
Tell, Dave 8
Temperance River State Park 141
Tennessee River 43
Tennessee Valley Authority 48, 49n3
termination policies 41–42
Tettegouche State Park 141
Texas 104–106; Alamo 108; cultural values 109–112, 116; monuments 108–109; race 109; *see also* Texas Revolution (1835-6)
Texas Democracy Foundation 109
Texas Independence Trail Region 104
Texas Revolution (1835-6) 104–108; heritage sites and museums **110**; values celebrated at heritage sites **110**; websites 110–115
thanatourism 90
Thomas, Cyrus 40
Thomas, Deborah 56, 58, 61
Thomas, Lynnell L. 88
Thousand Eyes Archaeological Stewardship program 48
Till, Emmett 8
Timothy, Dallen J. 10, 73, 75
Tippecanoe County Historical Association (T.C.H.A.), Feast of the Hunters' Moon *see* Feast of the Hunters' Moon
Tom's Wall 43
Toni Morrison Society 18, 26, 28
tourism 1–2, 73, 80, 81, 139; apps as intervention in urban landscape 91–94; British tourism 127; dark tourism 90; heritage tourism *see* heritage tourism; Indigenous Native American heritage tourism 140; Jamaica 52–53; plantation tourism 87; sustainable Indigenous heritage tourism 140; thanatourism 90
tourism authenticity 87
tourism imaginary 53, 58, 61
tourist-cum-ethnographers 104–105
tourists 1–2
Toy, Katherine 25
traditional presentations of slavery in tourist sites 86–88
Trail of Tears Commemorative Motorcycle Ride 43, 49n6
Treaty of Chickasaw Council House (1816) 49n4
Treaty of Fort Jackson 39
Tremoulet, Bernard 96
tribal labels 71
Trofanenko, Brenda 75
Trump, Donald 155
Turtle Island 142
Tybee Island (Georgia) 21, 29
Tyler, Edward 127–128

uncertainty avoidance 109, 111
unsettling settler colonialism 81
Urry, John 9

virtual ethnography, heritage tourism 112–115
Vivian, Bradford 8
voiced participant 150

Waayaahtanonki 71, 78
Wabash Indians 71
Wabash River 71–72
War That Was Lost 104–105, 117
War That Was Won 108, 117
Wateron, Emma 1–2, 11, 127
Watson, Steve 1–2, 11
Wea 70–73
websites: San Jacinto Museum of History 117; Texas Revolution (1835-6) 110–115
Webster, Peletiah 24
Werner, Emmy E. 20
Wheeler, Roxann 5
"Whistler's Walk" 61
white-dominated narratives 130; Bulloch Hall 127

whiteness 6, 63, 125
white supremacy, Alamo monuments 109
White Witch, Rose Hall Great House (Jamaica) 55–57, 64
Whitney Plantation (Louisiana) 89–90
Wilkes, Karen 64
Wilson, Erica 68, 80
Wilson, Miriam 87
Witcomb, Andrea 126
Woodside, Arch G. 111, 115

Wright, Donald R. 3–4
Wu, Ming-Yi 110

Yankholmes, Aaron 126
Yuhl, Stephanie E. 19, 87
Yung, Judy 25

Zahedi, Fatemeh Mariam 110–111, 115
Zelizer, Barbie 8
Zinn, E.F. 41

Printed in the United States
by Baker & Taylor Publisher Services